Compliments
of
Opies

Metrics and Case Studies
for Evaluating Engineering Designs

PRENTICE HALL INTERNATIONAL SERIES
IN INDUSTRIAL AND SYSTEMS ENGINEERING

W.J. Fabrycky and J.H. Mize, Editors

AMOS AND SARCHET *Industrial Safety and Health Management, 2/E*
AMOS AND SARCHET *Management for Engineers*
AMRINE, RITCHEY, MOODIE AND KMEC *Manufacturing Organization and Management, 6/E*
ASFAHL *Industrial Safety and Health Management, 3/E*
BABCOCK *Managing Engineering and Technology, 2/E*
BADIRU *Comprehensive Project Management*
BADIRU *Expert Systems Applications in Engineering and Manufacturing*
BANKS, CARSON AND NELSON *Discrete Events System Simulation, 2/E*
BLANCHARD *Logistics Engineering and Management, 4/E*
BLANCHARD AND FABRYCKY *Systems Engineering and Analysis, 2/E*
BROWN *Technimanagement: The Human Side of the Technical Organization*
BURTON AND MORAN *The Future Focused Organization*
BUSSEY AND ESCHENBACH *The Economic Analysis of Industrial Projects, 2/E*
BUZACOTT AND SHANTHIKUMAR *Stochastic Models of Manufacturing Systems*
CANADA AND SULLIVAN *Economic and Multi-Attribute Evaluation of Advanced Manufacturing Systems*
CANADA, SULLIVAN AND WHITE *Capital Investment Analysis for Engineering and Management, 2/E*
CHANG AND WYSK *An Introduction to Automated Process Planning Systems*
CHANG, WYSK AND WANG *Computer Aided Manufacturing*
DELAVIGNE AND ROBERTSON *Deming's Profound Changes*
EAGER *The Information Payoff: The Manager's Concise Guide to Making PC Communications Work*
EBERTS *User Interface Design*
EBERTS AND EBERTS *Myths of Japanese Quality*
ELSAYED AND BOUCHER *Analysis and Control of Production Systems, 2/E*
FABRYCKY AND BLANCHARD *Life-Cycle Cost and Economic Analysis*
FABRYCKY AND THUESEN *Economic Decision Analysis*
FISHWICK *Simulation Model Design and Execution: Building Digital Worlds*
FRANCIS, MCGINNIS AND WHITE *Facility Layout and Location: An Analytical Approach, 2/E*
GIBSON *Modern Management of the High-Technology Enterprise*
GORDON *Systematic Training Program Design*
GRAEDEL AND ALLENBY *Industrial Ecology*
HALL *Queuing Methods: For Services and Manufacturing*
HANSEN *Automating Business Process Reengineering*
HAMMER *Occupational Safety Management and Engineering, 4/E*
HAZELRIGG *Systems Engineering*
HUTCHINSON *An Integrated Approach to Logistics Management*
IGNIZIO *Linear Programming in Single- and Multiple-Objective Systems*
IGNIZIO AND CAVALIER *Linear Programming*
KROEMER, KROEMER AND KROEMER-ELBERT *Ergonomics: How to Design for Ease and Efficiency*
KUSIAK *Intelligent Manufacturing Systems*
LAMB *Availability Engineering and Management for Manufacturing Plant Performance*
LANDERS, BROWN, FANT, MALSTROM AND SCHMITT *Electronic Manufacturing Process*

LEEMIS *Reliability: Probabilistic Models and Statistical Methods*

MICHAELS *Technical Risk Management*

MOODY, CHAPMAN, VAN VOORHEES AND BAHILL *Metrics and Case Studies for Evaluating Engineering Designs*

MUNDEL AND DANNER *Motion and Time Study: Improving Productivity, 7/E*

OSTWALD *Engineering Cost Estimating, 3/E*

PINEDO *Scheduling: Theory, Algorithms, and Systems*

PRASAD *Concurrent Engineering Fundamentals, Vol. I: Integrated Product and Process Organization*

PRASAD *Concurrent Engineering Fundamentals, Vol. II: Integrated Product Development*

PULAT *Fundamentals of Industrial Ergonomics*

SHTUB, BARD AND GLOBERSON *Project Management: Engineering Technology and Implementation*

TAHA *Simulation Modeling and SIMNET*

THUESEN AND FABRYCKY *Engineering Economy, 8/E*

TURNER, MIZE, CASE AND NAZEMETZ *Introduction to Industrial and Systems Engineering, 3/E*

TURTLE *Implementing Concurrent Project Management*

VON BRAUN *The Innovation War*

WALESH *Engineering Your Future*

WOLFF *Stochastic Modeling and the Theory of Queues*

Metrics and Case Studies for Evaluating Engineering Designs

Jay Alan Moody
William L. Chapman
F. David Van Voorhees
A. Terry Bahill

To join a Prentice Hall PTR internet mailing list point to
http://www.prenhall.com/register

Prentice Hall PTR
Upper Saddle River, New Jersey 07458
http://www.prenhall.com

Library of Congress Cataloging-in-Publication Data

Metrics and case studies for evaluating engineering designs / Jay
    Alan Moody…[et al.].
        p.   cm.
    Includes bibliographical references and index.
    ISBN 0-13-739871-9
    1. Systems engineering—Evaluation—Case studies. 2. System
design—Evaluation—Case studies. I. Moody, Jay Alan.
TA168.E93 1997
620'.001'171—dc21   96-4491
                                                                   CIP

Editorial/production supervision: *Nicholas Radhuber*
Cover design: *Bruce Kenselaar*
Cover design director: *Jerry Votta*
Manufacturing manager: *Alexis Heydt*
Acquisitions editor: *Bernard Goodwin*
Marketing manager: *Miles Williams*
Editorial Assistant: *Diane Spina*

© 1997 by Prentice Hall PTR
Prentice-Hall, Inc.
A Simon & Schuster Company
Upper Saddle River, New Jersey 07458

The Publisher offers discounts on this book when ordered in bulk quantities.
For more information, contact:

> Corporate Sales Department
> Prentice Hall PTR
> 1 Lake St.
> Upper Saddle River, NJ 07458
> Phone: 800-382-3419 Fax: 201-236-7141
> E-mail: dan_rush@prenhall.com

Printed in the United States of America

10 9 8 7 6 5 4 3 2 1

ISBN 0-13-739871-9

Prentice-Hall International (UK) Limited, *London*
Prentice-Hall of Australia Pty. Limited, *Sydney*
Prentice-Hall Canada Inc., *Toronto*
Prentice-Hall Hispanoamericana, S.A., *Mexico*
Prentice-Hall of India Private Limited, *New Delhi*
Prentice-Hall of Japan, Inc., *Tokyo*
Simon & Schuster Asia Pte. Ltd., *Singapore*
Editora Prentice-Hall do Brasil, Ltda., *Rio de Janeiro*

CONTENTS

Preface   **xi**

1 **Design Difficulty and Resources Metrics**   **1**
Introduction   1
Case Study Approach   2
Design Difficulty   2
Resources   6
Case Studies   7

2 **Design of Resistor Networks**   **10**
Design Difficulty and Resources Scores   12

3 **SIERRA Train Controllers**   **13**
Design Difficulty and Resources Scores   14

4 **Bat Chooser**   **16**
Design Difficulty and Resources Scores   17

5 **Scheduling a Pinewood Derby**   **19**
Design Difficulty and Resources Scores   23

6 **Second Opinion**   **24**
Design Difficulty and Resources Scores   26

7 **American Airlines Scheduling**   **27**
Design Difficulty and Resources Scores   29

8 **Superconductors**   **30**
Design Difficulty and Resources Scores   32

9 **Incandescent Light Bulb**   **33**
Design Difficulty and Resources Scores   36

10   Boeing 777   **37**
Design Difficulty and Resources Scores   39
11   The Apollo Moon Landing   **41**
Design Difficulty and Resources Scores   45
12   Building a House   **47**
Design Difficulty and Resources Scores   49
13   Central Arizona Project   **50**
Design Difficulty and Resources Scores   51
14   The Great Pyramid at Giza   **53**
Design Difficulty and Resources Scores   55
15   An Automobile Factory   **56**
Design Difficulty and Resources Scores   58
16   The GM Impact—An Electric Car   **60**
Design Difficulty and Resources Scores   62
17   Batteries for Electric Vehicles   **63**
Design Difficulty and Resources Scores   66
18   C3PO from the *Star Wars* Film   **68**
Design Difficulty and Resources Scores   69
19   Velcro   **70**
20   The Manhattan Project   **71**
Resources   71
Objectives and Requirements   72
Description   72
The Alternatives   72
Uncertainties   75
Los Alamos   76
Analysis   77
Design Difficulty and Resources Scores   80
21   The Polaris Program   **81**
Resources   81
Objectives   82
The Special Programs Office   82
Analysis   85
Design Difficulty and Resources Scores   86
22   The Hubble Space Telescope   **87**
System Description   88
Costs   89
Total Life-Cycle Cost   89
Requirements   89
The HST Life Cycle   91
The Primary Mirror   91
The HST Jitter   93
Design Difficulty and Resources Scores   93

23 Lessons Learned from the Simple Case Studies   95
The Metrics Summary Tables   95
The System Design Process   104

**24 What Is Systems Engineering? A Consensus
of Senior Systems Engineers   122**
Abstract   122
The Process   123

**25 Metrics for Systems Engineering
and the Developmental Environment   132**
Performance   136
Systems Engineering Fundamentals   138
Development Environment   143

26 The Boeing 777 Commercial Airplane   148
Development History, Design, and Performance   149
Systems Engineering Fundamentals   151
Development Environment   154
Summary   156

27 Lockheed F-117 Stealth Fighter   160
Development History, Design, and Performance   161
Systems Engineering Fundamentals   164
Development Environment   166
Summary   169

28 Northrop B-2 Stealth Bomber   172
Development History, Design, and Performance   173
Systems Engineering Fundamentals   177
Development Environment   181
Summary   184

29 McDonnell Douglas C-17 Military Transport   187
Development History, Design, and Performance   188
Systems Engineering Fundamentals   193
Development Environment   198
Summary   202

30 Learjet Model 60 Business Jet   206
Development History, Design, and Performance   207
Systems Engineering Fundamentals   209
Development Environment   211
Summary   212

31 McDonnell Douglas MD-11 Commercial Airplane 215
Development History, Design, and Performance   216
Systems Engineering Fundamentals   220
Development Environment   224
Summary   227

32 Comparison of the Aircraft Case Studies   **230**
Validation of Methodology   237
33 Other Metrics   **238**
The INCOSE Metrics Working Group   238
The San Francisco Bay INCOSE Chapter   239
Technical Performance Measures   242
34 General Comments   **245**
Index   **247**

PREFACE

This book presents metrics designed to assess the design difficulty, required resources, systems engineering efficacy, and developmental environment for system design. We think that creating metrics to assess the engineering design process is very important. As Harrington (1991) put it, "Measurements are key. If you cannot measure it, you cannot control it. If you cannot control it, you cannot improve it. It is as simple as that."

First we present two simple metrics: Design Difficulty and Required Resources. Then we present case studies to show how these metrics can be used. Several of these designs were done by our group. The advantage of this is that we can point out the mistakes that we made. The first score of case studies is simple. Creating them taught us two things: formal systems engineering is seldom used on small projects, and these simple metrics can be used to detect projects that will have high technological risk or high political risk. The metrics presented in the first part of the book, Chapters 1–23, are simple and general. We think each company should develop its own metrics that are tailored to its organization.

The second half of this book, Chapters 24–34, is devoted to metrics for systems engineering efficacy and the developmental environment for system design. The first chapter of this part of this book is entitled "What is Systems Engineering?" Bahill has delivered this lecture dozens of times. At the end of each lecture, someone comes up and suggests a different title. Project managers say, "What you have just described is really Project Management." Quality engineers say, "You have just described Quality Engineering." People who have served as Lead Engineers on projects say,"You have just described the job of a Lead Electrical Engineer." Design engineers say it describes design engineering, etc. The point is that many different types of people do systems engineering and all good engineers do systems engineering. So in this book we often use the term *Systems Engineer*. The reader may substitute any other desired term. It is not important what it is called; it is only important that all of the tasks get performed.

The last six case studies in this book show how to use our complex metrics. All these case studies are airplane development examples, so the design process is similar. They show that successful systems can be developed if there is good systems engineering and a good developmental environment. We hope that they illustrate good and bad systems engineering principles. They should also show that the systems engineering process can be measured and monitored; because if you can measure and control it, then you might be able to improve it.

We thank the following students at the University of Arizona who studied these cases and made comments that are included in this book: Bo Bentz, Brian Croyle, Jeremy Duke, Cassie Fleetwood, Allan Jaegers, Bill Karnavas, John Kneuer, Gary Knotts, Dennis Shephard, and Eric Taipale. We also thank Bruce Gissing, retired Vice President of Operations for the Boeing Company, for his helpful comments.

REFERENCE

HARRINGTON, H.J., *Business Process Improvement: The Breakthrough Strategy for Total Quality Productivity, and Competitiveness.* New York: McGraw-Hill, 1991.

1

DESIGN DIFFICULTY AND RESOURCES METRICS

INTRODUCTION

The ability to create technical designs quickly, accurately, and cost-effectively makes companies successful. It is important for companies to understand the process for designing technical systems. There are many books, short courses, standards, handbooks, and manuals that explain various facets of the system design process. In addition, we think that studying examples of successful and unsuccessful design efforts will help engineers assess the feasibility of design projects for their companies. We present metrics that can be used to assess risk of project failure. Then we present case studies to show how the metrics are used. We propose that such case studies and metrics can be developed by other companies as appropriate for their products. Thus we hypothesize that engineers can develop company specific metrics for the quantitative assessment of design feasibility. For example, Figure 1-1 shows the four regions

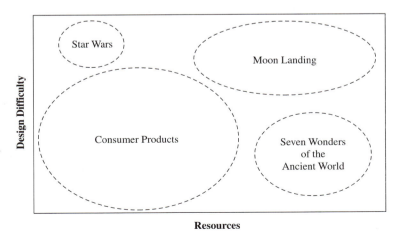

Figure 1-1   The four regions of the Design Difficulty versus Resources plane.

that our case studies encompass. If a small consumer products company was asked to design and build a system that fell into the Star Wars region, the systems engineer should be able to determine that there is virtually no feasibility of this design effort succeeding.

CASE STUDY APPROACH

Through the use of case studies, we can create a bridge between systems theory and actual design efforts. Figure 1-1 compares the design difficulty versus the resources used to create the designs. To set a common limit, we have decided that the system design process ended when the first production unit was built. The areas named reflect the type of design needed. The largest area, Consumer Products, is characterized by a design difficulty that is small to moderate and requires a small to moderate amount of resources. One area that requires the maximum amount of resources, Seven Wonders of the Ancient World, has a design difficulty that is small to moderate. The upper left quadrant is called Star Wars after the 1977 movie. It indicates items that we can imagine, but probably not design and build because of the complexity of the product. The designs are so difficult that it is impossible to solve these problems; thus they remain intractable. The final region is for high design difficulty coupled with massive resources. This quadrant is called Moon Landing to indicate the enormous nature of both the design effort and the resources needed.

The values for design difficulty and resources were computed by summing scores for their constituent parts. Each constituent part is an ordinal ranking within the category. We recognize that ordinal rankings are not necessarily additive, however in this case, we have adjusted the categories so that the answers pass a reasonableness test. Extreme examples may not fit these rankings; this scale fits these specific case studies, although it is not an unassailable system.

DESIGN DIFFICULTY

The scores for the vertical axis of the graph, Design Difficulty, represent a combination of the following categories:

1. design type, which is a continuum from redesign to original innovative design and, finally, to breakthrough design,
2. complexity of the knowledge needed to create the design,
3. number of steps needed to complete the design,
4. quality implementation effort,
5. process design, and
6. aggressive goals for selling price.

Each case study was scored using the scale illustrated in Table 1-1. Many more categories can be created. For example, we found that the expected system life was another useful and orthogonal metric, but we chose not to incorporate it here. We decided to derive a minimal set that would be useful for engineers embarking on a new design project.

By choosing ranges for these categories we have, in effect, created weights of importance for each.

A. **Design type** reflects whether feasible solutions exist and how much original thought goes into the project.

14 or 15 points are given for a breakthrough design effort.

7-13 points are given for original innovative design.

0-6 points are given for continuous improvement.

B. **Knowledge complexity** needed to create the design is based on an estimate of the number and availability of the people with the necessary knowledge to do the design.

9 or 10 points are given for undiscovered knowledge that can be found only by specialists.

6-8 points are given for complex knowledge held by few people.

3-5 points are given for complex knowledge held by numerous people.

0-2 points are given for common knowledge held by many people.

C. The number of **steps** is defined as the number of major process steps that are needed to assemble the system. It is related to the number of major components.

9 or 10 points are given for systems with greater than 10,000 steps or components.

5-8 points are given for systems with more than 500 but less than 10,000 steps or components.

TABLE 1-1   Design Difficulty Scores.

Metric	Range	Score
Design type	0-15	
Knowledge complexity	0-10	
Steps	0-10	
Quality	0-10	
Process design	0-5	
Aggressive selling price	0-5	
Design difficulty total	0-55	

3 or 4 points are given for systems with up to 500 steps or components.

0-2 points are given for any system with fewer than 50 steps or components.

D. **Quality** represents the desired level of quality in the product. It could come from the customer's inherent expectations or it could be enhanced by the company. It could be quantified with defect rate, reliability, maintainability, etc. Evidence that the company is serious about quality includes programs such as Zero Defects, Six Sigma, total quality management (TQM), ISO-9000, the Baldridge Award criteria, quality circles, gathering customer feedback, Taguchi methods, Quality Function Deployment (QFD), and Deming's 14 points. But be aware of Deming's 10th point: "Eliminate slogans, exhortations, and targets for the work force asking for zero defects and new levels of productivity. Such exhortations only create adversarial relationships, as the bulk of the causes of low quality belong to the system and thus lie beyond the power of the work force."

7-10 points are given for a system whose developer places high emphasis on implementing or continuing quality-related programs and techniques on the system development effort.

4-6 points are given for a system whose developer places medium emphasis on implementing or continuing quality-related programs and techniques on the system development effort.

0-3 points are given for a system whose developer places little or no emphasis on implementing or continuing quality-related programs and techniques.

E. **Process design**: is crucial because Systems Engineering designs both a product and a process to manufacture it. Sometimes the design of the process adds to the difficulty of the design of the product. Difficulty in designing the manufacturing process includes the **complexity** of the fabrication processes and the **quantity** of items produced. For example, the manufacturing process to produce one or a few large, complex systems can be as extensive as those established to mass produce small, less complex systems. Quantity is normalized between different items by partly basing the measure on the extent of national market share met by the output of a system's manufacturing operations.

5 points are given for highly complex manufacturing operations that are designed to produce systems in quantities to meet a large national market share.

4 points are given for:
1. highly complex manufacturing operations that are designed to produce systems in quantities to meet a moderate national market share, or
2. manufacturing operations of moderate complexity that are designed to produce systems in quantities to meet a large national market share.

3 points are given for:

1. highly complex manufacturing operations that are designed to produce systems in quantities to meet a small national market share, or
2. manufacturing operations of moderate complexity that are designed to produce systems in quantities to meet a moderate national market share, or
3. manufacturing operations of low complexity that are designed to produce systems to meet a large national market share.

2 points are given for:

1. manufacturing operations of moderate complexity that are designed to produce systems in quantities to meet a small national market share, or
2. manufacturing operations of low complexity that are designed to produce systems in quantities to meet a moderate national market share.

1 point is given for manufacturing operations of low complexity that are designed to produce systems in quantities (of greater than one unit) to meet a small national market share.

0 points are given for manufacturing operations of low complexity that are designed to produce only one system.

Note: This is not a good metric by itself, because it is dependent on other metrics: design type, complexity of knowledge, number of steps, and quality.

F. **Aggressive** goals for **selling price** is the degree to which the system design is driven and constrained by unit sales price requirements or goals. These requirements and goals are based on the competition level in the market. In general, the greater the competition, the greater the constraint. The sales price requirements and goals for government systems can be determined by design-to-cost requirements or goals, as well as by the existence of equivalent commercial systems already on the market.

4-5 points are given for very challenging unit sales price requirements or goals driven by a highly competitive market.

2-3 points are given for moderately challenging unit sales price requirements or goals driven by a moderately competitive market.

0-1 points are given for little or no challenge to meet unit sales price requirements or goals due to lack of competition or lack of unit sales price requirements or goals.

Note: Aggressive goals for time to market might also be a useful metric. Reducing time to market will increase profit and will make the design more difficult.

The scores are provided in a table at the end of each case study similar to that illustrated in Table 1-1.

RESOURCES

The scores of the horizontal axis of Figure 1-1, Resources, represent a composite score of the following categories:

1. costs to develop the product through the first production unit,
2. time from the beginning of the effort through the first production unit, and
3. infrastructure required to complete the design.

The score for each case study is on the scale illustrated in Table 1-2.

A. **Cost** is the amount needed to pay for development, including salaries, utilities, supplies, and materials, through the first production unit. This is not in absolute dollars, but in terms of the payer's ability to pay. For example, the Internal Revenue Service may consider a Cray computer to be low cost, but you or I may consider a Pentium PC to be expensive.

14 or 15 points are given for massively expensive systems requiring major sacrifices.

9-13 points are given for very expensive systems that are rarely developed.

3-8 points are given for moderately expensive systems.

0-2 points are given for affordable systems.

Note: This metric considers only design and manufacturing costs. Another interesting metric would be total life cycle cost.

B. The **time** score is for time spent from the beginning of the effort to define the customer's needs through the first production unit.

10 points are given for more than eight years.

8 or 9 points are given for five to eight years.

4-7 points are given for one to five years.

3 points are given for six months to a year.

TABLE 1-2   Resources Scores.

Metric	Range	Score
Cost	0-15	
Time	0-10	
Infrastructure	0-10	
Resources total	0-35	

2 points are given for three months to six months.

1 point is given for one to three months.

0 points are given for less than a month.

C. **Infrastructure** required to achieve the design is also hard to quantify. Infrastructure is described as the physical resources needed for construction (including machine tools, process shops, and assembly workstations), transportation, communication, utilities, laws and legal protections, skilled managers, and the education system available. Infrastructure must be judged in regard to the designer's ability to get and use the infrastructure over the needed design time.

Infrastructure is relative to the time the system was designed. Thomas Edison did not need a lot of scientific support. He invented everything he needed, like the world's first good vacuum pump. So he has a low infrastructure score. The Apollo program used every available engineering tool. We gave it the maximum score for infrastructure. In contrast, the Boeing 777 used vastly more complex computer aided design tools, but we did not think they pushed the limits of availability, so we only assigned that project an 8.

9 or 10 points are given for a massive infrastructure requiring major portions of the available labor force and the available equipment.

6-8 points are given for large complex infrastructures requiring large portions of the cost of the entire project

3-5 points are given for moderate infrastructures requiring people on the project to support it.

0-2 points are given if it is a common, low cost infrastructure (e.g., clean tap water in the U.S.)

The scores are given in a table at the end of each case study similar to that illustrated in Table 1-2.

All of our metrics depend heavily on the context of the design. It is impossible for a person in a primitive country to obtain the resources necessary to build a telephone in a reasonable time. However, it is relatively simple to do this in America. It may be impossible for a small company to obtain $10 million to fund a new product. But it is easy for General Motors. At the end of every case study, the context for the scores will be given to help explain the rational for the given scores.

CASE STUDIES

In the following paragraphs, we give a brief description of our first case studies. References and a full discussion are given in subsequent chapters.

1. Resistor Networks—A network of up to four resistors connected in series and/or parallel must be designed to produce a specific resistance value.

2. SIERRA Train Controllers—University students have developed numerous versions of a controller to run two HO gauge model trains. The controller must prevent collisions and can be built with three to six state designs. Despite being limited to nine components, students have found dozens of successful solutions.

3. Bat Chooser—Bat Chooser is a small consumer product developed to determine the Ideal Bat Weight for an individual baseball or softball player. By measuring the swing speed of a given bat, the ideal weight of bat for the player can be calculated.

4. Pinewood Derby—A Pinewood Derby is a Cub Scout race of wooden cars. Creating schedules for these races was a difficult problem.

5. Second Opinion—Second Opinion is a personal computer based decision support system that helps with the diagnosis and prognosis of young children who may have begun to stutter.

6. American Airlines Scheduling—American Airlines schedules its aircraft and crews using computer algorithms. These sophisticated algorithms search for a good solution, but not necessarily the optimum solution.

7. Superconductors—Superconductors are materials that exhibit no electrical resistance when very cold. Recent development of advanced copper oxides was a breakthrough design effort. In four months, Paul Chu of the University of Houston raised the world record from 30° K to 90° K.

8. Incandescent Light Bulb—In 1879 Thomas Edison developed the first commercially viable light bulb. He was ridiculed throughout the effort by the mainstream press, engineering, and scientific communities. His breakthrough occurred in two months and increased the life of a bulb from 13 hours to 560 hours.

9. Boeing 777—The 777 is a commercial aircraft designed by the largest airplane manufacturer in the world. Boeing spent $4 billion using a new design process centered on teaming and computer models.

10. Apollo Moon Landing—The Apollo moon landing was one of the most difficult and costly projects humanity has ever undertaken. The rockets were a major portion of the design effort. The development of the Saturn V rocket used only two prototype launches before manned flight, compared to 91 prototypes for the Atlas rocket.

11. House—The family home in America is easy to design, but it is a major investment. Modifying existing designs is the normal design approach.

12. Central Arizona Project—The CAP is a 336 mile aqueduct built from the Colorado river to the central Arizona cities of Phoenix and Tucson. It cost $4.7 billion and took more than 20 years to build.

13. Great Pyramid at Giza—One of the Seven Wonders of the Ancient World, the Great Pyramid is still admired for its engineering. It was built around 2575 B.C. and took 20 years and 50,000 laborers.

14. New Car Factory—The design of new cars is one of the most costly ventures in modern industry. Japanese and American corporations do it differently. The Japanese spend an average of 46 months while the Americans take over 60 months. The difference can be attributed to the Japanese use of rapid prototyping; the seamless relationship between the suppliers, the design engineers, and production engineers; and the overall efficiency of their system.

15. Electric Vehicle—The General Motors Impact is an electric vehicle with impressive specifications for a battery operated car.

16. Batteries for Electric Vehicles—Batteries are preventing the widespread use of electric vehicles. Incremental design changes may eventually produce a satisfactory battery. However, a breakthrough in energy storage might be needed.

17. C3PO—This handy robot in the *Star Wars* film is an intractable design problem for Americans in the twentieth century.

18. Velcro—This unique fastener was created by serendipity, not by engineering design.

19. Manhattan Project—During World War II, our scientists were convinced that Hitler had the scientists and resources to design and build an atomic bomb. To counter this threat, the Americans designed and built the first atomic bombs.

20. Polaris Program—This case chronicles the development of the submarine ballistic missile fleet and the invention of project management and systems engineering.

21. Hubble Telescope—This beautiful instrument cost about a billion dollars to build and about a billion dollars to store. During its years of storage, no one ever tested it to see if it worked, i.e., there was no total system test. As a result, it cost about a billion dollars to fix.

REFERENCE

DEMING, W. EDWARDS, (1982), *Out of the Crisis*, Cambridge, MIT Center for Advanced Engineering Study.

2

DESIGN OF RESISTOR NETWORKS

In this case study, we design a network of resistors that will produce some specified resistance value. This problem has no efficient solution. Selecting the proper values of the resistors and the output of the network are important because of the difficulty in getting an exact value. Axial leaded resistors only come in fixed values (1.0, 1.2, 1.5, 1.8, 2.2, 2.7, 3.3, 3.9, 4.7, 5.6, 6.8, and 8.2 ohms). These values are then multiplied by a power of 10 to obtain a full range of possible resistance values. For the resistor network design problem, a given number of resistors is selected from the fixed list of values and then combined in parallel and/or serial networks to form a specified output. The problem then becomes: Can a resistance value R_1 be obtained from the available values? For example, using four resistors with the values given above, design a 19.8 Ohm network.

If we restrict our attention to only resistors in series, then the sum of the resistors would have to match some fixed value that would be set by the engineering requirements. If we consider the additional combinations possible from parallel connections, finding a solution will be more difficult, although the possibility of finding a feasible solution also becomes more likely. By enumerating all the possible combinations of resistance networks achievable in series or parallel using the 12 resistance values previously mentioned, the results in Figure 2-1 were obtained.

As the number of resistors available to build the network increases, so does the number of feasible solutions. This highlights an important aspect of design. As the complexity of a system increases, the chances of obtaining a feasible solution increases. This is why initial designs of most products are so complex. Engineers find it difficult to obtain a solution that meets all the necessary requirements, so they add complexity to the system until they find a system that does meet the requirements. (A good, "bad" example is a Rube Goldberg machine!) This often has a negative impact

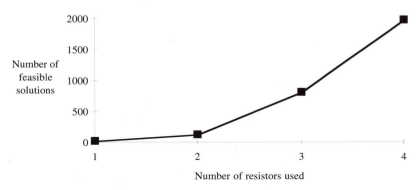

All combinations of 1, 2, 3, and 4 resistors in parallel and/or series

Number of feasible solutions

Number of resistors used

Figure 2-1 Number of possible solutions within 0.01 ohms.

on other resources and performance criteria for the problem. More resistors means higher cost, larger power requirements, larger physical space requirements, and decreased reliability. This is illustrated by Figure 2-2. The top graph shows all possible solutions in the range of 0.5 to 1.5 ohms using any two resistors from the list of 12. The presence of a bar means a solution within 0.01 ohms can be found. The middle graph shows the results using three resistors and the third shows the number of solutions found using four resistors.

Figure 2-3 shows how the feasible solution set grows. The percentage of feasible solutions obtainable within the given range increases with complexity.

As the complexity of the system increases so does the feasible solution space.

All combinations of 1 or 2 resistors in series or parallel.

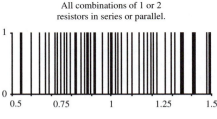

All combinations of 1, 2, or 3 resistors in series or parallel.

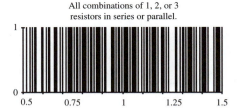

All combinations of 1, 2, 3, or 4 resistors in series or parallel.

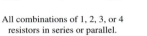

Figure 2-2 Solutions using a different number of resistors.

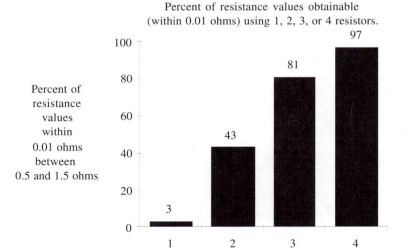

Figure 2-3   The feasible solutions grow with the number of resistors.

DESIGN DIFFICULTY AND RESOURCES SCORES

The following scores are from the viewpoint of an engineer wanting to compute and sketch one simple resistor network. For example, the 19.8 Ohm network described on the first page of this case study could be formed by connecting an 8.2 Ohm resistor in series with another 8.2 Ohm resistor in series with two 6.8 Ohm resistors connected in parallel.

Design Type	Knowledge Complexity	Steps	Quality	Quantity and Complexity	Aggressive Selling Price	Design Difficulty Total
1	1	1	1	1	1	6

Cost	Time	Infrastructure	Resources Total
1	1	1	3

REFERENCE

Handbook of Electrical Engineering. New York: McGraw Hill, 1992.

3

SIERRA TRAIN CONTROLLERS

Over the last two decades, more than 1000 students in Dr. Bahill's classes at Carnegie Mellon University and the University of Arizona have designed and built controllers to prevent two HO gauge model trains on overlapping loops from colliding. The system has two circles of track that intersect at two places. Four sensors have been mounted around the crossings to detect when a train has entered or exited the common area. Power can be turned on or off for each ring of track. The students must design and build controllers to monitor the sensors on the tracks and control power to the tracks in order to avoid collisions. The students build three different types of controllers. One design uses integrated circuits, wires, resistors, and a protoboard to form a hard wired controller. Another design uses an assembly language program. A final design uses a high level language, such as Pascal or C. In their final reports, students compare and contrast these divergent technologies. This project is called the Systems and Industrial Engineering RailRoad Assignment (SIERRA). The equipment that the students use in this assignment was designed and built by William J. Karnavas.

This case study will only discuss the hardware controllers. The components from which the students may select is unlimited if they purchase the parts themselves. However, most students opt to use the components in the laboratory. A list is given in Table 3-1.

The students first create a state diagram to satisfy the functional requirements. The simplest of these diagrams contains four states and the most complex built to date has six. The students choose their components and wire them on a protoboard. These systems are then subjected to tests by the laboratory's teaching assistant. All systems from two recent classes were different, and yet they all fulfilled the functional requirements provided to the students. Table 3-2 lists the number of states and

TABLE 3-1   Available Components
in the Lab.

Component Name	Description
SN7400	Quad 2 input NAND
SN7402	Quad 2 input NOR
SN7404	Hex inverters
SN7408	Quad 2 input AND
SN7420	Dual 4 input NAND
SN7421	Dual 4 input AND
SN7430	8 input NAND
SN7432	Quad 2 input OR
SN7473	Dual JK flip flops

the components used in five of these systems. Note that even the machines using the same number of states used different components.

From a collection of only nine components, the students designed five non-identical working systems. From an optimality viewpoint, some of the systems were cheaper than others and some did a better job of ensuring safety. However, all were in the feasible solution set and achieved the results of the lab work.

This highlights the difficult nature of the design process. The allocation of hardware components to functions can provide a large number of feasible solutions even when the system is simple and limited in scope. Because each potential customer may value a different feature provided in one system over another (i.e., cost versus maximum laps), recommending the best system becomes a multiobjective decision problem.

DESIGN DIFFICULTY AND RESOURCES SCORES

The following scores are from the viewpoint of the students beginning to design their controllers.

TABLE 3-2   Student Solutions.

Students Initials	Number of States	Components
R&L	5	7404, 7408, 7432, 7432, 7473, 7473
D&B	4	7408, 7432, 7432, 7473, 7473
S&B	6	7400, 7404, 7408, 7432, 7473
D&T	5	7408, 7421, 7421, 7432, 7473, 7473
D&K	5	7400, 7400, 7408, 7421, 7473, 7473

Design Type	Knowledge Complexity	Steps	Quality	Process Design	Aggressive Selling Price	Design Difficulty Total
2	2	1	1	1	1	8

Cost	Time	Infrastructure	Resources Total
1.5	1.5	1	4

REFERENCES

CHAPMAN, W.L., A.T. BAHILL, and A.W. WYMORE, *Engineering Modeling and Design*, Chapter 6, Boca Raton: CRC Press Inc., (1992).

4

BAT CHOOSER

Bat Chooser™ is a product developed by Bill Karnavas and Terry Bahill to determine the Ideal Bat Weight™ for a given baseball or softball player. It is an outgrowth of their studies on eye-hand coordination. It represents a product of moderate design difficulty developed by a very small company with limited resources.

Bat Chooser measures the speed of the bat at the point where it would meet the ball. It does this by positioning two parallel light beams in the path of the bat. By measuring the time it takes for the bat to pass between the two beams, Bat Chooser computes the speed and then the momentum of the bat.

The original prototype was built in May 1988. The frame supporting the structure was made of wood. It took approximately 80 hours to build this prototype over a one month period. The materials cost $500. This prototype was used to verify the functionality of the system as well as the form.

The measured bat speed was used in the conservation of momentum equation and the coefficient of restitution equations to compute the amount of energy transferred to the ball by the bat. The equation for the conservation of momentum is:

$$W_{ball} V_{ball-before} + W_{bat} V_{bat-before} = W_{ball} V_{ball-after} + W_{bat} V_{bat-after}$$

where W represents weight, V represents velocity, and *before* and *after* mean before and after the bat-ball collision. Next we used a property associated with the energy loss in a collision, a property called the Coefficient of Restitution (CoR). One popular definition of CoR is the ratio of the relative speed of the objects after the collision to their relative speed before the collision:

$$CoR = \frac{V_{ball-after} - V_{bat-after}}{V_{ball-before} - V_{bat-before}}$$

When the equations are combined, the velocity of the ball after it is hit by the bat becomes:

$$V_{ball-after} = \frac{(W_{ball} - CoR\ W_{bat})V_{ball-before} + (W_{bat} + CoR\ W_{bat})V_{bat-before}}{W_{ball} + W_{bat}}$$

Using these equations, the maximum batted ball speed for a given player is computed. This is then converted into the Ideal Bat Weight for each batter.

The prototype successfully measured the swing speed, so plans were made for a preproduction unit. This one was made with a metal frame. The San Francisco Giants baseball team tried it out in February 1989, during spring training. Ideal Bat Weight recommendations were made for all the players. Over 70% of the players were using a bat in the recommended range.

A production version was then built. This unit exchanged the light bulbs (used to measure bat speed) with lasers. This was a continuous improvement change because the lasers were easier to aim and did not need to be focused. The signal to noise ratio was also better; it provided more consistent results. The production unit cost $2,000 to manufacture and was marketed to a baseball bat manufacturer. Bat Chooser is ideally set up in a sporting goods store or a sports park. A potential buyer of a baseball bat is measured by Bat Chooser and told the Ideal Bat Weight.

Systems Engineering Mistakes

Bat Chooser was designed because the engineers thought they could do it. They thought that the technology push could make it a commercial success. This is seldom the case. Rather, market pull usually produces success. Bat Chooser was a technical success, but a market failure. The professional baseball players would not use it. They implied, "I earn a million dollars playing ball for six months. Why should I accept advice from a poor professor? Besides my grandfather used a 33 ounce bat and I expect my grandchildren to also use a 33 ounce bat." Furthermore, the professional baseball teams do not have money to spend on research, training, or development. All of their money is tied up in player salaries. And Little League players and common folk could not afford it. Before designing a new product, you should make sure that someone wants to buy it and has the money to do so.

DESIGN DIFFICULTY AND RESOURCES SCORES

The following scores are from the viewpoint of Karnavas and Bahill when they began designing a machine to recommend the ideal baseball bat.

Design Type	Knowledge Complexity	Steps	Quality	Process Design	Aggressive Selling Price	Design Difficulty Total
6	5	1	3	1	2	18

Cost	Time	Infrastructure	Resources Total
2	3	2	7

Bat Chooser is protected by U.S. Patent Number 5,118,102 issued June 2, 1992.

REFERENCES

BAHILL, A.T., and M. MORNA FRETIAS, "Two methods for recommending bat weights." *Annals of Biomedical Engineering,* vol. 23: pp. 436–444 (1995).

BAHILL, A.T., and W.J. KARNAVAS, "Determining ideal baseball bat weights using muscle force-velocity relationships." *Biological Cybernetics,* vol. 62: pp. 89–97 (1989).

BAHILL, A.T., and W.J. KARNAVAS, "The Ideal Baseball Bat." *New Scientist,* vol. 130, no. 1763: pp. 26–31 (1991).

WATTS, R.G., and A.T. BAHILL, *Keep Your Eye on the Ball: The Science and Folklore of Baseball,* New York: W.H. Freeman and Co., 1990.

5

SCHEDULING A
PINEWOOD DERBY

Since the 1950s over 80 million Cub Scouts have built five-ounce wooden cars and raced them in Pinewood Derbies. Pinewood Derbies have traditionally been single elimination tournaments where only the winner from each race proceeded to the next round. This pleased scouts with fast cars, but for the unlucky majority it meant a single race, waiting for the awards to be announced, and then going home.

Karnavas and Bahill changed the race format for their Cub Scout pack to a round robin, as shown in Table 5-1, where each car is identified with a letter, e.g., A, B, C, ..., L. The objective was to allow each scout to race more often and race throughout the whole event. We decided to use six rounds, because that would give each car two runs in each lane and still keep the whole event reasonably short. Switching from an elimination tournament to a round robin produced two side benefits: the scouts raced more of their friends; and lane biases were ameliorated, because each car ran in each lane the same number of times.

This schedule looks simple, but it took us eight years to derive it. Let's see why. Originally we asked for schedules where each car raced in each of six rounds, each car raced twice in each lane, and no cars raced each other more than once. We used many programs and many computers (including six uninterrupted weeks of searching on an AT&T 3B2), but we could not find a perfect schedule. Five different experts in scheduling theory were consulted. All said they could find a solution. In fact, they all claimed to have already solved a similar problem at some point in their careers. They were asked to provide the solution to this problem, but none did. Subsequently, we discovered that there is no schedule that meets the above requirements for 12 cars.

To see why, let us first examine the requirement that no car race another car more than once for a 12 car derby. Consider first car A.

**TABLE 5-1 12 Car Round
Robin Schedule.**

	Lane 1 Car	Lane 2 Car	Lane 3 Car
Round 1:			
Race 1	A	B	C
Race 2	D	E	F
Race 3	G	H	K
Race 4	I	J	L
Round 2:			
Race 1	C	L	E
Race 2	B	H	J
Race 3	F	G	I
Race 4	K	D	A
Round 3:			
Race 1	K	I	C
Race 2	G	E	B
Race 3	J	F	A
Race 4	H	L	D
Round 4:			
Race 1	B	D	I
Race 2	L	A	E
Race 3	J	K	G
Race 4	H	C	F
Round 5:			
Race 1	C	J	D
Race 1	F	B	K
Race 1	E	I	H
Race 1	A	G	L
Round 6:			
Race 1	E	K	J
Race 2	L	F	B
Race 3	D	C	G
Race 4	I	A	H

In the first round, let car A race cars B and C.

In the second round, let car A race cars D and E.

In the third round, let car A race cars F and G.

In the fourth round, let car A race cars H and I.

In the fifth round, let car A race cars J and K.

In the sixth round, let car A race cars L and Who?

There is no one left for car A to race. Therefore, it is impossible to schedule a 12 car round robin where no car races another car more than once. Although it is harder to prove, it is also impossible to have every car race every other car.

When we were making schedules, we did not know that a 12 car schedule was impossible; we only knew that we could not find it. But we had to have some schedule, because the Pinewood Derby was going to be held and we had to run it. So we relaxed our requirements in order to get an acceptable, but not perfect, solution to the problem.

A lesson can be learned from this case study. During the design process, when it becomes clear that an easy solution is not at hand, the best approach is to relax the requirements and obtain any suboptimal solution. The continuous improvement approach is applied to this suboptimal solution to try to move it toward optimality. Brainstorming to achieve a breakthrough which produces a perfect schedule will require lots of time with possibly no deliverable product. The best approach is to obtain a deliverable first, then iterate the design to get a better solution. If something is infeasible by the statement of the problem, then a solution can only be found by changing the problem statement, not by investigating many possible solutions.

We now understand this scheduling problem better, so we can state the requirements better. As the cars arrive, each is assigned a letter, e.g., A, B, C, ..., L. If there are only 10 cars in a divisional race, then a 12 car schedule is used, but no cars are labeled K or L. For a 12 car round robin there are six mandatory requirements:

1. each car shall race in each of six rounds,
2. each car shall run twice in each lane,
3. there shall be three cars in each race,
4. no cars should race each other more than twice,
5. even if cars K and L are missing, no car will ever race without at least one opponent, and
6. every car shall race every other car, except cars K and L shall not race each other.

The first round should be almost in alphabetical order so that the scouts have some control over whom they race. The schedule of Table 5-1 satisfies these requirements.

Table 5-2 shows a schedule for a 15 car, six round divisional race. As the cars arrive, each is assigned a letter, e.g., A, B, C, ..., O. If there are only 13 cars in a divisional race, then the 15 car schedule is to be used, but no cars will be labeled N or O. There are six mandatory requirements:

1. each car shall race in each of six rounds,
2. each car shall run twice in each lane,
3. three cars shall be scheduled in each race,
4. no cars should race each other more than once,
5. even if cars N and O are missing, no car will ever race without at least one opponent, and
6. cars N and O shall not race each other.

The first round should be almost alphabetical so that the scouts have some control over whom they race.

The 12 and 15 car schedules were difficult to generate. Most of our scheduling techniques failed to find such schedules. The schedules of Tables 5-1 and 5-2 were

TABLE 5-2 15 Car Round
Robin Schedule.

	Lane 1 Car	Lane 2 Car	Lane 3 Car
Round 1:			
Race 1	A	B	C
Race 2	D	E	F
Race 3	G	H	I
Race 4	J	K	N
Race 5	M	L	O
Round 2:			
Race 1	H	A	E
Race 2	B	O	G
Race 3	K	L	C
Race 4	I	F	J
Race 5	N	M	D
Round 3:			
Race 1	L	F	H
Race 2	G	D	J
Race 3	C	E	N
Race 4	A	I	O
Race 5	K	M	B
Round 4:			
Race 1	D	C	I
Race 2	F	N	A
Race 3	E	G	M
Race 4	J	B	L
Race 5	H	O	K
Round 5:			
Race 1	N	G	L
Race 1	O	C	F
Race 1	E	I	K
Race 1	M	J	A
Race 5	B	D	H
Round 6:			
Race 1	L	A	D
Race 2	O	J	E
Race 3	I	N	B
Race 4	F	K	G
Race 5	C	H	M

generated by Van Voorhees using genetic algorithms. For round robin races with 18 or more cars, deriving schedules was easy, and such schedules are given in Chapman, Bahill, and Wymore (1992). The requirements for schedules for 18 or more cars are the same as for 15 cars.

Systems Engineering Mistakes

The major Systems Engineering mistake that we made on this project was a failure to validate the requirements. That is, we did not prove that it was possible to satisfy the system requirements before we started designing. We were trying to design an impossible system.

DESIGN DIFFICULTY AND RESOURCES SCORES

These scores are from the viewpoint of the two naive engineers starting to create schedules for a Pinewood Derby.

Design Type	Knowledge Complexity	Steps	Quality	Process Design	Aggressive Selling Price	Design Difficulty Total
3	2	2	2	1	1	11

Cost	Time	Infrastructure	Resources Total
2	2	1.5	5.5

REFERENCES

BAHILL, A.T., and W.J. KARNAVAS, "Reducing State Space Search Time: Scheduling in the Classic AI Challenge." *AI Expert*, pp. 29–35, Sept. 1993.

CHAPMAN, W.L., A.T. BAHILL, and A.W. WYMORE, *Engineering Modeling and Design*. Boca Raton: CRC Press Inc., Chapter 5. (1992).

6

SECOND OPINION

Childhood Stuttering: A Second Opinion™ is a decision support system that was designed to assist speech language clinicians, or students in training, to evaluate and arrive at an appropriate diagnostic decision for young children who are suspected of stuttering. Richard F. Curlee was the domain expert and K. Bharathan was the knowledge engineer. *Second Opinion*® went through a nine year period of occasional development with a panel of clinicians, who had extensive experience in childhood stuttering, and computer programmers who were skilled in artificial intelligence techniques (Bahill, Bharathan, and Curlee, 1995).

Work on the decision support system began in 1985. The goal was to have enough case studies with diagnoses in the knowledge base to allow comparison of a wide range of situations. The first system was built in a few months and tested using an expert in childhood stuttering. This required a large portion of his time, so a validation technique that relied on test cases was used. Using this method, the programmers could test the design. The goal of any test system is to create test trajectories that will exercise every state. In the case of decision support systems, it is the rule base that is exercised. The cases from the experts did not always use extreme data so artificial cases had to be created to test the entire system. This initial prototype was abandoned after some use.

The second system was developed in 1987. The system was more sophisticated than the first and much more complete. In addition, the programmers used a different programming language. Graduate students contributed to system development and as they changed, the character of the system changed. This is a common trait of any system with a long development cycle. Once again, testing the system became a major concern. It is estimated that half of the system design process was test and validation. This is not common for hardware systems, but it is for software systems. This is because software systems are large finite state machines. To truly test the system, each state must be tried. A system with thousands of possible states requires sophisticated testing. The Analytic Hierarchy Process (Saaty, 1980) was used to extract knowledge from the expert. The technique forced the experts to exhaustively compare attributes relative to each other. This knowledge was then used to test the systems.

The third version of Second Opinion was ready in 1989. This system was again larger and more sophisticated than its ancestors. The testing was done using an automated program called Validator. This product checked for syntax errors, unused rules, facts and questions, incorrectly used legal values, redundant constructs, rules that used illegal values, wrong instantiations, and multiple methods for obtaining values for expressions. Validator helped to decrease the time spent debugging the third version.

The fourth version of Second Opinion was ready in 1991 and was also tested using Validator. In addition, five experts in speech diagnosis checked the system's results and recommended changes.

A half-million dollar grant from the National Institutes of Health (NIH) financed the fifth version of Second Opinion, which was completed in 1992. The testing revealed wide divergence between experts in their evaluations of the cases. To better test the system, 25 case studies were mailed to the five experienced clinicians. Based on their evaluations, it was proven that Second Opinion gave as good an evaluation as the experts. In fact, the experts did not all agree on cases and there was actually a wider divergence between the experts than between the experts and the software. The software was validated, packaged, and put on the market.

This case illustrates two important elements of system design. The first is that design is iterative. Each prototype developed was more acceptable to the customer and a better product. The second is that validating the system to the customer's requirements is essential to ensure product satisfaction. When the system must satisfy a wide variety of customers, it is difficult to fully define and accurately reflect all of the requirements. Indeed the experts themselves changed their opinions from one prototype to the next (Bahill, Bharathan, and Curlee, 1992). However, most companies can never afford to develop five versions of the product as was done here. The average is four. The first is often called the alpha version (or the model), the second is the beta version (or the prototype), the third is the preproduction unit, and the last is the production version. Some software companies skip the preproduction model. This usually results in a version 1.1 released a short time after the initial offering. This is done to get a quicker financial return but it often leaves inferior products with some customers.

Systems Engineering Mistakes

Formal Systems Engineering was not performed on Second Opinion, because it was a small project and the requirements were all in the head of the knowledge engineer. However, just before the system was released commercially, it was discovered that an important rule had disappeared from the rule base. We did not expect rules to disappear as the system was updated and enlarged. Formal configuration management might have prevented its disappearance.

DESIGN DIFFICULTY AND RESOURCES SCORES

The following scores are from the viewpoint of Bahill and Curlee at the beginning of the effort to design a decision support system to help with the diagnoses and prognoses of young children who may have begun to stutter. They did not intend to finance the project out of their pockets. They knew that they would have to get a grant from the NIH in order to complete the project.

Design Type	Knowledge Complexity	Steps	Quality	Process Design	Aggressive Selling Price	Design Difficulty Total
5	6	3	5	3	2	24

Cost	Time	Infrastructure	Resources Total
2	8	3	13

REFERENCES

BAHILL, A.T., *Verifying and Validating Personal Computer-Based Expert Systems.* Englewood Cliffs: Prentice Hall, 1991.

BAHILL, A.T., K. BHARATHAN, and R. F. CURLEE, "How the testing techniques for a decision support system changed over nine years." *IEEE Transactions on Systems, Man and Cybernetics Society* SMC 25: pp. 1533–1542 (1995).

BAHILL, A.T., K. BHARATHAN, and R.F. CURLEE, "Making an Expert System Changes the Expert." *Recent Trends in Research, Education, and Applications,* ed. M. Jamshidi, R. Lumia, J. Mullins, and M. Shahinpoor. New York: ASME Press, vol. 4, pp. 711–716. Paper presented at the proceedings of the 4th International Symposium on Robotics and Manufacturing, Santa Fe, November 11–13, 1992.

JAFAR M., and A.T. BAHILL, "Interactive verification of knowledge-based systems." *IEEE Expert,* vol. 8, no 1: pp. 25–32 (1993).

SAATY, T.L., *The Analytic Hierarchy Process.* New York: McGraw-Hill, 1980.

7

AMERICAN AIRLINES
SCHEDULING

American Airlines is the largest air carrier in the United States. It uses optimization techniques to schedule crews, gates, and airplanes. Large Integer Programming models are used extensively for scheduling. This approach works well because the system of routing crews, gates, and airplanes is robust and flexible. American Airlines personnel can change many parameters easily and implement a solution almost immediately.

American Airlines has an Operations Research Department that creates algorithms for scheduling flights and crews for the airline. Because of the demand on resources, the more complicated algorithms are run in a relaxed simplex mode (which is not NP-complete) rather than the Integer Programming mode (which is NP-complete).

NP-complete (also called NP-hard) means that the problem cannot be solved by brute force with an algorithm that generates a solution in nonpolynomial time. Or if you wish a trite analogy: if you had an infinite number of monkeys, working on an infinite number of typewriters, they probably could not find a solution.

The solutions generated by American Airlines' computers are much better than manual scheduling, although American Airlines concedes that they are not optimal. The programs they use for scheduling are not innovative or complicated. It is the *size* of the problem that makes solutions difficult to find.

American Airlines has over 2,300 flights per day to over 150 different cities utilizing over 500 jet aircraft. Assigning aircraft types to routes is the most critical and sophisticated of problems.

"Except for the smallest fleets, it is not possible to obtain a globally optimal solution because the problem is too large. Combinatorial problems begin to explode for problems

larger than 100 segments and become unmanageable for 200 or more. It is therefore necessary to work in sub problems small enough that a reasonably-sized matrix can be built and solved optimally. To a large extent, it is desirable to solve as large a sub problem as computer resources will allow. The limit on size will depend on the software design or on constraints of available storage or processor power." (Abara, 1989)

Crew assignments are another complex problem. Hotel and per-diem costs for crews (when not at their home airport) are a large portion of the costs of the airline. Yet restrictions based on FAA rules, union rules, and experience of pilots and attendants make this a difficult problem to optimize cost-effectively. The pairing of crews with airplanes is a major scheduling effort that requires another relaxed simplex solution (rather than an attempt for optimality). In this case, each airplane fleet is broken into separate sub problems and then the routes within the fleets are reduced even further so that the computer can handle the scheduling. The selection of the pairings within the sub problems is very difficult.

"Intelligent selection of pairings to comprise the sub problem has been surprisingly difficult. A random selection is unbiased and assures that a particular pairing will be used in many sub problems in a long run. The perplexing aspect is that we have not been very successful in finding a selection strategy better than random." (Gershkoff, 1989)

The problem of partitioning is also difficult. At the beginning, a solution was needed and a random ordering turned out to be a good starting point. Once a sub problem solution is found, finding a better one is not any easier. This part of the problem is not robust.

"A major concern using any sub problem approach is that different sequences of sub problems can lead to different solutions because of the presence of local minima. There is no way of knowing a priori which sequence will provide the best solution." (Anbil, Gelman, Patty, and Tanga, 1991)

Table 7-1 shows the savings from running their relaxed Integer Programming sub problems on an IBM 3090 for 300 minutes. The human scheduling department continued to create their schedules while the software was developed and tested. The solutions achieved by the software were compared later to the manually developed schedules in use. The computer algorithms would have saved money if they had been

TABLE 7-1   Results of Computer Scheduling.

Monthly Schedule	Manual Solution	Computer Solution After 300 Minutes	Missed Savings
Jan. 1986	$2,025,390/mo.	$1,801,890/mo.	$222,000/mo.
Feb. 1986	$2,073,930/mo.	$1,942,980/mo.	$129,450/mo.
Mar. 1986	$2,003,190/mo.	$1,857,030/mo.	$144,660/mo.
Apr. 1986	$2,120,610/mo.	$1,966,800/mo.	$153,810/mo.

implemented. With this type of problem, even better solutions can be obtained with more resources (more computer time yields better solutions). This situation is highly complex and resource bound. The number of design steps to create the schedule grows exponentially and eats up the available resources.

Clearly a solution to solve these difficult problems is not within reach. The design of these schedules is no less complex and no less relevant than the design of the hardware. Indeed the operation of an existing system is often (though not always) a difficult problem in itself. Design can be for schedules, services, and manpower, as well as for hardware. In this case study, if American Airlines had put more money into the design effort, they would have yielded little additional benefit. Instead, placing money into more powerful computers was the answer to get better solutions, although there is a cost-effective limit here as well.

DESIGN DIFFICULTY AND RESOURCES SCORES

The following scores are from the viewpoint of American Airlines preparing to develop new scheduling algorithms.

Design Type	Knowledge Complexity	Steps	Quality	Process Design	Aggressive Selling Price	Design Difficulty Total
6	4	4	2	2	1	19

Cost	Time	Infrastructure	Resources Total
3	5	5	13

REFERENCES

ABARA, J., "Applying Integer Programming to the Fleet Assignment Problem." *Interfaces,* vol. 19, no. 4: pp. 20–28 (1989).

ANBIL, R. E., GELMAN, B. PATTY, and R. TANGA, "Recent Advances in Crew-Pairing Optimization at American Airlines." *Interfaces,* vol. 21, no. 1: pp. 62–74 (1991).

GERSHKOFF, I., "Optimizing Flight Crew Schedules." *Interfaces,* vol. 19, no. 4: pp. 29–42 (1989).

V. MARQUEZ, A., "American Airlines Arrival Slot Allocation System (ASAS)." *Interfaces,* vol. 21, no. 1: pp. 42–61 (1991).

8

SUPERCONDUCTORS

Superconductors are materials that exhibit no resistance to the flow of electrical current when cooled. They were first discovered by Onnes in 1911 when he cooled Mercury to 4 K.

Research into finding superior superconductors is a good example of the breakthrough system design process. After the initial discovery, there was steady but limited interest displayed in superconductors. The problem was that the low temperature was too costly to maintain and the usefulness at such temperatures was limited. From 1911 to 1970, work had progressed so that the critical temperature was raised to 23 K using an alloy of the exotic metal niobium. Most commercial research was limited to actual products and few researchers spent any real time or money on the problem. In 1975, a researcher at DuPont discovered a barium alloy that exhibited superconduction at 13 K. Although this was a lower temperature than previously recorded, it was important because it did not use niobium. Using this information, two IBM researchers in Switzerland, Bednorz and Müller (working without the backing of their own company), discovered an alloy of barium-lanthanum in 1986 that exhibited superconduction at 30 K. This result was published in November 1986. The actual time spent to make major improvements using this breakthrough was remarkably short once a clue to superconduction became known. See Figure 8-1.

Paul Chu at the University of Houston immediately saw the value of the barium copper oxide. He stopped all other work, got several helpers, and worked night and day on finding a better superconductor. Within four months Chu had developed a superconductor that worked at 90 K. Researchers at AT&T, IBM, and other laboratories replicated these results. By 1993 Chu developed an alloy that became a superconductor at 153 K. This shows a typical breakthrough; he had little progress for years then suddenly he had numerous improvements in a short time. The steady

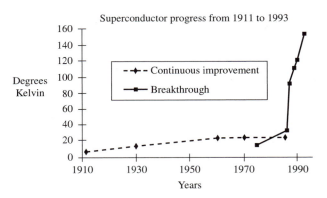

Figure 8-1   Superconductor history.

progress was achieved by methodical research on many types of alloys. Many varieties of copper oxides were tried, yielding improvement after improvement. This was a breadth, rather than a depth, search. The product was stuck at a local minimum with niobium. By moving away from this minima down to 13 K, a clue on a new alloy led to an amazing breakthrough. In the superconductor case study, the resources of many researchers and companies were exhausted, but the persistence of a few (the IBM researchers) led them to a Nobel Prize.

From an engineer's viewpoint, superconductors have three important temperatures: Above 77 Kelvin, because they can use liquid nitrogen (a cheap coolant); above 160 K, because they can use inexpensive Freon driven refrigeration units; and at room temperature, where no cooling is necessary. Essentially, all technologies in between these temperatures become less important. Once the copper oxides with critical temperatures above 77 Kelvin were discovered, the manufacturing requirements became important. At 77 K there are problems with the flexibility of the material and magnetic vortices that are caused by magnetic fields introduced from outside the superconductor that disrupt the free flow of current. To solve this, a variant using yttrium-barium-copper oxide was developed. This worked well but wasn't flexible enough to be used to make wire. After three years of research, bismuth-strontium-calcium-copper oxide was developed. However, it was a failure because the alloy required cooling to 25 Kelvin to be free of magnetic vortices. Hence, thallium-barium-calcium-copper oxide was developed. This is currently the most promising alloy for manufacturing, although with a critical temperature of 80 Kelvin, it does not hold the temperature record.

The search for manufacturability was essentially a multicriteria decision problem. After a feasible solution to the major limiting constraint, i.e., temperature, was found; the search for solutions around other constraints began. In this case, flexibility and the magnetic vortices. The optimum configuration of these constraints translates into an economic concern for any company wanting to develop a product. The search of the feasible design space will continue in a predictable way.

In the superconductor race, Paul Chu was able to duplicate the results of IBM in less than a week. AT&T took two weeks to duplicate the results. After that, both teams began a breadth search around the new alloy. Sometimes 15 or 20 new alloys were tried in a single week. All of these could have been tried before the breakthrough but nobody knew to search in this area.

The breakthrough by Müller and Bednorz was possible because Müller was an IBM fellow who could research anything he wanted, and Bednorz was a graduate student (or a postdoc assigned to Müller) and he could research anything they chose. Although Holton et al. (1996) pretend that this is a typical case of scientific discovery, we would like to point out that breakthrough designs are extremely rare, because few people have the freedom to investigate whatever they want.

In searching for superconductors, the same shotgun search approach continued to be used. In 1996 *Discover* magazine gave their first prize for technical innovation to Xiang and Schultz, who developed a technique for making and testing up to 10,000 new potential superconductors at the same time on a one-inch-square grid (*Discover*, 1996).

DESIGN DIFFICULTY AND RESOURCES SCORES

The following scores are from the viewpoint of the engineers in 1986 trying to find materials with superconduction temperatures above that of liquid Nitrogen.

Design Type	Knowledge Complexity	Steps	Quality	Process Design	Aggressive Selling Price	Design Difficulty Total
15	10	2	3	2	1	33

Cost	Time	Infrastructure	Resources Total
2	2	4	8

REFERENCES

"Micro-managing." *Discover* p. 72, July 1996.

HAZEN, R.M., *The Breakthrough, The Race for the Superconductor*. New York: Summit Books, 1988.

HOLTEN, G., H. CHANG, and E. JURKOWITZ, "How a scientific discovery is made: a case history." *American Scientist,* vol. 84: pp. 364–375 (1996).

YAM, P., "Trends in Superconductivity: Current Events." *Scientific American,* pp. 119–126, December 1993.

"TRW Superconductor Reduces Satellite Power." *Aviation Week & Space Technology,* p. 56, December 6, 1993.

MALOZERNOFF, A.P., "Superconducting Wires Get Hotter." *IEEE Spectrum,* pp. 26–30, December 1993.

"Fact vs Fantasy: Ceramic Superconductors Scrutinized." *IEEE Spectrum,* vol. 25 no. 5: pp. 30–41, (May 1988).

THE INCANDESCENT
LIGHT BULB

Thomas Alva Edison was America's most prolific inventor. He earned 1,093 U.S. patents. In the fall of 1878, he was on a hunting trip in the western United States when talk around the campfire turned to the electric light. His current inventions were the telephone switchboard and the phonograph, neither of which he enjoyed due to his near deafness. He became captivated with the idea of creating a commercially successful light and vowed he would succeed.

The electric light was nothing new. The first was invented in 1808 by Humphrey Davis. This was an arc lamp; it used high amperage sparks that arced between two pieces of coal. By 1844 these flickering and smelly lights were used to light the Paris Opera, and in 1858 they were used in light houses in England. Due to the high amperage current needed for the light and the easy availability of natural gas, the gas lamp was much more useful and economical. In 1876, an American named Jablochkoff used 200 carbon rods in an inert gas to create a glowing lamp that lasted only a few hours. The press was ecstatic, but the system destroyed the carbon rods quickly (which was why there were 200 of them). Nothing practical would come of this attempt and cynicism set in. Many said Ohms law ($E = I \times R$) prohibited the creation of an electric lamp, because all available generators created very high amperage, which would waste a lot of power in the transmission line.

The leading man in arc lamps at that time was Moses Farmer. In 1877, Edison wrote Farmer and said he knew nothing about the subject, but was interested. When Edison returned from his hunting trip at the end of 1878, he set out to develop an electric light; but he still had no background in the area and only a vague idea of Farmer's work. The 32 year old Edison had two main assistants, who were really co-inventors: 34 year old Charles Batchelor and 26 year old Francis Upton (plus another 15 or so technicians). They were able to develop five working ideas in two weeks.

Based on nothing but his ideas, Edison interested some New York bankers and they capitalized him at $300,000 because of his reputation. But, despite his bragging, he had no prototypes and had never built a light before. He quickly ran into trouble. The largest problem was that the metals he used as filaments (he called them "burners") melted quickly. Although he was able to get a bulb working, he was unable to keep it working for more than a few minutes. So he concentrated on platinum filaments, since they had the highest melting point of any metal then available. Upton told Edison that a light would have to sell for $97 (in 1879 dollars) with the platinum filament, but that did not deter him. Edison spent several days calling mining companies, trying to convince them they could get platinum cheaper if they only looked for more mines! As his biographer later wrote about Edison,

> *"That his scheme was impractical was not as important as it might seem—more frequently than not, his innovations started out technically in the wilderness."* (Conot, 1979)

One of the first critical insights was that a low resistance filament (< 0.1 ohms) required a high amperage that wasted power in the transmission lines. Therefore Edison sought materials with a higher resistance. Then, in order to get a decent amount of light, he had to invent a new high-voltage low-amperage generator. Edison put his assistant Batchelor to work on this new generator. It was developed by February 1879. Until then, Siemens built the best generator, which was 55% efficient. This new generator was 80% efficient and could easily handle the load of an entire house by putting out a higher voltage.

The next major breakthrough was the realization that the element should burn in a vacuum. At the time, vacuum pumps were not good; so Edison's other assistant, Upton used some of Edison's ideas, and invented a new pump that was vastly better than any available. Despite the vacuum, the platinum filaments, now coated with an assortment of oxides to keep them from disintegrating, wore out quickly. The investors were disheartened, and Edison was out of money. His critics crowed about how little he knew about electricity and science. Indeed Edison himself said,

> *"I do not depend on figures at all. I try an experiment and reason out the result, somehow, by methods which I cannot explain."*

He depended on Upton, who was college educated, to keep him from doing anything stupid. In essence, he tried anything unless Upton could prove that it was totally infeasible.

Edison spent a fruitless summer of long nights with no progress and little contact with his family. Then, on September 26, 1879, Edison was finally able to get a $2^1/_2$ inch platinum-iridium spiral wire coated with magnesium oxide to burn in a vacuum at 8 candela for 13 hours and 38 minutes. It was a world record—and the end of the road for platinum.

At the time, gas lamps produced about 12 candela. This was roughly Edison's goal for the electric light. (By comparison, a modern 100 Watt electric light bulb produces 140 candela by heating a Tungsten filament to 3000 K).

Knowing he needed a higher resistance element, Edison reluctantly switched to carbon filaments on October 11, 1879. Many people used carbon in arc lamps. However, the carbon always burned up in the atmosphere. The decision to try carbon was based on parallel work being done on telephones, plus the results of a little known experiment done in England in 1860. Edison's team immediately discovered an amazing fact: As the temperature in carbon increased, the resistance decreased. In essence, there was a built in temperature regulator to keep the element from burning out. The element could glow at an amazingly high temperature of over 5300 K. The next month was a mad rush. With only a few hours' sleep, Edison and his entire staff built lamp after lamp trying to find the magic formula. Dozens of prototypes relied only on intuition with little science or math backing each effort. Finally, on November 28, 1879, Lamp #89 burned at 16 candela for over 14 hours.

Giddy with delight, Edison staged a massive demonstration on Christmas night 1879. Using over 60 lamps manufactured hurriedly over three weeks (with less than a 30% yield), he lit six houses, his laboratory, and an entire street. The age of electricity had arrived. By the end of January 1880, he had a bulb that lasted for 560 hours. (Modern bulbs last an average of 2,000 hours.) Edison's one year effort took electric bulbs from 10 minutes to 33,600 minutes. In the 100 years since, engineers have managed only an additional gain of a factor of four. Figure 9-1 summarizes Edison's success.

In retrospect, Edison and his team developed at least three major inventions. A generator good enough for commercial use, the best vacuum pump in the world, and the electric light. Any of these inventions would have been remarkable. However, they were of little interest to Edison because they were only developed to meet his goal.

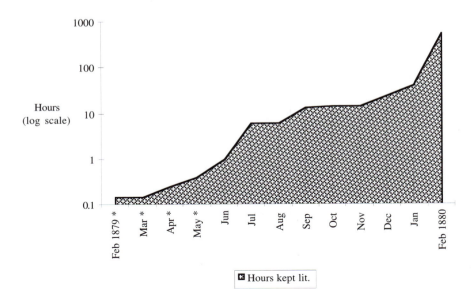

Figure 9-1   Hours Edison kept a light lit.

As with the case of the superconductor a century later, Edison and his team worked night and day to solve a problem that others said could not be done. They were not the first to work in the area, nor was the scientific community behind them. They groped for solutions and built hundreds of prototypes on nothing but intuition and guesswork. They were extremely motivated and inventive, but not well funded. Indeed the project almost bankrupted Edison.

Breakthroughs appear, not when they are well funded and reasoned, but when a group of talented and dedicated people are determined to solve a problem. The implication for the system design process is that the only way to achieve a massive improvement in technology is to motivate talented people, give them some resources (although not everything they want), and then leave them alone. There were no managers, no finance people, and no marketing people: only engineers and scientists with clearly defined goals for success and a try-anything atmosphere. For a computer to attempt this seems impossible. Yet the probabilistic jumps in some algorithms (simulated annealing, fuzzy sets), if backed by a sufficient knowledge base (artificial intelligence), may prove to be the right formula to solve the most intractable problems.

DESIGN DIFFICULTY AND RESOURCES SCORES

The following scores are from the viewpoint of Edison embarking on the project in 1878. We did not include the invention of the vacuum pump and the high-voltage generator.

Design Type	Knowledge Complexity	Steps	Quality	Process Design	Aggressive Selling Price	Design Difficulty Total
14	5	4	2	4	4	33

Cost	Time	Infrastructure	Resources Total
5	3	2	10

REFERENCES

CONOT, R., *A Streak of Luck, A Biography of Thomas Alva Edison*. New York: Seaview Books, 1979.

FRIEDEL, R., "Great Inventions That Changed The World." *American Heritage,* pp 26–32, 1994.

10

BOEING 777

In 1995 the Boeing Aircraft Company delivered their first 777, which is between the size of the 767 and the huge 747. Competition forced Boeing to enter this market. They were not interested in creating another product that competed with their other lines. However, the Airbus consortium in Europe came out with the A-340 and McDonnell Douglas came out with the MD-11, both of which are larger than the 767. Since Boeing is the number one manufacturer of commercial aircraft in the world, they had to respond to the competitive push. The new aircraft needed to sell for about $100 million per production copy.

The initial desire of Boeing was to create a stretch version of the 767. They called this the 767-X. After interviewing their major customers, Delta, American, United, and Nippon Airways, Boeing decided that this was not a large enough airplane. The customers wanted an aircraft with at least 350 seats, but they wanted it smaller than the 747. The wingspan on the 747 is so large that it cannot be accommodated at many airports. Boeing decided they needed a new airplane that would have several versions, which could span the range between the 767 and the 747. The largest version of the aircraft would rival the smallest 747; therefore, they needed a large wingspan of 197.7 feet. But this wingspan is still too large for many airports; so to keep the size down (so the plane would fit in as many taxiways as possible) and still retain the seating capacity, Boeing decided on a folding wing option similar to that used by Navy airplanes on aircraft carriers. By hinging the wings at the ends so they can fold up when landed, the wingspan is reduced to 155.2 feet. Nippon Airways did not like this design, so they forced Boeing to consider a version without folded wings. Boeing responded with two wing designs: one fixed and one capable of folding.

One of the major advantages Boeing hoped to gain from the 777 over its potential rivals was fuel economy. The 777 has two engines, the MD-11 has three, and the

A-340 has four. The use of newer engine technologies, light weight metals, and composite materials on the horizontal tail has reduced the 777's weight by 20% compared with a 747 of similar size. The light metals are new. Alcoa developed a new aluminum alloy that provides slightly better strength with less weight. However, most of the aircraft's weight savings come from titanium. Although more expensive than aluminum, titanium is lighter. This results in savings in fuel cost over the expected life cycle of the aircraft. New alloys with higher strength will be used on the engine exhaust nozzles, the main landing gear, and the flap tracks on the wings. The use of composite materials is also new for Boeing. Until the 777, the use of composites has been infrequent and the cost of working with the new materials has made them expensive. Composites offer weight savings, so the decision to try composites on the tail rather than metal was weight driven and not production cost driven. The risks were high, but Boeing was confident that they had worked out all the engineering problems.

In 1989, Boeing decided to proceed with a preliminary design of the 777. The traditional design process at Boeing takes four years. But they decided to take an extra six months to design and build the first 777, and to use a different design strategy. They made another risky decision by going with fewer mockups and prototypes. In essence, they wanted a "paperless airplane" that was designed entirely on a computer aided design system called CATIA. Never before had a major commercial aircraft been built without drawings and mockups. The desire at Boeing was to use their new design approach called Continuous Quality Improvement. This is a teaming arrangement where design teams are responsible for each subsystem. The top integration level consists of 30 teams, which break the system into an additional 217 teams to work on the subsystems. The teams are grouped around parts, not functions. The reason is simple: engineers design parts. It is the systems engineer's job to allocate the requirements that implement the system functions. The function "Stop Aircraft" integrates hundreds of different parts from braking to hydraulic boosters to engine controls. The teams are multidisciplinary. The part designers, customer representatives, service personnel, and manufacturing engineers are all represented. Each of the teams uses the CATIA system to create their drawings and to compare their designs with other team's work. Special software was written to help look for fit problems between the different design efforts. By using the software model, Boeing hoped one of the initial mockups (or prototypes) would skip saving development time that could later be used for testing.

Figure 10-1 compares the schedules of the 767 design to the 777 design.

With the new design teams, the modeling available on CATIA, and strong support from the factory and suppliers, Boeing released the drawing package 18 months ahead of the 767's schedule. Their goal was not a faster design cycle. A comparison of the two charts shows that the 777 schedule is six months longer. Rather, their goal was to get the design to the factory without any problems or design changes. The flight test was even a month longer to ensure that there were no design problems after delivery. To partly make up for the longer build cycle, Boeing created the simulators for the flight deck sooner in the process. The flight deck resembles that of the

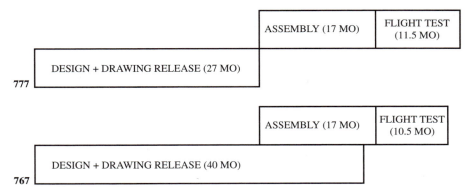

Figure 10-1   777 versus the 767 design and build schedule.

767, which allows a faster coding of the simulator. The pilots were able to get simulator time for the aircraft before the first unit was built.

For a commercial company, this was a risky adventure. Boeing was using untried design practices, untried metals, untried composites, and a folding wing, and doing it with faster drawing delivery dates.

DESIGN DIFFICULTY AND RESOURCES SCORES

The following scores are from the viewpoint of Boeing Aircraft Company in 1989 when deciding to proceed.

Design Type	Knowledge Complexity	Steps	Quality	Process Design	Aggressive Selling Price	Design Difficulty Total
9	6	9	8	4	4	40

Cost	Time	Infrastructure	Resources Total
12	7	8	27

REFERENCES

"777 Revolutionizes Boeing Aircraft Development Process." *Aviation Week & Space Technology,* pp. 34–61, June 3, 1991.

ASHLEY, S., "Boeing 777 gets a boost from Titanium." *Mechanical Engineering,* vol. 115, no. 7: pp. 60–65 (1993).

"Boeing Selects Design for 777 Candidate." *Aviation Week & Space Technology,* pp. 106–107, December 18, 1989.

BROOKS, D., "Engineering Simulators Enhance 777 Development." *Aerospace America,* vol. 31, no. 8: pp. 30–32, 41 (1993).

TENNING, C.B., "Evolution of the Boeing 777 electrical power system," *Proceedings of the 27th Intersociety Energy Conversion Engineering Conference.* San Diego, CA, August 3–7, 1992.

There is a world wide web address for a site with information about the 777:
http://bofh.its.rmit.edu.au/richard/777

11

THE APOLLO MOON LANDING

The Apollo moon landing program began in 1961. Thousands of new products had to be developed to achieve the overall objectives of sending a man to the moon and returning him safely. This required a massive expenditure of capital that only a government could afford. The space program began in 1956 with primarily military goals. The Soviet Union's launch of the Sputnik on October 4, 1957 convinced the United States that there were military and political goals to be achieved with a manned space program. Work began on the Mercury mission in 1958. The Soviet Union beat the Americans again with the orbit of the earth by Yuri A. Gagarin on April 12, 1961. The Mercury did not fly until May 5, 1961. On May 25, 1961, President Kennedy took the initiative by challenging Congress and the nation to

"achieve the goal before this decade is out of landing a man on the moon and returning him safely to the earth."

This became the top level system function for the entire moon landing project. There were three mandatory requirements for the mission to be successful:

1. Land a man on the moon,
2. Return him safely to the earth, and
3. Do it before the end of the decade.

There was one major constraint missing: cost. The public was expected to pay any price to achieve the three mission goals. All large projects of this magnitude are government sponsored. Private companies need a return on investment. Space projects do not yield a return in cash, but rather in glory or benefits for future generations.

The cost of the space program was over $24 billion (1962 dollars). It is rare that a nation embarks on such a costly adventure, but the military applications of space were stressed far more then is remembered today.

The first step in any system design process is to evaluate the alternatives. Three major concepts for accomplishing the mission were carefully considered. The program manager made a point of not expressing an opinion because he felt that would sway the analysis. The options were:

1. Launch a spacecraft directly to the moon, where it would land. After an excursion, the astronauts would blast off the moon and return directly to the earth. This was called the direct ascent method. It required a rocket that could develop 12 million pounds of thrust and carry the 75 ton Apollo all the way to the moon. This was Jules Verne's version of the moon launch, which he had written in a novel 100 years earlier.

2. Make two launches from the earth. The first rocket would become an orbiting gas tank that would circle the earth. The second would contain the astronauts, who would fuel up in the earth orbit then proceed to land directly on the moon. After an excursion collecting rocks the astronauts would blast off the moon and return directly to the earth. This was called the Earth Orbit Rendezvous (EOR).

3. The final alternative was to make one launch directly to the lunar orbit. A small craft would then land on the moon, leaving the larger craft with its fuel and one astronaut in orbit around the moon. Two astronauts would land on the moon in the smaller craft and then blast off into the lunar orbit to rendezvous with the "command module" in orbit around the moon. They would then all return in the command module to the earth. This was called the Lunar Orbit Rendezvous (LOR).

NASA wisely took a full year to do the concept selection. The process cost over one million man hours of study. (If you assign 2,200 man hours per man year, then this would be 455 people working full time.) All of the alternatives were fully developed as programs and actual contracts were given to companies to begin work. In this way, no time was lost in the selection process. The major driving constraint for the entire mission was the rockets needed to lift the weight into orbit. The largest then proposed was called the Nova. It was a monster rocket that had 12 million pounds of thrust and could send 150,000 pounds to the moon and back. However, the development time for the Nova would delay the mission until 1972. Kennedy's speech became a driving force at NASA. They had to get to the moon by 1969, or even better 1968, then if Kennedy were reelected he would still be president during the moon landing. As crazy as these reasons seem, it was the driving factor for decision making. Because the direct ascent approach would have required the Nova rocket, this approach was scrubbed.

The EOR could use two Saturn C5 rockets. The Saturn C5 was under development and would be ready within the time frame. This was still a major effort, as shown in Figure 11-1. It had 8.7 million pounds of thrust and could take 45 tons to the moon and back. An Apollo vehicle that landed on the moon would weigh 75 tons, therefore two C5s were needed. The first would be a gas tank with 95 tons of fuel; it would be added to a second vehicle containing the astronauts. The major drawback was that two C5 launches were needed. The success rate for launches was so bad that it was decided that the probability of mission failure was high.

The last option was LOR, which could use one Saturn C5. It could take 45 tons, including fuel, to the moon. Since the initial design of the Apollo would weigh 75 tons, a new design was needed. A Lunar Excursion Module (LEM) was developed that could take two astronauts to the moon. It was a small, light spacecraft that would need only a small amount of fuel to escape the moon's gravity when the astronauts left the surface. The new Apollo with the LEM fit within the weight limits, although its complexity was higher. It became the option of choice. When feasibility cannot be achieved, an approach often taken is to increase complexity until a solution is found (as was also shown in the resistor network case study).

The final decision was made in July 1962. By the end of the year, every major component of the moon landing mission was under contract and design except the LEM. Per Congress, almost every major aerospace company in the United States was working on a large piece of the project. In addition to the usual pork barrel politics, there was a concerted effort to develop an aerospace industry. Satellites, space planes, and even bombs and factories in space were envisioned and a large industry would be needed to support all of these products.

The Saturn C5 rocket was developed by the rocket genius Wernher von Braun. It had three stages developed by three companies. Boeing had the booster, North American had the second stage, and Douglas Aircraft had the third stage. It stood 364 feet tall and weighed 6,200,000 pounds fully fueled. The first test launch was on

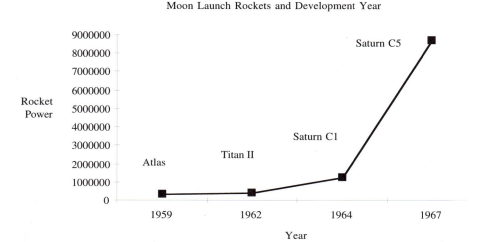

Figure 11-1   Development of the rockets for the space program.

November 9, 1967 and was a phenomenal success. Because of budget cutbacks (due to the cost of the Vietnam War), only the third stage had been tested prior to launch. The first and second stages were making their maiden flight together. This, despite 2,000,000 functional parts in the C5 and a total of 95 separate engines in the entire Apollo apparatus! This very risky approach was needed because of the shrinking time window. In an amazing strike of good fortune, the entire mission was nearly flawless and the C5 worked great. There was only time for nine Saturn test flights before a moon launch and the success of the first launch gave NASA the opportunity to go to the moon in 1969.

The second test flight had problems with both the second and third stages due to vibration from the booster stage. A fix for this was accomplished and on the third flight test, NASA made the decision to go with a manned spacecraft called the Apollo 8. Never before had such a risk in rocketry been taken. In full view of the world, the lives of men were in danger, safty was based only on the firm belief that both the advances in computer modeling, and the testing of the rocket during construction and on the launch pad, were adequate to skip the prototype testing. See Figure 11-2. By monitoring the rocket on the launch pad seconds before it was started, confidence in the launch was raised significantly. This confidence was a major development in man's history of developing complex systems. Of course, the political reality of finishing the project before the end of the decade helped encourage NASA to take the risk too. The Saturn C5 was successful and never failed in a manned space flight.

On July 16, 1969, the ninth Saturn C5 rocket with the Apollo 11 spacecraft on board left the earth for the moon. On July 20, 1969, the Apollo 11 spacecraft divided into two parts with two astronauts going to the moon's surface in the LEM. The two astronauts landed on the moon with no major problems and all systems functioning.

Total Number of Flight Tests Before Manned Flight

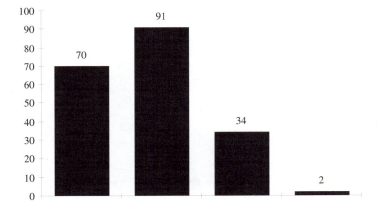

Figure 11-2   Flight tests for the space program rockets.

This fulfilled Kennedy's vow to land a man on the moon before the end of the decade. The astronauts left 23 hours later in the LEM and rendezvoused with the command module in lunar orbit as planned. All three astronauts returned safely to the earth on July 24th. Thus, all three major system functions were satisfied.

How was NASA able to achieve this complex mission after the concept was selected? The major ingredients combined continuous improvement with break-through excitement. Many of the projects, including the rockets, had never been built or developed. However, all were deemed feasible by the best scientific and engineering minds around. This is a key ingredient that did not make this a true breakthrough project. All breakthroughs in other fields were not deemed feasible by anyone but the few people working the problem. The moon landing was highly risky, but was technologically feasible. The existing rocket technology had to be scaled larger and more complex, but there was more redesign than new design for most of the work. The major constraint was time, not whether it was possible.

The excitement around the program was highly contagious. Most companies made little money and even lost money just to be involved. Engineers and technicians worked hundreds of hours of free overtime just to be able to say they worked on the Apollo mission. For example, the director of the NASA Manned Space Flight program was 41 year old D. Brainerd Holmes who was responsible for two-thirds of the total Apollo budget. He was an important executive at RCA who took a huge pay cut to take the job, because he felt he would not be able to explain to his grandchildren why he did not work on the moon landing (Lewis, 1969). This dedication and job interest is not found on consumer projects.

In addition, advances in modeling, especially the digital computer, allowed prototype testing to be reduced and mathematical modeling to be enhanced. This is critical if expensive prototype testing is to be avoided. For projects with inexpensive prototypes, this is not as important. However, the space program would not have met its goals if the modeling and on-line computer monitoring testing were not possible.

DESIGN DIFFICULTY AND RESOURCES SCORES

The following scores are from the viewpoint of the United States government during the early 1960s.

Design Type	Knowledge Complexity	Steps	Quality	Process Design	Aggressive Selling Price	Design Difficulty Total
12	7	10	9	2	1	41

Cost	Time	Infrastructure	Resources Total
15	9	10	34

REFERENCES

Apollo 13, a United Artists movie, 1995.

Editors of *Time* Magazine, *The Space Industry, America's Newest Giant*, Englewood Cliffs, NJ: Prentice-Hall, 1962.

LEWIS, R. S. (1969), *Appointment on the Moon*. New York: Viking Press, 1969.

PELLEGRINO, C.R., and J. STOFF, *Chariots for Apollo: The Making of the Lunar Module*. New York: Atheneum, 1985.

WOLFE, T., *The Right Stuff*. New York: Farrar, Straus & Giroux, Inc., 1979.

12

BUILDING A HOUSE

Single family homes are popular and affordable in America. A typical family can afford one by financing the cost of the home for up to 30 years. Approximately 1.2 million homes are built every year. Although it is the most costly investment most families make, the design of a home is simple.

The first step is to pick a piece of land. Custom lots are easy to find, though the prices vary widely. Site preparation depends on the floor plan. Complete home floor plans are available by the thousands for a nominal fee (around $200). For an additional $2,500, a home buyer can hire an architect to modify an existing floor plan. After a floor plan is selected, it must be approved by the local planning board. The approval process includes permit fees, lot plans, etc. Then the owner decides how to go about the construction. There are three basic options:

1. hire a contractor,
2. do the contracting yourself and hire subcontractors to do the labor, and
3. do as much of the construction as possible by yourself.

However it's done, the same steps must be completed. The following list shows the various tasks needed to be performed to construct a home.

1. land survey
2. insulation
3. water well or water connection
4. excavation
5. dry wall or plaster

6. electrical connection
7. footings and foundation
8. floor topping—finished hardwood, underpayment
9. bath, kitchen tile
10. steel beams and columns
11. kitchen and bath—appliances, cabinets
12. interior finish—paint, wallpaper, stain, varnish
13. rough carpentry—sills, framing, sheathing, windows
14. heat registers, baseboards
15. hardwood floor sanding, finishing
16. roofing
17. furnace
18. linoleum, floor tiles
19. siding
20. finish carpentry—doors and frames, baseboards, stairways
21. carpeting
22. exterior paint
23. finish plumbing
24. exterior steps, porch
25. rough plumbing
26. finish electrical
27. caulking
28. rough electrical
29. sewer connection
30. exterior painting, staining
31. rough heating
32. septic system
33. grading
34. chimney and fireplace
35. water
36. grass, landscaping

Home building is not a difficult design task because the major design work has all been done. Ask the local planning board how large the footings must be for a 2,000 square foot home with a tile roof and they will tell you in minutes. All the electrical codes, plumbing codes, and heating and air-conditioning regulations, are already determined and approved. No home builder will have to compute these numbers. The inspectors will make sure you use the correct numbers and so will the insurance and mortgage companies.

An expert software system has been designed in Japan to allow customers to custom order prefabricated homes. The knowledge base contains over 300,000 potential parts. The typical home has 5,000 parts after the system completes the design. Clearly, the major job in the design of any home is selecting the parts from the thousands of options available. If you consider size and color, it truly looks impossible to get the right choices. That is why there are interior designers, architects, and contractors to help the home buyer. Ask anyone who has ever built a home and they will tell you hundreds of things they would do differently. There is no optimum home. However, the design and manufacture of a home is easy enough for a person with an eighth grade education to build a quality home that meets all the codes.

Systems Engineering Mistakes

The most common mistake made by amateurs designing homes is failing to freeze the system requirements before manufacturing is begun. Changing the requirements during manufacture is costly.

DESIGN DIFFICULTY AND RESOURCES SCORES

The following scores are from the viewpoint of the home buyer getting ready to custom build a new home, doing most of the work himself.

Design Type	Knowledge Complexity	Steps	Quality	Process Design	Aggressive Selling Price	Design Difficulty Total
2	1	4	3	1	3	14

Cost	Time	Infrastructure	Resources Total
12	3	6	21

REFERENCES

HOTTON, P., *So You Want to Build a House*. Toronto: Little, Brown & Company, 1976.

Projects and Plans. Elmhurst, Illinois: Craft Pattern Studios, 1976.

13

CENTRAL ARIZONA PROJECT

The Central Arizona Project (CAP) is the largest single water-delivery project ever authorized by Congress. The CAP is a 336 mile aqueduct built from the Colorado River at Lake Havasu, Arizona (elevation: 482 feet above sea level) to the major cities of Phoenix (elevation: 1,083 feet) and Tucson (elevation: 2,375 feet) in central Arizona. The aqueduct will cost an estimated $4.7 billion by its completion in 1999.

A concern of both of these Arizona cities is a reliable source of water for future growth. Phoenix has relied primarily on groundwater and the Salt River Project. The Salt River Project is the oldest reclamation project in the United States. It began in 1903 and consists of 1,280 miles of canals and ditches that deliver water from the Salt and Gila Rivers, which are fed from Arizona's White Mountains. Tucson has relied almost exclusively on groundwater and has severely impacted the water table under the city and outlying areas. Both cities knew as early as 1960 that future growth would depend on more reliable and economical sources of water. After much lobbying, the United States Congress passed the spending bill to begin construction for the CAP in 1973.

The design of the project required detailed surveying of the route. Aerial photographs, land surveys, and other geographic data had to be accumulated. To speed this data collection and access, a new database information system was created. It is called the Geographic Information System (GIS). Tapping this system helped ensure accurate and timely access to the engineering data needed. Examples of the type of data stored in the system includes: drill-hole coordinates, geologic strata coordinates, profiles, canal alignment, dams and structures positioning, section lines, right-of-way, distance and area measurements, and reservoirs capacities.

The Central Arizona Project has three major aqueducts: Hayden-Rhodes, Salt-Gila, and Tucson. The project has 14 relift pumping plants, 39 radial gate check structures, and 33 turnouts. A major dam, the Waddell Dam, was constructed north of Phoenix using the GIS extensively. The entire system is controlled from a central location in Phoenix. The Programmable Master Supervisory Control System is used to remotely monitor all of the pumping stations and control them. Using the system, operators monitor the flow of the entire canal. They can schedule the rate of flow and respond to remote alarms. The peak flow rate of the canal system is 3,000 feet^3/second. Though this peak is only reached during the summer, it illustrates the size of the entire project. It is a huge system that provides water throughout central Arizona. As of 1994, additional construction to outlying farmers and small towns was still in progress. As of January 1994, Tucson was receiving all the allotted water and so was Phoenix. Total system completion, including the water processing plants, will be completed around 1999.

Systems Engineering Mistakes

The problems with the CAP system are water quality, environmental damage, and cost. The CAP water has a different chemistry and flows in a different direction in the water mains. Consequently household tap water tastes bad and looks rusty. As a result, Tucsonians do not want it. The city of Tucson is dumping its share of the CAP water into washes and wells to recharge the groundwater. The farmers are not buying the CAP water because they can pump water out of the ground at less than half the cost. The project's cost is double the initial estimate. The state of Arizona must repay $2 billion to the federal government as part of the original agreement. A taxpayer bailout (rather than increased usage fees) is the only option to pay for this massive government project. The CAP planners overestimated the demand for the water and underestimated the cost of the project. In Systems Engineering terminology, they did not mitigate the cost risks.

DESIGN DIFFICULTY AND RESOURCES SCORES

The following scores are from the viewpoint of the federal and state governments who authorized the project in 1973.

Design Type	Knowledge Complexity	Steps	Quality	Process Design	Aggressive Selling Price	Design Difficulty Total
4	2	5	2	1	1	15

Cost	Time	Infrastructure	Resources Total
12	9	6	27

REFERENCES

Arizona Department of Water Resources, "Impact of groundwater management act and CAP water supply on agricultural water conservation programs." *Proceedings of the 20th Anniversary Conference on Water Management in the 90's*, Seattle, WA, 1993.

PAUL, D.B., S.B.M. MCDONALD, "Use of geographic information systems for design and construction of new Waddell Dam." 1992. *International Symposium on Mapping and Geographic Information Systems*, San Francisco, CA, June 21–22, 1990, pp. 183–192, 1992.

ROGERS, D.C., T.F. KACEREK, R.S. GOOCH, "Field data for verifying canal unsteady flow models." *Journal of Irrigation and Drainage Engineering,* vol. 199, no. 4: pp. 679–692 (1993).

"Who will pay for CAP?" *Tucson Citizen*, Dec. 11, 1993.

14

THE GREAT PYRAMID AT GIZA

The Great Pyramid at Giza in Egypt is one of the seven wonders of the ancient world. It was built to be the eternal resting place of their pharaoh Cheops, around 2575 B.C. As such, the resources expended were for his benefit and for the religious character of the nation as a whole. Construction of this pyramid employed over 50,000 men, which would have been about 2% of the total population of the country. In comparison, the United States military comprises about 1% of the U.S. population. Construction took about 20 years, although most people probably only worked from July to November, when the Nile was flooded, and no planting could occur. The Great Pyramid rises 482 feet high and each side is 755 feet long at the base. It consists of thousands of limestone blocks seven feet high and up to 18 feet long.

As an engineering feat, the Great Pyramid is amazing given its antiquity. Only copper and stone tools were available. The quarry where the high quality limestone blocks were cut was over eight miles away. Although there are many theories on how the builders moved these heavy stones without automation, their method is still a mystery. The most popular theory involves a crew of 25 men that cut each stone at the quarry and then used ropes and logs as levers to place the huge stone on wooden sleds. The sled was then dragged to a barge. The barge was used only when the Nile was at flood stage during the summer. This was done to limit the amount of dragging necessary. Very few beasts of burden are assumed to have been available, so men had to do the labor. Once at the pyramid site, the men dragged the sled up an earthen ramp that was built around the pyramid as it rose from the ground. The surface of the ramp was covered with logs. By wetting the logs there was reduced friction on the sled. When the men got to the location where the stone was to be placed, they dragged the stone off the sled with ropes and levers and pushed it into place. There are many problems with this theory. Where did all the wood come from? How was the placement so exacting? The problem is that all of the archeological evidence reveals no other tools available.

The actual engineering design probably took less than a year. The references for surveying and clearing the site were done using simple surveying tripods and the stars. Since their religion was based on the stars, the ancient Egyptians were good astronomers. Most of the work was not in designing the actual burial chamber and pyramid, but in the infrastructure needed to manufacturer the pyramid. Since this was a custom design, the first unit built to this design was the only one built, therefore the system design process encompassed the entire construction phase of twenty years. Other pyramids existed in that area, so the design and construction was not innovative or new.

What are the lessons to be learned from such an ancient effort? First, only a government can undertake such an enormous task. However, from an engineering viewpoint, the resources necessary to do a thorough job were available. Modern Euclidean geometry was not yet invented, so simple measurements based on the stars were used. The task was feasible because similar, but smaller pyramids had been constructed by the Pharaoh's predecessors. The time frame was also feasible, as long as the Pharaoh lived a normal life span and did not die at an early age. In that event, it would be up to his successor to finish the job, which wasn't likely if it prevented him from creating his own magnificent tomb!

The second lesson here was that an infrastructure has to exist to do a design. If it does not exist then it becomes part of the design effort. A blueprint is not the end of a system design. It is when a unit has been built and validated to those plans. Without validation, I can claim to have developed the warp drive for the Starship *Enterprise!* The infrastructure to build a validated unit is part of the design process and is comparable to the software needed to run a scheduling algorithm. Until the solution is produced the software is worthless. All the processes must be proven before the system design process is complete. More engineering effort went into training middle managers, building the barges and ramps, and placing the blocks than into the relatively simple job of clearing the site and creating the drawings.

A modern Great Pyramid is the Apollo space launch (see the case study), where billions of dollars were spent to create a unique experience without any profit motive. The infrastructure of the test facilities, the factories, the launch facilities, and even the ships that took place in the recovery were far more extensive and consumed more effort than the big rockets and the spacecraft.

Infrastructure is often feasible but consumes many resources. The glamour is not in the infrastructure, but the effort is. Without infrastructure, a modern engineer would be almost worthless on a primitive island. His education and training is based on the tools, specialists, transportation system, and communication system that make up his environment. The entire system design process must take into account the infrastructure in order to be successful.

DESIGN DIFFICULTY AND RESOURCES SCORES

The following scores are from the viewpoint of the Pharaoh's engineers.

Design Type	Knowledge Complexity	Steps	Quality	Process Design	Aggressive Selling Price	Design Difficulty Total
4	4	5	10	1	1	25

Cost	Time	Infrastructure	Resources Total
15	10	9	34

REFERENCES

"Pyramids." *Encyclopedia Britannica*. New York, 1972.

MACAULAY, D., *Pyramid*. Boston: Houghton Mifflin Co., 1975.

15

AN AUTOMOBILE FACTORY

Most design is redesign. Companies spend most of their design efforts trying to incrementally improve an existing product to conform to some new or tighter requirement. One of the largest ongoing industrial design efforts is the redesign of automobiles. Companies typically spend $2-3 billion and 6–10 years to design these consumer products.

The book, *The Machine That Changed the World,* is about the development of automobiles and their factories. The book describes the design, manufacturing, and assembly techniques for Japanese, American, and European car makers. The American and European manufacturers use a matrix organization with a weak project manager. Engineers are assigned for specific design efforts. When an engineer's efforts are complete or on hold, he returns to his own department for reassignment. Teaming with a strong project leader is the preferred method of the Japanese. Engineers are assigned to the project leader for the life of the design effort. The Japanese appear to achieve similar or better results with less expense using this method. See Figure 15-1.

The average development time for Japanese manufacturers is 46.2 months and for American producers is 60.4 months. The reason usually given for this discrepancy is the strong central project manager. Since the designers are assigned directly to the manager, they work with more direction. There is also less chance that the engineers will move to another job before completing the redesign.

A close look at the design numbers highlights another issue. The Japanese get their prototypes in 6.2 months while the Americans take 12.4 months. This accounts for 40% of the Japanese advantage. Design is an iterative process. The more cycles a designer performs before the product design is complete, the better the product adheres to the requirements. By obtaining their prototypes earlier, the Japanese can get the changes needed to the drawings before the design is finalized.

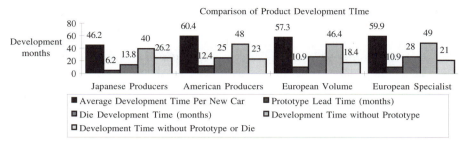

Figure 15-1   Development time for various producers.

The next major difference between the Americans and Japanese is the die development time. Dies are large fixed metal stamps that are used to pound out the shapes of the fenders, doors, etc. They are the most expensive tooling on the project and require exacting precision. A design change done to the car body after the dies are set will require long delays and large expense. The Japanese get their dies in 13.8 months while the Americans take 25 months. This one year head start is probably the most significant Japanese advantage for the redesign of cars. In fact, comparing the development hours, without the prototypes or dies, shows the Japanese spend 26.2 months to develop a car and the Americans only 23 months. The extra three months' design time may well account for some of the quality difference in the two products.

Another Japanese advantage is their design teams have only 485 members and spend 1,700,000 hours per new car, while the American teams have 903 members and spend 3,100,000 hours. See Figure 15-2. The difference is in the suppliers. The Japanese allocate almost 50% of their design work to their suppliers while the Amer-

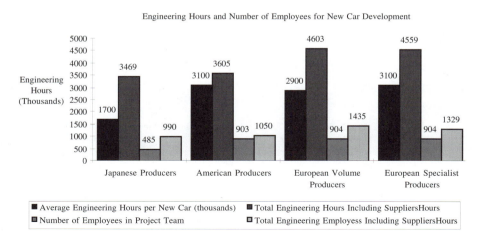

Figure 15-2   Hours for various producers.

icans only allocate 18%. Once this is factored, the total number of engineering hours is almost identical. The only technical advantage may be that the Japanese suppliers are experts in their specialty, such as brakes, power steering, etc., while the American team members are often more general in their application. The advantage in time may be more important. By performing their work in parallel, with hundreds of little suppliers, the actual Japanese design time is reduced. Separate units are built simultaneously at hundreds of locations and then combined quickly to create the prototype. This technique requires very strict interface specifications so that the integration will go smoothly. The Americans complete the design and then send it to a supplier who often requests design changes before they can produce a working prototype.

This approach is analogous to a strong central algorithm flowing down localized optimization parameters for sub problems to solve (Karp, 1977). Each of the sub problems (transmissions, doors, seats, radios, etc.) has fixed interfaces and firm requirements. Optimization within the requirements is done for each sub problem. As will be seen when discussing the Traveling Salesman Problem in Chapter 23, this approach gives consistent results but takes longer than some other methods.

A faster design approach is to use a tree search, which would require keeping many more solutions open longer. This takes less time than the sub problem approach, but costs more money (see the Apollo case study). The team approach that the Japanese use keeps more options open far longer into a program. This is why the change rate is high early in the design process for a Japanese design team. The Americans have high rates at the end of a design because it is only after integration and test that they catch the problems created by dividing the system into sub problems early. Keeping more options open longer also permits a better chance of finding superior solutions (or alternative minima) rather than locking in the design early in the system design process.

DESIGN DIFFICULTY AND RESOURCES SCORES

The following scores are from the viewpoint of a modern automobile manufacturer beginning the design of a new model automobile and a factory to build it in.

Design Type	Knowledge Complexity	Steps	Quality	Process Design	Aggressive Selling Price	Design Difficulty Total
7	4	6	5	5	5	32

Cost	Time	Infrastructure	Resources Total
9	7	6	22

REFERENCES

DeVera, D., T. Glennon, A.A. Kenny, M. Kham., M. Mayer, "An Automotive Case Study." *Quality Progress* pp. 35–38, June 1988.

Halberstam, D., *The Next Century*. New York: William Morrow & Co., 1991.

Halberstam, D., *The Reckoning*. New York: William Morrow & Co., 1986.

Karp, R.M., "Probabilistic Analysis of Partitioning Algorithoms for the Traveling Salesman Problem." *Mathematics of Operations Research,* vol. 2: pp. 209–224 (1977).

Womack, J.P., D.T. Jones, D. Roos, *The Machine That Changed the World.* New York: Rawson Associates, 1990.

16

THE GM IMPACT—AN
ELECTRIC CAR

Electric cars are not new. The most popular automobiles in America in 1900 were electric. The motors were simple, but their range was limited. Improvements in the internal combustion engine, coupled with the low price of the Model T Ford, convinced most people to go for the power and range of the gas engine. Electric cars just could not keep up with performance requirements, and fell out of favor.

Hobbyists have kept the idea alive for years. Many people have built small electric cars from converted automobiles but the range is always poor. A typical kit provides a small subcompact car a range of about 40 miles. Batteries are the problem. Their ability to store energy is small compared to gasoline, even though electric motors are 95% efficient and internal combustion engines are only 15% efficient. Typical batteries provide 1% as much power per weight as does gasoline.

Air pollution is a major problem in California. The increasing population density and a naive belief in technology convinced the California Air Resources Board to set down rules that require 2% of any automobile manufacturers' fleets to be zero-emissions by 1998. The only feasible zero-emission vehicles are electric cars. California is the largest single car market in North America. To lose this market is unthinkable for large manufacturers.

General Motors analyzed the situation and turned to two high technology companies to try and break free from current thoughts and constraints of car design. They contacted Paul MacCready, a 65 year old Cal Tech professor who invented the light weight solar airplane, Solar Challenger, and helped GM create an all solar car, Sunraycer. His company, AeroVironment, is expert in using light weight materials and practical systems engineering. The second company is a subsidiary of GM called Hughes Aircraft Company. Although an aerospace giant, Hughes was not involved in transportation. However, Hughes has done a lot of work with light weight power supplies. The result of Hughes' and AeroVironment's efforts was the 1990 GM Impact. The Impact is a two seat electric car with very impressive performance even when compared to an internal combustion engine. It accelerates from 0 to 60 in 7.9 seconds, and has a top speed of 110 miles per hour. It travels 120 miles on an 8 hour charge using 32 standard lead-acid batteries. When asked about the Impact's success, MacCready answers:

> *"Everyone is looking for the gimmick, the gadget, the special ingredient that makes the Impact succeed. There isn't any. This worked because of something that isn't glamorous. It worked because of systems engineering."* (Discover, 1992)

AeroVironment's area of expertise is weight reduction. The typical subcompact car weighs 2,500 pounds. Electric car batteries weigh almost 1,000 pounds. Consumers are not concerned about the weight of the vehicle. They want range and performance. The job of the systems engineer at AeroVironment was to translate a range requirement of 120 miles into a weight requirement. AeroVironment carefully considered the possible technologies that could be used on the project. The weight goal became 2,050 pounds. Instead of trying to find better batteries, the Impact would use standard batteries, better. When the final version of the Impact was fielded, it weighed 2,200 pounds. Most of the extra weight came from nonoptimum tires, heat pumps (instead of air conditioners), glass, etc. The extra weight stole about 25 miles from the range of the car on a single charge.

The Impact uses alternating current (AC) motors, so the direct current (DC) energy in the battery has to be transformed into AC energy. Hughes contributed the power inverter. The typical conversion devices available off the shelf weighed 300 pounds. The major weight was in the bulky switches that changed the direction of the current. The solution was to replace all the switches with transistors and repackage the entire setup in light casing. The final product weighed 60 pounds.

The Impact's introduction in 1990 was an instant success with the public. It was sporty and had good performance specifications. GM was asked when it could deliver the vehicle to market. They made plans to rush the design into mass production. By 1993, GM had realized that the production cost would exceed $40,000 per car. They changed their plans and decided to build only 50 prototypes. The cost of the technology, which in the case of the Impact was the light materials, was still too much for the consumer. Automakers are now looking for government subsidies to sell these cars.

All the engineering innovations required to develop the Impact were well within the technology available. Repackaging of existing technology is redesign. Continuous improvements along a known technology path are the most common design projects. As seen with the Impact, performance can be doubled with commitment to innovatively improve along the same path. Repackaging is the major reason for improvements made in consumer electronics (TVs, camcorders, radios, CDs) and in the fuel economy of existing cars.

The system design process for continuous improvement is predictable. The success hinges on good systems engineering teamed with a solid grasp of the technology.

Improvements, not major breakthroughs, are needed to achieve ever more stringent requirements. If coupled with innovation, the jump can be significant.

DESIGN DIFFICULTY AND RESOURCES SCORES

The following scores are from the viewpoint of GM when they asked MacCready to design an electric car. We did not consider the batteries.

Design Type	Knowledge Complexity	Steps	Quality	Process Design	Aggressive Selling Price	Design Difficulty Total
10	7	5	3	2	3	30

Cost	Time	Infrastructure	Resources Total
7	4	4	15

REFERENCES

DVORAK, P., "The Shocking Truth about Electric Vehicles." *Machine Design*. pp. 86–94, September 21, 1989.

Electric and Hybrid Vehicle Advancements, Society of Automotive Engineers, 400 Commonwealth Dr., Warrendale, PA, March 1993.

"Electric Car Pool." *Scientific American*. pp. 126–127, May 1992.

"Electric Vehicles." *IEEE Spectrum*. pp. 18–24, November, 1992.

"EV Watch." *IEEE Spectrum*. p. 65, December 1993, and p. 72, September 1995.

"GM Drives the Electric Car Closer to Reality." *Business Week*. pp. 60-61, May 14, 1993.

"GM IMPACT." *Discover*. pp. 91–98: March 1992.

IEEE Spectrum. July 1993.

RIEZENMAN, M.J., "Road test: the Impact electric car." *IEEE Spectrum*. pp. 73–75, September 1995.

WYEZALEK, F.A., "Heating and Cooling Battery Electric Vehicles—the Final Barrier." *IEEE AES Systems Magazine*. pp. 9–14, November 1993.

17

BATTERIES FOR
ELECTRIC VEHICLES

Electric vehicles are feasible design projects if you limit the performance requirements to below those expected by the customer. Vehicle power (especially when accelerating) and total vehicle range are the main obstacles to viable electric cars. The general goal is to use the electric energy available at home to recharge the car and then have the power discharge satisfactorily over a normal commute based on the rigorous demands of the road. Basically, current technology limits the consumers to about 25% of the range and 50% of the power (including headlights, heating, cooling, stereos, etc.) that they have come to expect from modern automobiles.

The dream is alluring. Compare the emissions data shown in Table 17-1. These numbers represent the total emissions including the delivery of the gasoline or electricity to the user. The only real loser is sulfur dioxide, which is a byproduct of coal burning power plants. Carbon dioxide levels are also higher but are still acceptable. Power plants are generally not in the urban areas and thus, the impact on humans is minimal. Note that other types of power plants, such as nuclear, hydroelectric, or solar would not create such air pollution. The California Air Resources Board is responsible for the air quality in the Los Angeles basin. With a desire to convert to electric vehicles, the board established rules that require 2% of any automobile manufacturers' fleet to be zero-emissions vehicles by 1998. The only feasible zero-emission vehicles are electric cars. The Air Resources Board added no additional restrictions on power generation. The hope is that by creating a demand for electric vehicles, the resources necessary to develop the product will be dedicated.

What is needed to create a viable electric vehicle is well known. Customers want roughly the same performance for speed and acceleration as today's subcompacts. The range of a typical 1993 subcompact is over 300 miles. An electric car that could provide a range of 150 miles would be marketable, since 90% of daily trips by

TABLE 17-1   Impact on the environment from
generating electricity for a car versus a gas
powered engine. (*Business Week*, 1993)

Emissions	Electric	Gas
Volatile Organic Compounds	0.003	0.5
Nitrogen Oxide	0.03	0.6
Carbon Monoxide	0.003	7.0
Carbon Dioxide	105.0	7.0
Sulfur Dioxide	1.0	
0.08		

American urban dwellers are under 100 miles. The last major hurdle is cost. To capture up to 10% of the market share with an electric vehicle's limited performance, the cost of the vehicle would have to be less than $25,000. This is about the price of a comfortable, mid size car, such as an Oldsmobile Cutlass Supreme.

To produce a vehicle by California's deadline will require advances in battery performance similar to those listed in Table 17-2. The battery technologies listed are the most promising that were known in 1992.

The goals set for 1994 were missed. GM, BMW, and Mercedes decided not to use the sodium sulfur batteries. They are dangerous because they must be kept at 850° K and they may cause fires in an accident. Ford is betting on solving the problem with better design. They have incorporated a computerized security system that monitors temperature. This, combined with better structural support, should prevent any serious problems with the battery. The major problem that continues to exist is cost. Currently, it costs $40,000 just for the batteries. This for a power source that de-

TABLE 17-2   Goals for advanced batteries. (*Scientific American,* May 1992)

	1992 Lead Acid	1994 Sodium Sulfur, Nickel Metal Hydride	2000 Lithium Polymer, Lithium Aluminum/ Iron Disulfide
Energy Capacity (watt-hours per kilogram)	25–40	80–100	200
Range (miles)	40–100	150–200	300
Peak Power (watts per kilogram)	110–150	150–200	400
Recharge Time (hours)	6–8	4–6	3–6
Life (years)	3–5	5	10
Cost (40-kilowatt hour battery)	$3,000–5,000	<$6,000	<$4,000

livers less range, is harder to refuel, and has worse peak performance than existing internal combustion engines (*Wall Street Journal,* December 17, 1993).

Table 17-3 lists what is known about various existing technologies. A careful examination of Specific Energy shows that the only technology close to the gas engine is lithium-air. This is an exotic battery that cannot be recharged. The user would have to go to a service station and replace a chemical pack, which would be sent back to a factory for reconstitution. It is unlikely this technology will catch on. The next choice of many companies is sodium-sulfur. The specific energy is within acceptable limits, but the number of cycles that can be recharged is only 810. This represents three to four years for most users. Therefore, at least one complete change of batteries (at $40,000) would be needed during the car's expected life. Consequently, this is not a popular choice of automobile manufacturers.

In fact, none of the technologies listed in the table appear to be feasible yet. Other options for storing energy are still being tried, including: flywheels (Chrysler has a race car powered by one), ultracapacitors, and various fuel cells. However, nothing promising has been found. Without some major new breakthrough, the battery technology will not outperform gasoline powered engines for at least another generation.

This breakthrough is waiting to happen. Yet, no one seems to be going about the discovery process as with other breakthroughs (superconductor, electric light, etc.). A large consortium of major automobile manufacturers has gotten together to

TABLE 17-3 How the new batteries stack up (*Machine Design*, September 1989).

Battery Type	Specific Energy (watt-hour/kilogram)	Specific Peak Power at 80% depth of discharge (watt/kilogram)	Projected Operating Cost (1986 $/kilowatt-hour)	Cycle Life (cycles to 80% depth of discharge)
Lead acid types				
(flow through)	47	105	72	181+
(tubular)	36	80	—	800 to 1,000
(monopolar)	35	200	63	600
(bipolar)	57	—	—	1,200(est.)
Nickel-Iron	49	103	125	2,000
Nickel-Cadmium	44	110	72	700
Zinc-Bromide	55	88	75	50+
Lithium aluminum-iron sulfide	83	100	91	350 to 1,000
Sodium-sulfur	136	180	91	810+
Iron-air	70	83	91	48+
Zinc-air	200 to 300	—	—	6 to 12 months
Lithium air	800 to 1,200	—	—	Does not recharge
Gas-engine power train	400 to 500	—	—	—

collectively study battery technology. The government is handing out grants to favorite institutions to conduct studies. The problem is that everyone seems to be looking where the light is best, that is, where everyone else has looked. This guarantees that nothing new will be found. To develop the incandescent light, Edison tried hundreds of methods until he found a solution (see the case study). With the superconductor, Bednorz and Müller discovered a new alloy because they were trying anything interesting that came along. The willingness to strike out in a different direction is mandatory for a breakthrough.

Another key attribute is the fixation on the problem. These were not temporary sojourns into the field, but people who were fascinated with the problem and worked constantly for years with little reward. They were poorly funded, but highly motivated. In fact, the best laboratories rarely come up with breakthroughs. The comfort level is too high and the number of problems they are assigned are too many to achieve a true breakthrough.

If battery problems for electric vehicles are solved, it will probably be by a small company working with little support and with talented people in an area that is ignored or even rejected by other scholars (such as ultracapacitors).

DESIGN DIFFICULTY AND RESOURCES SCORES

The following scores are from the viewpoint of a moderate size company working to develop a new battery for electric vehicles achieved through continuous improvement.

Design Type	Knowledge Complexity	Steps	Quality	Process Design	Aggressive Selling Price	Design Difficulty Total
8	6	3	2	4	4	27

Cost	Time	Infrastructure	Resources Total
3	10	4	17

The following scores are from the viewpoint of a moderate size company writing proposals for government research and development grants to develop a new energy storage system for electric vehicles to be achieved with the breakthrough design approach.

Design Type	Knowledge Complexity	Steps	Quality	Process Design	Aggressive Selling Price	Design Difficulty Total
15	6	3	3	5	4	36

Cost	Time	Infrastructure	Resources Total
5	6	5	16

REFERENCES

"Chrysler Corporation Plans to Show a Model of Flywheel Auto," *Wall Street Journal*, pp. 10, January 3, 1994.

DVORAK, P., "The Shocking Truth about Electric Vehicles." *Machine Design*, pp. 86–94, September 21, 1989.

Electric and Hybrid Vehicle Advancements, Society of Automotive Engineers, 400 Commonwealth Dr., Warrendale, PA, March 1993.

"Electric Car Pool." *Scientific American*, pp. 126–127, May 1992.

"Electric Vehicles." *IEEE Spectrum*, pp. 18–24, November 1992.

RIEZENMAN, M., "The Search for Better Batteries." IEEE Spectrum, pp. 51–56, May 1995.

SURIS, O., "Ford Plans Rely on a Battery Seen as Risky." *Wall Street Journal*, p. B2, December 17, 1993.

WYEZALEK, F.A., "Heating and Cooling Battery Electric Vehicles—The Final Barrier." *IEEE AES Systems Magazine*, pp. 9-14, November 1993.

"GM Drives the Electric Car Closer to Reality." *Business Week*, pp. 60–61, May 14, 1993.

18

C3PO FROM THE
STAR WARS FILM

In the science fiction movie *Star Wars*®, C3PO is a protocol droid (robot). This case study has been included to show systems that we can imagine, but cannot design and build.

C3PO is anthropomorphic in appearance and movement. The machine can see, hear, and move at will. It was programmed to understand and speak 6,000,000 galactic languages and can converse with its owner in excellent English. In this science fiction land, other droids are available on the market and are easily affordable. In one scene, a family farmer buys C3PO and his more able companion, R2D2, from a junk dealer with about the thought or interest one would give when buying a television or a bicycle. They are clearly easily affordable and are an expected part of any home or small business.

What would it take to design C3PO? Many areas of advanced engineering are required, but we will concentrate on three major areas:

1. Artificial Intelligence,
2. visual sensors and pattern recognition, and
3. speech sensors and speech recognition.

Artificial Intelligence consists of large amounts of knowledge stored in an accessible format by a computer that is able to draw conclusions from this data. It provides the computer with the ability to "reason" out a situation based on stored knowledge and a predetermined set of rules. Creating Second Opinion, a decision support system to diagnose childhood stuttering (see the case study), required at least five man years of work and a design difficulty rating of 20. For the abilities displayed by C3PO, many times the difficulty and resources would be required. Yet, in the movie this is a household appliance, requiring less thought to purchase than today's personal computers. Therefore, it is reasonable to assume that this version of robot did not require large amounts of resources to create. Each droid design must therefore be similar to our personal computers, where many components are cheap and easily available.

The ability to "see" is currently available in focal plane arrays. These can digitize a scene at almost the resolution and speed of a human eye (e.g., camcorders). It is likely that in the future these sensors will be very inexpensive and available. Currently, the ability to recognize and process the visual data is infantile at best. All the droids in the movie had sight, therefore, the algorithms for this are clearly inexpensive. However, considering the lack of progress currently made in handwriting detection, even with algorithms that are five megabytes, the sight algorithm must be highly complex.

Capturing and digitizing sound is also possible today and it is relatively inexpensive. However, analyzing these signals is very hard. Affordable technology on the best personal computers today can recognize a vocabulary of around 800 words. This is hardly equivalent to C3POs 6,000,000 languages with probably 30,000 words per language or 180 billion words! The database and systems access software must be huge for such a system, but must have existed prior to development of C3PO, therefore, resources are low and design complexity is high.

DESIGN DIFFICULTY AND RESOURCES SCORES

The following scores are from the viewpoint of a twentieth-century high technology corporation designing a droid for household or industrial use, but with the attitude about resources as portrayed in the movie.

Design Type	Knowledge Complexity	Steps	Quality	Process Design	Aggressive Selling Price	Design Difficulty Total
15	10	10	6	4	3	48

Cost	Time	Infrastructure	Resources Total
2	2	3	7

REFERENCES

Star Wars, a feature film by Twentieth Century Fox, 1977.

19

VELCRO

In 1948 Georges deMestral, an engineer in Switzerland, went for a walk in the woods with his dog. When he returned, he noticed his socks and his dog's fur were covered with thistles. He proceeded to pull them off his socks and the dog. After becoming frustrated with the amount of effort it took to untangle the burrs from his dog's coat, his engineering curiosity was peaked.

Why did they stick so well? Georges deMestral took the burr and put it under a microscope. What he saw were hundreds of tiny hooks that latched onto anything that was shaped like a loop. He spent the next few months trying to duplicate nature and eventually used a woven nylon. He called the creation Velcro® for velvet and crochet.

Georges deMestral was not initially engaged in the system design process. He was just curious and stumbled on a clever fastening technique. This is serendipity, not design. This approach cannot be evaluated or duplicated, so no analysis of the design difficulty is provided. The most that can be said is "Good Luck!"

REFERENCE

STONE, Judith, "Velcro: The Final Frontier." *Discover*, May 1988.

20

THE MANHATTAN PROJECT

During World War II, the United States government sponsored an unusual development effort known at the time by the code name *Manhattan Engineering District* and later as the *Manhattan Project.* This project was unprecedented in that it was conducted by the most qualified technical people available, using the best technical resources available, under conditions of absolute secrecy. The product of this development project was not the atomic bomb. It was the demonstrated capability to manufacture atomic weapons in high rate production. Although many of the scientists would have been satisfied with two or three weapons—enough to end the war—the government would not fund the project under these conditions. The system to be designed was not an atomic bomb, but a reliable process for making atomic bombs.

RESOURCES

The cost of the project was estimated at $2 billion (about $14.6 billion in 1990 dollars), making the project slightly more expensive than the Apollo project in terms of how much of the gross domestic product it consumed. The effort required three years once engineering-manufacturing development began. There were at least two occasions when the project, which amazingly was hidden within the War Department's budget as a series of miscellaneous expenses, was threatened with exposure because the bill-payers (congressmen) could not understand how anything could cost so much without tangible short-term results. Human resources included 200,000 American citizens in various capacities, among them large numbers of highly qualified scientists from Nazi-occupied Europe.

OBJECTIVES AND REQUIREMENTS

In 1939, Albert Einstein wrote President Roosevelt to explain that the construction of the atomic bomb was theoretically possible, and that the Germans were probably working on it. Roosevelt comprehended the urgency, and soon several low-level scientific development efforts were initiated. By 1942, the American effort was approximately where the Germans had been in 1939. About this time, General Leslie Groves was put in charge of the project. General Groves was directed to build and explode an atomic bomb and convince the world that we could build and explode more.

Heisenberg, another Nobel laureate and the best physics theoretician of the time, led the German nuclear weapons program. In 1939, Heisenberg told Bohr that a Nazi bomb was technologically feasible. But he overestimated the necessary critical mass of uranium and therefore thought a bomb would be prohibitively expensive. But until 1944, the Allies believed that the Germans were significantly ahead in bomb technology. They believed that the Germans would build a nuclear bomb and would use it. They felt that their only defense was to build an atomic bomb first. This made the Allied effort especially urgent. Therefore, General Groves's second objective was to develop this capability before Nazi Germany, which meant as fast as possible since Germany's progress was not well known.

DESCRIPTION

Demonstration/Validation and Full-Scale Development began concurrently in 1942. There were two main technical issues: obtaining a reliable and adequate source of fissionable material, and designing and building the atomic weapon itself. By this point, five alternative concepts were identified as potential sources for fissionable material. None of them appeared particularly likely to succeed. Usually for full-scale development (also known as engineering-manufacturing development), alternative selection has been completed. Based on their proven performance, none of the available alternatives would have been allowed to proceed to engineering-manufacturing development under ordinary circumstances. Because the need was urgent, and because no alternative seemed more promising than another, all of the alternatives were funded for further development.

THE ALTERNATIVES

None of the alternatives could initially demonstrate how they hoped to come to production, but the heads of four of the five were absolutely certain it would happen.

Although most of the technical leadership within each project was exercised within academic institutions, all production facilities for separating U-235 from U-238, and for separating plutonium from uranium, were built at the Oak Ridge site in Tennessee. The production reactor for producing the uranium-plutonium blend was constructed in Hanford, Washington.

Let us now examine each of the five alternatives.

1. University of Chicago

Leaders: Nobel Laureates Arthur Holly Compton (Dean of the Division of Physical Sciences at Chicago) and Enrico Fermi. Principle: Plutonium production by means of uranium fission in a graphite moderated reactor. Technical Difficulties: No one had built a self-sustaining reactor before, and graphite of the required purity did not exist in industrial quantities. Although this is the most famous of the Manhattan Project teams, this was not a breakthrough project; it was original innovative design.

Fermi built a series of very small prototype reactors to check his calculations. The first self-sustaining chain reaction was obtained December 2, 1942, underneath Staggs Field at the University of Chicago. The maximum power of this initial reactor was 200 Watts. It required about 10^9 W to get 1 kg of plutonium per day, so the Chicago reactor could not have produced more than 200 micrograms of plutonium per day, and it would have taken about 100,000 years to get enough material for the Hiroshima bomb. The army wanted 1 kg per day, with no intervening prototype; imagine scaling up any complex system by six magnitudes! Nonetheless, construction on the full-scale production plant at Hanford, Washington began in March 1943. On September 27, 1944, the Hanford reactor went critical for the first time. On the advice of industrial consultants, an additional 504 fuel elements had been added to the design to provide a 20% design margin. As it turned out, all of these were needed to overcome Xenon poisoning of the reactor; previous reactors had not been large enough to notice the effect of Xenon poisoning. In January 1945, the first batch of plutonium was available. This event is notable because the most experienced chemists of the day (represented by James Conant, the country's leading organic chemist and the president of Harvard) believed it would take years; however, under the direction of Glenn Seaborg, the 32 year old discoverer of plutonium, it took two months. Seaborg's progress must be described as a breakthrough.

2. University of Chicago

Leader: Arthur Holly Compton (Nobel laureate). Principle: Plutonium production by means of uranium fission in a heavy water reactor. This project was very similar to the first project, except it relied on heavy water. Although heavy water reactors were used for experimental purposes at Argonne National Laboratories, this project was never a serious contender in the U.S. The Germans and British invested heavily in heavy water research. Perhaps the belief was that if Fermi's graphite reactor did not work, the British scientists could provide adequate support to catch up on a large-scale heavy water reactor.

3. Columbia University

Leader: Harold Urey (Nobel Laureate). Principle: Gaseous diffusion process for separating U-235 and U-238. Uranium is converted to gas, then filtered through microscopic holes in a "barrier." Technical Difficulties: Uranium is a heavy metal. Gaseous uranium is extremely corrosive. No barrier was known with sufficiently fine holes. Even with an adequate barrier, the process required many thousands of filtration sequences to obtain adequate concentrations. This cannot be viewed as a component allocation problem, since many of the necessary components did not exist. A breakthrough design was required.

Two barrier alternatives were initially identified. Neither had adequate characteristics. One was high strength, but had poor separation characteristics and was not predictable. The other was brittle and had marginal separation characteristics, but was predictable. The final design was a breakthrough; characteristically, it occurred when many (including the team leader, Urey) had given up hope, and it surpassed all expectations in its design characteristics.

Also, the process required an entirely new pump design with no lubricants, a supersonic speed in high vacuum, and no measurable leakage. The pump design depended on the barrier characteristics, which were not known. Eventually, the pump design was decomposed in such a way that the only unachievable part was the seal design; by allocating the most difficult functions to the seal, more flexibility was obtained for the rest of the design. A shotgun approach to seal design was started. At first, no adequate testing conditions or equipment existed, so development continued based on models and experience. In the summer of 1943, the best designs were tested: all seals failed. The final seal design, which had been developed but not yet recognized, was a complete breakthrough, and is still classified!

The diffusion process required as much power as a major city. The frequency of the power depended on the pump design. So the world's largest power plant was built to support five different frequencies; and to accommodate uncertainties, the flexibility of the design was more important than the cost. Similarly, the diffusion plant had to be built before an adequate barrier design was found. Again, the design had to be flexible.

By April 1945, the K-25 gas diffusion plant at Oak Ridge was producing uranium in very small quantities. K-25 had 2,000,000 square feet and 6,000 employees. It was the largest automated plant in the world at that time.

4. Westinghouse Research Laboratory, Pittsburgh

Leader: Eger Murphree, from Standard Oil Company. Principle: Use centripetal force to separate heavier U-238 from U-235 while in a gaseous state. Technical Difficulties: No adequate centrifuge existed. This project was canceled in late 1942.

5. University of California (Berkeley)

Leader: Ernest Lawrence (Nobel Laureate). Principle: Electromagnetic separation of U-235 and U-238 using a calutron. The calutron is a type of cyclotron (invented by Lawrence), named for "California University" and "cyclotron." Uranium particles were accelerated to uniform kinetic energy in a calutron, then magnetic fields were used to separate the particles that now had different momenta. Technical Difficulties: No equipment of suitable size existed, and the process showed inadequate separation characteristics. In 1942, after the initial three years of development, the project had obtained three samples totaling 75 micrograms of 30% enriched uranium.

Lawrence's method was eventually adopted at Oak Ridge, except on a larger scale. Ten 122 foot by 77 foot "racetracks" (calutrons) were built in the plant known as Y-12. The electromagnets in each unit were the largest the world had ever known. Because of wartime shortages of copper, 14,000 tons of silver from the U.S. Treasury were used in them. The calutrons were controlled by hundreds of local young women with minimal training—they were taught to operate knobs to keep dial indications within specification. Neither these operators nor their immediate supervisors knew what was being controlled. Despite the careful planning, this process was just too slow—by spring 1944, after about a year of operation, essentially no usable U-235 had been produced. Then the scientists discovered that if the raw material were slightly more enriched than the normal 0.7% of natural uranium (for example, the 7% obtained by the gaseous and thermal diffusion plants), then the electromagnetic units could produce adequate amounts of U-235.

UNCERTAINTIES

Indications were that plutonium would be fissionable, but at the time they could not be certain. In fact, none of the material properties of plutonium, and few of uranium, were known. Some material properties were highly unusual. For example, a 2-inch uranium rod was demonstrated to permanently lengthen to 12 inches under a heating and cooling cycle. Plutonium underwent five phase transformations between room temperature and its melting point.

The program had numerous problems even in starting development. One major hindrance: initial production quantities of uranium ore were not available. After scouring the free world, a sufficient supply was found in a warehouse in New York! The Belgian national who owned the ore would sell it to the U.S. government only on the condition that it *would* be used for military purposes.

The scientists thought that a dozen kilograms would be a critical mass, but they had little idea how big the bang would be. There was only one prototype. It was exploded on July 16, 1945 at the Trinity site in New Mexico. Before it was exploded, the scientists involved organized a betting pool on the yield: yields between zero and 45,000 tons of TNT were selected by various bettors. Enrico Fermi was willing to bet with anyone that the test would wipe out all life on Earth, with special odds on the mere destruction of the state of New Mexico. On August 2, well after this test, Admiral Leahy, President Truman's aide, flatly told the King of England that the atomic bomb would not work.

LOS ALAMOS

The other leg of the development process concerned the actual design and prototyping to manufacture an atomic weapon once a supply of fissionable material had been obtained. The design and prototype facility at Los Alamos was established for several reasons: (1) the director, Robert Oppenheimer, liked the New Mexican desert area (he owned a ranch there for several years), (2) it was desolate and likely to remain so, and (3) security requirements made communication difficult, so it was easiest to collocate the scientists in one place. Security was essential, since sabotage could easily damage the program. In the efforts to provide greater security, each inhabitant of the new city was issued a driver's license with no name (just a number), the same occupation (engineer), and the same address, P.O. Box 1663. No one was allowed to go to court, so speeding tickets were ignored. We can only assume that the scientists took full advantage of this circumstance.

Those working on the fissionable materials projects did not understand the fuss over the design effort. Ernest Lawrence, a project team leader, commented that the bomb could be designed by 30 scientists in three months. This belief that other parts of the development effort are trivial is typical in development environments; therefore when people who are competing for resources (regardless of their technical, personal, or administrative capability) express opinions about other aspects of the development process, the opinions should be evaluated accordingly. Despite Lawrence's claim, the heaviest concentration of talent was based at Los Alamos. This was because the 39 year old Robert Oppenheimer possessed lavish quantities of charisma, administrative ability, and scientific genius, which together made him an exceptional recruiter and organizer. Despite his talents, Oppenheimer had at one time been sympathetic to communist groups and the security bureaucracy routinely refused to grant Oppenheimer's security clearances; General Groves was required to directly override his own security apparatus.

The difficulty of the design was due to several factors.

1. There was a scarcity of fissionable material. Subsequently, the final bomb design would be the smallest that would fission. Initial estimates by Fermi were 2 to 100 kilograms, the uncertainty of which caused great consternation with General Groves! This implied that no functioning prototype would be available during the design—the Trinity explosion occurred too late to affect the design. Its purpose was merely to prevent us from dropping a dud.
2. The state of explosives science was far too backward to analyze atomic explosions which occurred in microseconds.
3. Virtually all scientific instrumentation required upgrading to allow adequate testing and measurement of this device.
4. The nature of the weapon required a complete functional analysis. For example, the central development concept was the "gun," in which two pieces of fissionable material are shot toward each other within a gun barrel. This design was prohibitively heavy for the aircraft of the day, but then one of the scientists

realized that because the gun only had to work once it could be made much lighter.

5. Finally, the physical properties of the fissionable materials were not well known. It eventually became clear that the "gun" concept would not function with plutonium, because the reaction would not be sufficiently abrupt. Fortunately, there existed a successful design concept (implosion) that had been rejected by the military and scientific leadership, but which had been kept alive by the dedication of several scientists on the staff, including Neils Bohr, John von Neumann, and Robert F. Christy.

Numerous scientists who worked on the project had or would eventually receive Nobel Prizes, including Glenn Seaborg (age 32), Enrico Fermi, Neils Bohr, Hans Bethe (age 40, head of the Theoretical Division), and Richard Feynman (who in one-half hour was able to solve a math problem that the entire Chicago project had failed to solve in months). Other notables included Leo Szilar, John von Neumann (the founder of game theory and a major influence in the evolution of cybernetics), Edward Teller (who went on to create the hydrogen bomb), and Joe Kennedy (age 26, head of the Chemical Division).

ANALYSIS

The five projects to obtain fissionable material were very definitely in competition with each other. General Groves made this clear when he canceled the Pittsburgh effort for not having the right attitude (they were not planning to work on Sundays and holidays). Although they had only limited formal lines of communication, they definitely possessed a strong yet secure informal network. This is to be expected, since the leaders were all well known in their fields. Although they shared the same objective, the competing efforts were chosen to be as different as possible in their means of accomplishment. Three projects investigated uranium production and two investigated plutonium production. The projects all concentrated on different concepts; this paid off generously at the end when the methods, each with different strengths and weaknesses, could be used in tandem to provide the adequate yield.

Although industrial consultants made many valuable contributions to the project, the development strategy of industry at that time would never have been successful. Industry's method was to evaluate several alternatives, then choose only the best one for engineering-manufacturing development. The scientific development method advocated continued parallel development at least until a good prospect was found. The Manhattan Project would not have succeeded without the academic institutions of the United States.

The Manhattan Project was by any measure a breakthrough design effort. From the beginning, technical experts in academia and industry evaluated many technical requirements as simply impossible. If technical evaluations had been used as the basis for development (as in a design review, for example), then the program would never have been started. Because the bomb worked, we know it was feasible. However, nobody could have foreseen the design of the bomb and bomb-production system in 1942; it required numerous technological breakthroughs. The insistence and enthusiasm of a few scientific leaders, and the threat of the German bomb project, kept the project going in those periods when progress seemed slow.

Because of the vast uncertainties and short schedule, the typical strategy was to explore all possibilities simultaneously. This exploration necessarily took the form of a combinatorial search. For example, in one case, all elements of the periodic table were tested for properties as a tamper (reflector) for the bomb.

In the end, none of the alternatives was adequate. At least two of the initial alternatives were duds (although eventually all of them were used effectively for other purposes). Near the end, they reinstated an alternative that had been screened out initially and developed independently for the Navy's nuclear propulsion program: thermal diffusion. The Navy had no Nobel Prize winners on their program, yet the thermal diffusion approach was technically sound. This demonstrates some of the uncertainties associated with the development process. In the end, only by combining the products of gaseous diffusion and thermal diffusion processes, could the project obtain the necessary quantities of fissionable U-235. Figure 20-1 demonstrates the configuration that led to the successful production of U-235.

Technical decision making was concentrated in General Groves and Robert Oppenheimer, who worked well together despite their extremely different backgrounds and politics. However, each project had great latitude, as well as great responsibilities, within its stated task. There is no indication of any project being starved for resources. Groves and his very minimal staff concentrated on expediting the needs of the project teams, rather than managing them. They also provided a technical forum within which relevant issues might be discussed. Typically, when individuals had a defensible position for moving forward against the complaints of others, they were backed. There was by no means any attempt to gain a consensus on technical decisions.

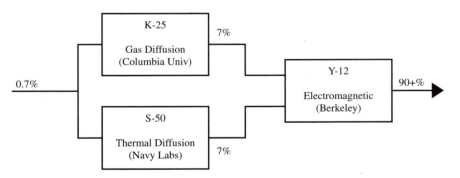

Figure 20-1   The final configuration at Oak Ridge successfully refined raw uranium ore into bomb grade U-235.

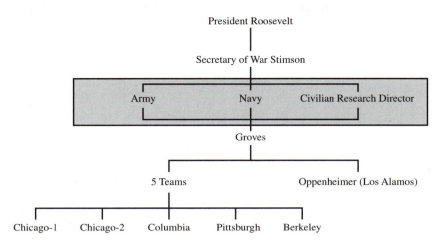

Figure 20-2 Chain of Command for the central parts of the Manhattan Project. In practice, Groves reported directly to Stimson.

The Manhattan Project was protected from normal government channels and other interference by the unique need for its product. Once, a strike threatened to shut down the Berkeley laboratory as the disgruntled workers negotiated to join a union. President Roosevelt interceded with the president of that union, and the laboratory workers were not even allowed to unionize! When congressional leaders got wind of the cost of the project, they wanted more information. Stimson, the secretary of war, interceded directly to give Congress confidence in the project without releasing details. There is no doubt that Roosevelt would have interceded if necessary. Several industrial giants were asked to risk their companies by overextending themselves on the effort. Only the CEO and hand-picked lieutenants were allowed to know anything about the project, but a surprising number of companies involved themselves anyway, including Du Pont (who would only accept a cost plus $1 contract). This ability to act autonomously without recurring interference from external authorities, public and private, played an enormous part in the eventual success of the project. Figure 20-2 shows the chain of command for the Manhattan Project.

Full scale engineering design of the atomic bomb began in 1942. In 1945, two atomic bombs were exploded three days apart, but they were entirely different devices. In the first, Little Boy, a cylinder of Uranium-235 was fired down a gun barrel into rings of U-235 forming a critical mass and producing an uncontrolled nuclear chain reaction. The second bomb, Fat Man, used plutonium. Because plutonium fissions spontaneously, the gun concept would not work. Therefore a sphere of plutonium was surrounded with high explosives. Implosion drove the plutonium together, which then produced the nuclear explosion. This project shows the use of alternative concepts right up to the end.

DESIGN DIFFICULTY AND RESOURCES SCORES

The following scores are from the viewpoint of top United States government officials near the beginning of World War II.

Design Type	Knowledge Complexity	Steps	Quality	Process Design	Aggressive Selling Price	Design Difficulty Total
14	10	7	6	2	1	40

Cost	Time	Infrastructure	Resources Total
14	5	7	26

REFERENCES

BROWN, A.C, and C.B. MACDONALD, ed., *The Secret History of the Atomic Bomb*. New York: The Dial Press/James Wade, 1977.

GROUEFF, S., *Manhattan Project*. Boston: Little, Brown, and Company, 1967.

LOGAN, J., "The critical mass." *American Scientist,* vol. 84, no. 3: pp. 263–277 (1996).

MORRISON, P., "Recollections of a nuclear war." *Scientific American*, vol. 273, no. 2: pp. 42–46 (August 1995).

RHODES, R., *The Making of the Atomic Bomb*. New York: Simon and Schuster, 1986.

SEABORG, G.T., *Nuclear Milestones*. San Francisco: W.H. Freeman and Company, 1972.

STOFF, M.B., et al., ed., *The Manhattan Project*. Philadelphia: Temple University Press, 1991.

21

THE POLARIS PROGRAM

In 1956, a new weapon system development program was launched by the United States Navy. Its purpose was to provide an invulnerable capability for retaliation in the case of nuclear attack, by placing strategic nuclear missiles on submarines. This program, called the Polaris Program or the Fleet Ballistic Missile (FBM) program, eventually cost $10.78 billion (about $46.7 billion in 1990 dollars), making it the most expensive development program up to that time. It was originally scheduled for completion in 1963, but development was advanced by three years after the Sputnik launch. Despite the aggressive schedule, the program came within 2% of original cost estimates; meanwhile, the defense industry at that time (circa 1962) averaged 220% cost overruns and 36% schedule overruns. Since it consisted of nuclear ballistic missile submarines, ballistic missile systems, and the deployment and logistics system to ensure proper operation and maintenance of all subsystems, this weapon system is one of the most complex ever deployed. The closest competitor (the U.S.S.R.) lagged at least five years behind, and even then could only copy the U.S.A.'s system. In order to deploy the system ahead of schedule and just about on budget, the Special Programs Office (SPO) created a policy of decentralization and competition within a strict framework.

RESOURCES

Each Fleet Ballistic Missile (FBM) submarine cost $110 million in 1962. The missiles and spare parts for each submarine cost $40 million. This deliverable product accounts for most of the cost of the program. In fact, research, development, test, and evaluation consumed only 24% of the funding. Eighty-five percent of the research and development and 75% of the funding went to the private sector, since the SPO did not trust government agencies to respond competitively.

During development, the SPO took up 50% of the Navy's budget for guided missiles, and up to 10% of the Navy's entire budget. Money for Polaris came directly out of other naval agencies since Eisenhower set a flat cap for each service. In succession the Triton, Regulus II, and Seamaster programs were canceled, and even operational units found their budgets reduced to obtain funding for Polaris. This made Polaris very unpopular with the rest of the Navy, who had to pay for it. Also, the head of the SPO, Admiral Raborn, was given authority by the Chief of Naval Operations, Admiral Arleigh Burke, to take any naval officer who could help the program. However, these unusual strategies paid off. At the end of development, the SPO turned in a $700 million surplus to the Navy.

OBJECTIVES

The Polaris weapon system was designed to ensure that even after suffering a full-scale nuclear attack the United States, would have the ability to destroy such a large percentage of any aggressor's military force, urban population, and industrial capacity that no country would consider a first-strike against the United States. Because all surface-based delivery systems were susceptible to a first-strike, the only feasible alternative was a launch platform that could not be detected or have its position given away. The only people who know the location of an FBM submarine are on the submarine, hence its advantage as a launch platform.

THE SPECIAL PROGRAMS OFFICE

The Special Programs Office, or SPO, was created to administer the Polaris program. Despite the amount of resources allocated to it, the SPO was always conscious of its precarious political position, and the need to manage its resources wisely. Its program office was limited to 45 naval officers and 45 civilians, and it always operated at a tiny fraction of the number of any conventional program. Civil servants within the SPO were not eligible to bump personnel in other parts of the federal civil service, so if the SPO failed, they would lose their civil service jobs. All civil service employees of the SPO were hired with this understanding, so it may be safely said that the SPO civil service employees were: confident in their abilities, not entrenched in bureaucracy, and somewhat risk-seeking.

The SPO differed from other programs in other ways. It prepared its own budget, and submitted it separately to Congress as an attachment to the Navy budget. It had no prime contractor. It required that all Polaris contractors set up separate organizations to which all Polaris work would be assigned. To the SPO, organizational autonomy was the number one objective. It recognized that it could not accomplish its task if it had to deal with bureaucratic interference from the government or its own contractors. In order to obtain autonomy, it had to ensure that the bill-payers

(Congress) recognized both the unique need for the program, and the unique management abilities of the SPO. To this end, the SPO originated the following management techniques: Project Management, Program Budgeting, Management and Control Centers (i.e., "War Rooms"), PERT,[1] Weekly Staff Meetings, Program Management Plans (Milestones, Tasks, etc.), and Line of Balance. These techniques are so standard in modern business that it seems strange that they should all have originated in a single program less than 35 years ago.

Most performance requirements were set by the technical director of the Special Programs Office in conjunction with technical experts, **not** directly by users. However, the user community was able to influence the requirements. For example, designers wanted to place at least 32 missile tubes on each of the new submarines. For the builders, this would be the best trade-off of cost versus performance. The minimum acceptable number by any cost-benefit analysis was 24 tubes per submarine. However, this conflicted directly with the desires and intuitions of the users, that is, the submarine personnel who would operate the system. Considerations of the users in this decision were:

1. tactical requirements of submarine maneuverability,
2. the large number of large hull penetrations, and
3. the desire to minimize the effect of a loss of one submarine ("too many eggs in one basket").

In order to ensure acceptance by the submarine community, Admiral Raborn directed that the design would be set at 16 missile tubes. Every navy in the world with ballistic missile submarines would adopt this same requirement despite its lack of a technical foundation.

Although adequate technology did not exist for any major subsystem, the SPO was careful not to let the necessary push for technology dominate the program. The program objective was the construction of a deployable system, not the advancement of technology. Although certain technologies had to be advanced to make the system deployable, almost all advances were predictable. Unlike the Manhattan Project and the Strategic Defense Initiative, no hard and fast physical limits had to be broken. It was comparable to the Apollo Program.

Central program issues were:

Fuel

The objective of weapon range, which implied a liquid-fueled rocket, conflicted with the objective of ship safety, which dictated a solid-fueled rocket. In 1955, Wernher von Braun, leader of the German rocket project during WWII and the American

---

[1]PERT stands for Program Evaluation and Review Technique. A PERT chart shows the events and activities that must be performed to finish a project. Time estimates are made for all activities. Events and activities are arranged so that as many activities are done in parallel as possible. It can then be determined which activites are most important in order to keep the project on schedule.

army rocket project thereafter, opined that the technical requirements of Polaris would be impossible to fulfill in the foreseeable future. However, this remark must be taken in context, since von Braun worked for the U.S. Army, which was in direct competition for funding with the U.S. Navy.

Guidance and Navigation Accuracy

The technical requirements were well beyond any components available at that time. This program produced enormous gains in inertial guidance and satellite navigation technology.

Warhead (Thermonuclear)

Eventually, a fractional megaton warhead was used; this decision was supported by the eventual accuracy of the weapon, and made possible by the extended range and the multiple warheads per missile. Such a warhead did not exist at program inception, but the Special Programs Office took Edward Teller's advice: "Why use a 1958 warhead in a 1965 weapon system?" Under current DoD guidance, such a technical decision would be unlikely, since it should increase the program risk. However, the implicit requirement for a sustainable advantage made this necessary.

Crew Rotation Cycle

Because of the high cost of each operational submarine, the Joint Chiefs of Staff wanted to keep them at sea full time. However, the Navy had learned that crews cannot be kept on station indefinitely without severely impinging on morale and effectiveness. Eventually, two crews were assigned to each submarine.

Communication

The Polaris system concept required the ability to order a strike at any time. However, in 1957, there was no effective way of maintaining communications with a submerged submarine, so technical advances were required in this area.

Launch

Eleven different launch alternatives were considered simultaneously.

Naval laboratories were specifically excluded from all Polaris development work. This was for several reasons, including:

1. the laboratories had unpredictable capabilities since they were ultimately controlled by congressional funding,
2. the laboratories were historically not responsive to program priorities, and
3. most importantly, other government agencies exerted control and influence in the naval laboratories.

Using such laboratories would violate the structured competition and autonomy on which this development program relied.

ANALYSIS

The program office focused on subsystem interrelationships, not components. A complete set of subsystem interfaces was defined very early in the program; but only those technical specifications associated with submarine physical constraints, and the program schedule, were fixed. The others were subject to negotiation with the SPO. The program office sought a disciplined flexibility with regard to interfaces, requirements, and specifications; but only the SPO had authority to change interface specifications.

Contrary to the custom of the time, there was no single weapon system contractor, which meant that no contractor held centralized systems engineering authority. Instead, the SPO retained complete control over all major interfaces and technical decisions. However, the SPO was, as previously mentioned, a very small organization compared to the overall technical effort. At a lower level, design authority was delegated in its entirety to the technical branches. Each technical branch had authority to develop its subsystem as it saw fit, subject to the interfaces; and each field office approved subsystem design changes that did not affect these interfaces. This ensured that technical decisions would be made by those closest to the problem. The rigorous competition among contractors that was structured into the program, along with the judicious use of independent design agents, such as the Massachusetts Institute of Technology and Johns Hopkins Applied Physics Laboratory, ensured that the technical branches and, when appropriate, the SPO, would receive the information that would allow them to make the best possible decisions.

Another important design philosophy was that the focus was on systems development, not technology. Once a design alternative was evaluated as adequate, with respect to system requirements and the prevailing uncertainties, it was more or less locked in. This policy was aided by the planned series of improvements to the original design. Any further progress would be incorporated in future versions. Each version of the system was to be complete, i.e., deployable on its own. The ultimate measure of technical success was to be the *operational* reliability of the Polaris Fleet Ballistic Missile system. To ensure this reliability, the SPO instituted subsystem testing, integrated system testing, tractability of discrepancies to the source, independent technical evaluations, and design redundancy.

Although the customers provided very few top-level requirements (for example, the number of missile tubes per submarine), almost all other requirements were generated by the technical organizations. This allowed a dynamic process of trade-offs, in which subsystem performance could be tailored to conform with the required schedules and the best available information from models and prototypes. In fact, with the exception of the physical submarine interfaces and the development schedule, the Polaris program is notable for its technical flexibility, which helped to avoid premature commitments to unrealistic or unnecessary performance goals.

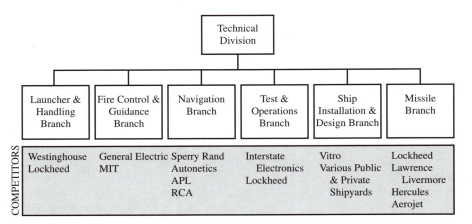

Figure 21-1   The technical organization of the Polaris program.

Perhaps the most important aspect of the SPO and the Polaris Program was its unique structure, which included a technical branch for every major subsystem, i.e., fire control & guidance, launcher & handling, navigation, ship installation & design, test & operations, and missile. Within each technical branch, every contractor had at least one direct competitor. Every contractor was placed in the position of looking for the design problems of the competitor to weaken the competitor's position, while at the same time working to avoid or mitigate its own problems. This prevented any complacency or collusion problems that might otherwise have resulted. Figure 21-1 shows the organization of the technical branches and the principal competitors within each branch.

DESIGN DIFFICULTY AND RESOURCES SCORES

The following scores are from the viewpoint of the United States government in the late 1950s.

Design Type	Knowledge Complexity	Steps	Quality	Process Design	Aggressive Selling Price	Design Difficulty Total
10	7	9	9	2	3	40

Cost	Time	Infrastructure	Resources Total
14	7	8	29

REFERENCES

Davis, V., *The Politics of Innovation: Patterns in Navy Cases*. University of Denver: 1967.

Sapolsky, H.M., *The Polaris System Development*. Cambridge, MA: Harvard University Press, 1972.

22

THE HUBBLE SPACE TELESCOPE

The Hubble Space Telescope (HST) was launched April 24, 1990, after over a decade of design, manufacturing, and testing that cost $1.5 billion. Freedom from atmospheric disturbances and high precision manufacturing was supposed to have given it 50 times the sensitivity of ground based telescopes. To achieve this sensitivity, the primary mirror was ground with a precision better than 150 angstroms. But it was ground in the wrong shape! This produced a telescope with significantly reduced sensitivity. Therefore it could not detect faint objects, such as planets of nearby stars, as originally specified. During the manufacturing process, there were many clues that something was wrong. In fact, a photograph taken in 1981 shows the flaw, but the test procedures directed the tester's attention to a different part of the photograph.

Satellites are generally partitioned into two subsystems: the bus and the payload. The bus is the portion of the satellite that provides the appropriate environment, such as power and suitable thermal conditions, for the payload. The payload is the reason the satellite is launched. The HST payload consists of two assemblies: the science instruments and the telescope components (including the primary mirror, the secondary mirror, and the tube). Each assembly seemed to work well by itself; the system failure was discovered when they were coupled together.

This failure could have been detected if a full system test had been performed, but such a test was not required. NASA specified tests to detect small errors, but not blunders of this magnitude. They thought a complete system test was unnecessary and would cost too much. However, the cost of a complete system test would have been much less than the $850 million it cost to fix the telescope in orbit.

SYSTEM DESCRIPTION

The HST is the most complex scientific instrument ever constructed. With 10 times finer resolution and 50 times greater sensitivity than any other optical mechanism ever constructed, it is truly a remarkable machine. It was designed and built between 1977 and 1986, but its launch was delayed four years due to the explosion of the space shuttle Challenger.

The heart of the HST is the telescope composed of the baffled tube and the primary and secondary mirrors. The 2.4 meter primary mirror was designed and manufactured between 1977 and 1981 by Perkin-Elmer Corporation. Despite its now-famous spherical aberration, the primary mirror is noted for an exquisite smoothness unsurpassed by any other surface of its size. If the mirror were scaled to the size of North America, the largest hill or valley would be like a small ant hill, while a typical eyeglass lens would have skyscraper-sized imperfections. The secondary mirror is 5 meters in front of the primary, and is 0.3 meter in diameter. The telescope tube extends another 3 meters beyond the secondary mirror to shield stray light.

The remainder of the HST's 13 meter length is occupied by the science instrumentation. The craft is 4.3 meters in diameter (12 meters in diameter with the solar arrays deployed), and weighs 11 metric tons. The HST's power requirements are supplied by solar arrays in conjunction with a battery storage system. The solar panels cover an area 2.4 meters by 12 meters, and consist of 48,800 solar cells producing 4,100 watts. The HST is composed of 400,000 parts and contains 26,000 miles of electrical wire.

Its Science Operations Ground Support Software System consists of nearly 4 million lines of Fortran and C code. By comparison, a supermarket scanner requires about 20,000 lines; a cellular phone needs about 30,000 lines; an average air-traffic control computer uses about 130,000 lines; and a typical ATM network contains about 600,000 lines. The only comparable systems currently deployed are military, e.g., the Seawolf submarines and the Aegis cruisers. For further comparison, the operators of the HST estimate that the Strategic Defense Initiative ("Star Wars") would require 10 times as much software. This ground support system is so complex because the onboard capability of HST is so modest. The two original onboard computers were about as powerful as a Commodore 64, although one has since been upgraded to 80386 capability at a cost of $3 million (not including delivery). This unequal partitioning of functionality is necessary because of the harsh radiation environment for orbiting satellites. Preflight simulations conducted to verify the HST computing system performance were the most exhaustive ever performed for a civilian space flight.

Although the HST is complex, it cannot be considered a technological breakthrough. Its performance gains, as well as its system weaknesses, are derived mainly from its location in orbit. Lacking the budget to field a fleet of satellites, NASA elected to place a relatively large number of science instruments on the HST, which made this the most complex satellite yet deployed. In other words, the technical issues were those of complexity management, rather than technical breakthrough. The spacecraft design itself is a variant of the design used for a series of intelligence satellites built under a program known as Keyhole. Interestingly, both Lockheed (the prime contractor), and Perkin-Elmer were familiar with the Keyhole program; yet neither company effectively used the lessons learned from Keyhole to avoid predictable problems with the HST. For example, it was well known in the intelligence-satellite community that flexible solar arrays of the type used by the HST would cause excessive jitter, as described below.

COSTS

The HST procurement cost was $1.5 billion, which was three times the amount originally budgeted. The costs were driven by an optical system of unparalleled complexity: a cutting edge guidance and control unit, and a modular design that allows replacement of up to 80 devices during a single servicing. The United States government starts systems of equivalent cost every few years.

TOTAL LIFE CYCLE COST

Our cost metric only includes design and manufacture, not operations and retirement. For some systems, such as the pyramids of Egypt, the cost and the total life cycle cost might be equal, because there are no operation, maintenance, repair, or retirement costs. However, the HST is not such a system. Maintenance costs are very high, because maintenance requires the space shuttle. Total life cycle costs have been estimated at $6 billion in 1990 dollars. This would represent 6 million man years of productivity for inhabitants of third-world countries, and is therefore on par with the cost of the pyramids.

REQUIREMENTS

The top-level requirements for the HST were stated by NASA:

> *"The optical image, including effects of optical wave-front error, pointing stability, and alignment of the scientific instruments to the Optical Telescope Assembly, shall satisfy the following on-axis requirements at 6,328 angstroms and be a design goal at UV wavelengths: Image resolution using the Rayleigh criterion for contrast of 0.10 second of arc. A full-width half-intensity diameter of 0.10 second of arc, 70% of the total energy of a stellar image must be confined within a radius of 0.10 second of arc. After correction for astigmatism, these specifications shall apply to the image quality over the entire usable field of Space Telescope."*

Due to the spherical aberration of the primary mirror, the HST does not come close to meeting these requirements; for example, only 15% of the total energy is captured within 0.1 second of arc. Therefore, a set of corrective mirrors (called COSTAR) was installed between the primary and secondary mirrors to allow the science instruments to effectively use the spherically aberrated primary mirror. The high speed photometer had to be removed to make room for COSTAR, and the high resolution spectrograph stopped working as a result of installing COSTAR. With the COSTAR spectacles in place, the top level requirement is nearly met by the Wide Field/Planetary Camera, and is exceeded by the Faint Object Camera. Unfortunately, this comes with the complete loss of two instruments, and a reduced field of view in a third. However, not many astronomers will complain about what was lost. They are ecstatic about its performance.

One of NASA's principal responsibilities was the specification of system requirements for HST. The partitioning of most system functionality to the ground resulted in a very complex ground support system that nevertheless seems to work very well. The functionality assigned to the primary and secondary mirrors does not seem to have been avoidable. In all, NASA seems to have adequately determined the requirements of both the spacecraft and the science instruments required for the Hubble Space Telescope. The top level requirements for the individual instruments are summarized in Table 22-1.

The four principal performance parameters for optical systems are: field of view, wavelength, resolution, and sensitivity. As shown in Table 22-1, the HST's observable wavelengths range from the deep ultraviolet to the far-infrared. Ultraviolet sensitivity was paramount, because the earth's atmosphere screens out most of the ultraviolet radiation that could provide useful astronomical information for earth bound telescopes. Only one of the instruments probes the infrared, because ground-based infrared telescopes already have HST's capabilities for these wavelengths.

The sensitivity of the HST is specified as the magnitude (or brightness) of the faintest objects it can see. The human eye can detect objects to the 6th magnitude, good binoculars can reach the 9th magnitude, a 6 inch telescope can make out objects of the 13th magnitude, and precision astronomical instruments such as the 200 inch

TABLE 22-1 Science Instrument Specifications.

Instrument	Field of View	Wavelength (A)	Resolution	Sensitivity
Wide Field/Planetary Camera	2.7; 1.1 min sq	1150–11000	0.1 sec; 0.04 sec	28
Faint Object Camera	11 sec; 22 sec sq.	1200–6000	0.02 sec; 0.04 sec	28
Faint Object Spectrograph	0.1–4.3 sec	1150–8000	3A;20A	22,26
High Resolution Spectrograph*	0.25–2 sec	1100–3200	0.03;.1;1A	11,14,17
High Speed Photometer**	0.4;1;10 sec	1200–8000	10μs	24
Fine Guidance Sensors***	0.69 sec sq	4670–7000	0.002 sec	18

Note: HST optical instruments are specified in arc-seconds or arc-minutes. 1 arc-second $\cong 4.848 \times 10^{-6}$ radians, and 1 arc-minute $\cong 290.9 \times 10^{-6}$ radians.

*stopped working soon after first service

**removed at first service to make room for COSTAR

***still using uncorrected aberrated source

telescope on Mount Palomar can detect objects of the 25th magnitude, which is a million times as sensitive as the human eye. With its optical fix in place, the HST can see objects as faint as the 30th magnitude.

The HST is also notable for its resolution. The best ground-based telescope can resolve objects of about 0.5 arc-second on exceptionally good nights. The HST can resolve to 0.05 arc-second, which is like being able to read a car license plate at 300 miles. As a result of its exceptional performance regarding both sensitivity and resolution, the HST is the largest step forward astronomically since Galileo's original telescope.

THE HST LIFE CYCLE

When originally planned in 1977, the Large Space Telescope program intended to return the HST to the earth for refurbishment and relaunch every five years, with on-orbit servicing midway between each refurbishment. As a result, hardware and system reliability requirements were based on a 2.5 year interval. Late in development, issues associated with contamination and structural integrity caused the program to eliminate the scheduled return of the HST to the earth. So the 2.5 year servicing cycle was extended to a 3 year cycle. It is fortunate that the HST was designed for on-orbit servicing because the shuttle astronauts used this capability beyond original expectations; in December 1993, they installed COSTAR, a set of mirrors that ameliorates the spherical aberration of the primary mirror. However, the change in life cycle servicing appears to have been driven entirely by resource considerations (i.e., bottom-up) rather than a well-reasoned balance between resources and requirements. Nevertheless, at this time HST is expected to serve adequately for its 15 year design life.

THE PRIMARY MIRROR

Following good engineering practice, Perkin-Elmer engineers designed, built, and used three separate measurement instruments during the fabrication of the primary mirror. These instruments were a reflective null corrector, a refractive null corrector, and an inverse null corrector. Each of these instruments was used to assess the performance of the mirror by producing a picture called an interferogram, which is a pattern of lines called fringes. A mirror that does not meet the specifications defined by the appropriate optical template will produce wavy fringes.

The reflective null corrector was the most sophisticated of the three measuring instruments. Even when the other two instruments showed conclusively that a flaw existed in the mirror, Perkin-Elmer placed its confidence in the reflective null corrector's incorrect measurements. This was bad systems engineering for two very important reasons. The first is that *undesirable* test results should not be dismissed arbitrarily in favor of *expected* test results. In fact, a knowledge of the relative accuracies of the test instruments would have led a competent evaluator to conclude that the probability of two null correctors independently showing false results was infinitesimally small. The second reason is that part of the apparatus used to polish the mirror was shared by the reflective null corrector, so the reflective null corrector was intrinsically incapable of detecting errors resulting from that part of the fabrication equipment. The primary mirror was ground in the wrong shape because this reflective null corrector was incorrectly assembled.

Not everyone at Perkin-Elmer was oblivious to the possibility of an error in the primary mirror's manufacture. An internal Perkin-Elmer audit team reviewed the optical performance evaluation of the HST primary mirror in 1981. The memo documenting this audit was introduced into hearings before Congress, and is especially noteworthy for two reasons. First, the technically-minded authors were clearly aware of the complex "long chain of analyses and tests" involved in the design and manufacture of the mirror, and referred to the very real possibility of "gross errors." Second, the authors specifically requested that additional testing be conducted to "eliminate every possibility of error." Interestingly, two anonymous reviewers derided this recommendation with the hand-written notations "Technically Questionable" and "Out of Scope!"

A key consideration in the decision not to conduct a total system test, also known as an end-to-end test, was the cost of the test. In the early days after the discovery of the spherical aberration, NASA estimated this testing cost as several hundred million dollars. When this figure was questioned by the technical community, NASA significantly reduced its estimate by an order of magnitude. In fact, the Air Force had the test equipment on hand. Worse, a simple "knife-edge" test commonly used by amateur astronomers could have detected the error for less than $100. But in fact such a test would have been meaningless, since the manufacturers already had plenty of reason to believe that the mirror was imperfect; they simply chose to ignore the evidence at hand.

The subsequent error in the mirror, up to 2μ or 20,000A, was over 100 times the amount certified to NASA by Perkin-Elmer. The optical impact was to substantially reduce the sensitivity of the telescope to approximately that of the best ground-based telescope. However, the judicious use of image processing and well-planned exposures allowed the HST to produce useful astronomical results even before the 1993 space shuttle service mission. The situation with the HST was never as bad as described in the popular media before the fix, nor as good as described after the fix. This is a lesson in the value of the perception of the bill-payer.

One of the greatest tragedies is that NASA had already recognized that the manufacture of the primary mirror was a critical and inherently risky task and, following good risk management practices, had Corning manufacture a backup mirror. This backup mirror was built and delivered, but was never tested. The manufacturing method of this backup primary mirror was completely different from that of the Perkin-Elmer mirror, and there is every reason to believe that the backup was within specification. Also notable is the fact that the backup mirror came in on schedule and within budget. However, the whole truth may never be known, as this backup mirror was apparently requisitioned for use as a U.S. national security asset.

THE HST JITTER

Another problem with the HST, not as well publicized as the spherical aberration of the primary mirror but in many ways just as consequential to its mission, was the one Hertz jitter experienced by the telescope as it crossed the day-night terminator on each 96-minute orbit. For about five minutes crossing into night and 10 minutes crossing into day, the HST's solar array experienced a relatively large amplitude (about one degree) vibration induced by thermal differences in its solar array. Although the effect of this vibration on the telescope itself was smaller (0.3 arc-second), it nonetheless greatly exceeded the required 0.007 arc-second requirement and seriously compromised the HST's high resolution and ability to acquire and track guide stars. Consequently, the HST's essential mission capability was significantly affected. This problem was significant for another reason: like the primary mirror, the original solar arrays were never adequately tested on the ground due to technical and financial reasons. It was only with the replacement of the solar arrays during the 1993 service mission that this problem was significantly mitigated, although the telescope still occasionally loses track for this reason.

Systems Engineering Mistakes

Although Lockheed is on record as the system integrator, it seems that the bill-payer, NASA, was responsible for the actual top-level system performance. NASA's systems engineering is an interesting contrast between very good approaches (such as using the backup primary mirror to mitigate risk, and developing thorough requirements specification), and very poor approaches (notably, relying on poor system and subsystem validation plans—as exemplified by the primary mirror and solar array subsystems—and lacking a total system test).

DESIGN DIFFICULTY AND RESOURCES SCORES

The following scores are from the viewpoint of top United States government officials and scientists in 1977.

Design Type	Knowledge Complexity	Steps	Quality	Process Design	Aggressive Selling Price	Design Difficulty Total
9	7	5	2	3	1	27

Cost	Time	Infrastructure	Resources Total
6	10	5	21

REFERENCES

ALLEN, L. ed., *The Hubble Space Telescope optical systems failure report.* NASA, NASA-TM-103443, NAS 1.15:103443 CASI HC A06/MF A02, November 1990.

CHAISSON, Eric J. *The Hubble Wars: Astrophysics Meets Astropolitics in the Two-Billion Dollar Struggle over the Hubble Space Telescope.* New York: Harper Collins, 1994.

FIELD, George, and Donald GOLDSMITH, *The Space Telescope.* Chicago: Contemporary Books, 1989.

FIENBERG, Richard T., "The Hobbled Space Telescope." *Sky & Telescope*, vol. 80, no. 3: p. 245, (September 1990).

FIENBERG, Richard T., "Hubble's Image Restored." *Sky & Telescope*, vol. 83, no. 9: pp. 21–22, (April 1994).

FIENBERG, Richard T., "Space telescope; picking up the pieces." *Sky & Telescope*, vol. 80, no. 4: pp. 352–358, (October 1990).

House Committee on Science, Space, and Technology. *Hearings on the Hubble Space Telescope Flaw,* 101st Congress: 81, July 13, 1990.

House Committee On Science, Space, and Technology. *Hearings on the Hubble Space Telescope,* 103rd Congress: 156, November 16, 1993.

SINNOTT, Roger W., "Mirror Testing for Non-Opticians." *Sky & Telescope*, vol. 79, no. 8: pp. 214–220, (February 1990).

LESSONS LEARNED FROM THE
SIMPLE CASE STUDIES

23.1 THE METRICS SUMMARY TABLES

Validating the Scores

Tables 23-1 and 23-2 show the summary scores for all of the case studies. Figure 23-1 plots all of the case studies together on one chart. Many more case studies could have been extracted from the literature. But we were trying to derive a minimal set that would cover the entire plane and be useful for systems engineers embarking on a new design project. We started by reading two or three books and numerous articles on each case study. Next, we condensed the system engineers' roles and the critical design requirements into a case study ranging from 3 to 10 pages in length.

The scores shown in Tables 23-1 and 23-2 were derived through multiple iterative discussions. First Chapman assigned scores based on his reading of the case studies. Then Bahill and Chapman discussed them: about 50% were changed by one or two points and 10% were changed by more than two points. A month later, Bahill and Chapman discussed them again and changed about 20% of them by one or two points. Next, the case studies were presented to eight students in a graduate class entitled "Model-Based Systems Engineering" at the University of Arizona. The consensus of the students caused about 10% of the scores to be changed by one point. The case studies were presented at a Systems and Industrial Engineering Departmental seminar and minor changes resulted. Then, Bahill presented the case studies to 25 senior systems engineers at Sandia National Laboratories. The consensus of these systems engineers was that one particular score should be changed by three points. After some discussion, Bahill and Chapman changed the score and also made changes of one or two points to two other scores. The following spring, nine graduate students (all of

TABLE 23-1   **Design Difficulty Scores for the Case Studies.**

Case Study	Design Type	Knowledge Complexity	Steps	Quality	Process Design	Aggressive Selling Price	Design Difficulty Total
Resistor Networks	1	1	1	1	1	1	6
SIERRA	2	2	1	1	1	1	8
Bat Chooser	6	5	1	3	1	2	18
Pinewood Derby	3	2	2	2	1	1	11
Second Opinion®	5	6	3	5	3	2	23
American Airlines	6	4	4	2	2	1	19
Superconductors	15	10	2	3	2	1	33
Light Bulb	14	5	4	2	4	4	33
Boeing 777	9	6	9	8	4	4	40
Apollo Moon Landing	12	7	10	9	2	1	41
House	2	1	4	3	1	3	14
CAP	4	2	5	2	1	1	15
Pyramid	4	4	5	10	1	1	25
Car Factory	7	4	6	5	5	5	32
Electric Vehicle	10	7	5	3	2	3	30
Improved Battery	8	6	3	2	4	4	27
Breakthrough Battery	15	6	3	3	5	4	36
C3PO	15	10	10	6	4	3	48
Manhattan Project	14	10	7	6	2	1	40
Polaris Program	10	7	9	9	2	3	40
Hubble Space Telescope	9	7	5	2	3	1	27

whom had industrial experience) studied and evaluated the case studies and the metrics. As a result, 15% of the scores were changed, on average, by 1.4 points. In areas where the standard deviations of evaluations were large, the metrics or the case studies were rewritten. The most significant changes were made in the end of each case in the section "from the view point of." These cases were then presented in a graduate systems engineering course at the University of Arizona and a systems engineering course at Sandia National Laboratories. No scores were changed. Therefore, we conclude that evaluations such as those presented in this book can be derived by obtaining a consensus from systems engineers. The consensus that develops is robust and is acceptable to engineers with broadly differing backgrounds. For more information on generating a consensus, see Bahill, Bharathan, and Curlee (1995).

Usefulness of System Design Metrics

This system of rating design efforts is valuable for several reasons. First, design is as much an art as a science and by studying how other design efforts were done, lessons can be learned and applied to future projects. The evaluation scheme presented here is one method of explaining different facets of design.

The second, and main reason, for such a system of measurement is to rate proposed design efforts before they even start. Corporations that must make a profit to

TABLE 23-2   Resource Scores for the Case Studies.

Case Study	Cost	Time	Infrastructure	Resources Total
Resistor Networks	1	1	1	3
SIERRA	1.5	1.5	1	4
Bat Chooser	2	3	2	7
Pinewood Derby	2	2	1.5	5.5
Second Opinion®	2	8	3	13
American Airlines	3	5	5	13
Superconductors	2	2	4	8
Light Bulb	5	3	2	10
Boeing 777	12	7	8	27
Apollo Moon Landing	15	9	10	34
House	12	3	6	21
CAP	12	9	6	27
Pyramid	15	10	9	34
Car Factory	9	7	6	22
Electric Vehicle	7	4	4	15
Improved Battery	3	10	4	17
Breakthrough Battery	5	6	5	16
C3PO	2	2	3	7
Manhattan Project	14	5	7	26
Polaris Program	14	7	8	29
Hubble Space Telescope	6	10	5	21

survive must only attempt those projects in the Consumer Products region. Any design effort outside this region will require resources outside the scope of most ventures. Those ventures in the Star Wars arena are best left to academics and research laboratories where lack of immediate success is not punished. If your customer asks you to build a system that fits into the Star Wars quadrant, you should tell them at the beginning that it cannot be done with the allotted resources. Projects that fit the Seven Wonders of the Ancient World region are strictly for governments. Not only do these ventures not pay for themselves, but they also require despotic power to implement, since there is so little reward for the citizens involved. And finally, those in the Moon Landing area require government and industry involvement to succeed, since it requires such a large share of the national resources.

We expect systems engineers to look at requirements for a new design; assemble an interdisciplinary team of customers, designers, manufacturing engineers, sales, product support, etc.; and develop a consensus for the amount of resources required and the design difficulty. We believe that an analysis, such as the ones presented in this book, would lead the system design team to decide the scope of the project and the appropriateness of the resources to the task.

We used Figure 23-1 to assess when formal systems engineering was used. We expected a nonlinear Pareto-optimal contour in the Design Difficulty versus Resources plane. Quite surprisingly, we found that all systems to the right of the project, Second Opinion®, used formal systems engineering; and all systems to the left of Second Opinion® did not. Second Opinion® did not use formal systems engineering, but it

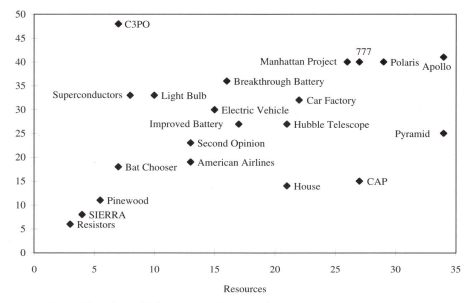

Figure 23-1   Design Difficulty versus Resources plane.

should have. It was thought that during the evolution from one prototype to the next, the rules used in the expert system model would be kept intact; but they were not. One important rule disappeared. There was no formal list of systems requirements, so the omission almost escaped detection. We conclude that in these case studies, the use of formal systems engineering was determined mostly by resources. Small projects, where the engineers tracked everything in their heads, did not use formal systems engineering; while large projects, where information had to be communicated between people, did use formal systems engineering. The boundary line between the two is a vertical line passing through Second Opinion®. So it seems that in the past, the decision of whether or not to do formal systems engineering has been based on resources. However, we think the decision should be based on risk.

Most of the points in Figure 23-2 follow a sequence from the lower left corner to the upper right corner. We tried very hard to get points in all parts of the plane. If we had not, then the points would have formed a dense cluster in this main sequence. A straight line drawn through Bat Chooser and Electric Vehicle separates the high technological risk projects from those in the Main Sequence. Risk mitigation using technical performance measures are a must for projects in this region. A parallel line going through Polaris separates the Main Sequence projects from the high political risk projects. These projects have a low return on investment and therefore probably need nonfinancial factors, such as patriotism (Apollo), religion (the Pyramids), national security (Polaris), pride of ownership (owning a house is the "American Dream"), government subsidies (the House), or overpopulation (CAP), to convince

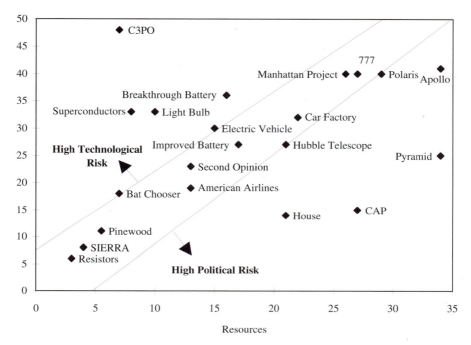

Figure 23-2   Risky projects in the Design Difficulty versus Resources plane.

people to support them through completion. Such projects are often canceled for political reasons.

The Superconductor Supercollider may be an example of a high political risk project that was canceled. The following evaluation of the Supercollider was done by T.J. Hippeli.

Design Type	Knowledge Complexity	Steps	Quality	Process Design	Aggressive Selling Price	Design Difficulty Total
7	4	7	6	1	1	26

Cost	Time	Infrastructure	Resources Total
13	10	9	32

This evaluation puts the Supercollider in the high political risk region as is shown in Figure 23-3. But its designers did not realize this. Nor did they realize its consequences. The Supercollider stopped being a science project and became a big

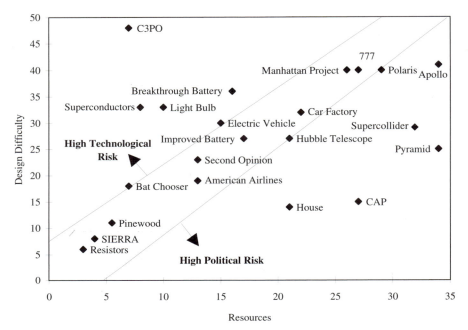

Figure 23-3   The Design Difficulty versus Resources plane with the addition of the Supercollider.

physics project. It stopped being an American project and became a Texas project. It stopped being a good project and became a poorly managed project. It lost its image as a good American, science project and therefore lost patriotic support. Consequently, it was canceled. If your project is in the area of high political risk, you must identify its source of support, and work very hard so that you do not lose it.

If your project turns out to be in the area of high political risk, then you should design your system so that it has stable intermediate forms. That way, if the project gets canceled, you will still have something useful. If the CAP were canceled in midstream so that it brought water to Phoenix, but not to Tucson, then it would have still been a useful system. In contrast, when the Supercollider was canceled, there was nothing useful for humanity, except for some huge concrete tunnels in the Texas desert.

Two important insights were noted from the case studies. First, successful projects always have clearly defined criteria for success. The engineers knew where they were going and were able to judge their success themselves. The systems engineer plays an important role here. It is the systems engineer's job to set up the criteria for success on all subsystems of large projects. By flowing down the requirements clearly and correctly, the probability of project success is greatly increased.

Each law passed by any political body should define its criteria for success. For example, a crime bill might state that it will reduce crime by xx% as measured with yy statistic within zz years. If it fails, the law would automatically be rescinded.

Another major feature of these projects was not under the control of the systems engineers. Successful design projects always had motivated workers who cared about the outcome of their efforts. By motivating the workers with a "vision" or "reward," the management ensured dedicated people who would find some way to get the job done. This motivation affected the systems engineers as much as anyone else. Motivated systems engineers did great jobs (see the Apollo Moon Landing and the electric vehicle case studies for good examples). The fact that great systems engineers cannot motivate the workers severely limits their ability to ensure a successful project. Obviously the project leader, as the chief motivator and planner, must also understand the system design process and use it wisely.

Conclusions about the Design Difficulty Versus Resources Plane

The analyses of our case studies would have to be tailored by individual companies. Analyses similar to those we have presented in this book are being done throughout the world. This is often referred to as "bench marking." For each new project a company contemplates, the engineers gather and compare it to previous company projects. They discuss the lessons learned from previous projects and discuss the similarities and differences between the current and previous projects. However, these comparisons are usually informal and qualitative. We are suggesting that they should be more formal and quantitative. Our nine metrics and two axes could be enlarged and customized using in-house data for each company. We suspect that the resulting conclusions will be similar. If a project is too complicated for that company, it should be rejected. If the design life of the project is too long for stockholder or voter appreciation, it should be rejected or modified. Such analyses will help reject high-risk projects, and modify the requirements for acceptable projects.

Invention on the Critical Path

Both PERT charts and work breakdown structures are used to help keep projects on schedule (Kerzner, 1995). All tasks are listed, along with their predecessor and successor tasks. Some tasks can be done in parallel, but others have to be done in series. The tasks are laid out with as many tasks in parallel as possible. Then the path that has no slack time is identified. This is called the critical path. If any task on this path slips behind schedule, then the whole project slips behind schedule. The systems engineer should make sure that invention (or basic research) is not being done on the critical path. Table 23-3 analyzes invention on the critical paths of the case studies described in this book.

The Manhattan Project and the Hubble Space Telescope were high risk projects. But they did not appear in the region of high technological risk or in the region of high political risk in Figure 23-2. We can now see what caused their high risk: they had invention on the critical path.

TABLE 23-3   Invention on the Critical Path.

Case Study	Invention on the critical path?
Resistor Networks	No invention was involved.
SIERRA	Yes. The students thought that their designs were innovative. Most students are always on their critical path. Consequently, some students failed to meet the schedule.
Bat Chooser	No. There was no scheduled completion date. Therefore, there was no critical path.
Pinewood Derby	Yes. We were trying to invent schedules on the critical path. This project would have failed if we did not stop.
Second Opinion®	No. There was no scheduled completion date. Therefore, there was no critical path.
American Airlines	No. Little invention was involved.
Superconductor	No. There was no scheduled completion date. Therefore, there was no critical path.
Light Bulb	No. There was no scheduled completion date. Therefore, there was no critical path.
Boeing 777	No. Most of the innovation involved building the computer design software, and that was not invention.
Apollo Moon Landing	Maybe. There was not a lot of invention in this project, but there was a hard schedule requirement.
House	No. Architects do a lot of innovation, but never on the critical path.
CAP	No. There was no innovation on this project.
Pyramid	No. There was probably no scheduled completion date. Therefore, there was no critical path.
Car Factory	No. There was not a lot of invention in this project.
Electric Vehicle	Maybe. But there was no hard scheduled completion date.
Improved Battery	No. There was no invention on this project.
Breakthrough Battery	No. There is no scheduled completion date. If breakthrough batteries are not discovered, then we will continue to use traditional batteries.
C3PO	Who knows?
Manhattan Project	YES, and this is the highest risk project we have studied!
Polaris Program	No. There was little technical invention on this project.
Hubble Space Telescope	Yes. The control and guidance system was on the cutting edge and it sapped resources from Systems Engineering. As a result, a total system test was never performed.

Other Metrics

The metrics used by any company to evaluate project risk will have to be tailored to that company. Many other metrics are available. For example, we considered using design life as another measure of design difficulty.

Design Life
(The operation and maintenance phase of the system life cycle, the life span.) The longer the system is supposed to last, the harder it will be to design and build it. Points are assigned for design life according to the following equation:

$$\text{Design Life Score} = \log_{10} (\text{Design Life in years}) + 4$$

Table 23-4 shows the Design Life scores for the cases we have studied so far.

Some other potential cost metrics include the amount of scrap materials and waste generated during production, the cost of the scrap and waste, and the cost for disposing of the scrap and waste.

Attributes of a Good Metric

A good metric should measure aspects of the process that can be controlled; provide information that can be used to initiate change; provide insight into how well goals and objectives are being met; be simple, understandable, repeatable, and measurable; and have inexpensive methods to collect and analyze data.

Design for Recyclability

When designing a system, it is very important to consider the whole system life cycle, including retirement and replacement. Design engineers should design systems so that they can be easily recycled at the end of their useful life. Germany has a law that all television sets shall be returned to their manufacturer at the end of their useful life. Table 23-5 shows how the designs in these case studies are recycled.

TABLE 23-4   Design Life Metric .

Case Study	Design Life	Design Life Score
Resistor Networks	1 hour	0
SIERRA	3 days	2
Bat Chooser	1 year	4
Pinewood Derby	3 days	2
Second Opinion®	3 years	4
American Airlines	1 year	4
Superconductors	1 hour	0
Light Bulb	1 month	3
Boeing 777	30 years	5
Apollo Moon Landing	1 month	3
House	100 years	6
CAP	100 years	6
Pyramid	1000 years	7
Car Factory	10 years	5
Electric Vehicle	10 years	5
Improved Battery	2 years	4
Breakthrough Battery	10 years	5
C3PO	10 years	5
Manhattan Project	1 year	4
Polaris Program	30 years	5
Hubble Space Telescope	15 years	5

TABLE 23-5   Design for Recyclability.

Case Study	Recyclability
Resistor Networks	Resistors are often recycled.
SIERRA	These controllers were built on breadboards. After system test, all components were removed and they were used by subsequent students.
Bat Chooser	It would be difficult to recycle anything from Bat Chooser.
Pinewood Derby	This system is dismantled after each Derby and is set up again a year later.
Second Opinion®	Software systems have little recyclability (but modules may be reusable).
American Airlines	Software systems have little recyclability.
Superconductors	Artifacts of basic research have little recyclability.
Light Bulb	Artifacts of basic research have little recyclability.
Boeing 777	We suspect that the aluminum, titanium, and composites can be easily separated and recycled.
Apollo Moon Landing	We know of no attempts to reuse the command modules or lunar landers, except to put them in museums.
House	Large buildings are sometimes demolished and thrown away, but houses are often disassembled and sold in salvage yards.
CAP	We know of no retirement and disposal plans.
Pyramid	There were no plans for retirement. The pyramids were supposed to last forever.
Car Factory	Unknown.
Electric Vehicle	The GM Impact was modular and was, therefore, probably quite recyclable.
Improved Battery	Batteries for electric cars are expensive and have a limited life. Therefore, they are being designed to be returned to the factory for refurbishing.
Breakthrough Battery	Unknown.
C3PO	In the movie, C3PO was bought in a recycled robots shop.
Manhattan Project	There were no plans for retirement and disposal. We are still cleaning up radioactive material near Hanaford.
Polaris Program	Because of their expense, materials are being removed from warheads and used in new weapons.
Hubble Space Telescope	It will probably drift into the earth's atmosphere and burn up.

23.2 THE SYSTEM DESIGN PROCESS

The System Design Process is NP-Complete

The system design process is NP-complete (Chapman, Rozenblit, and Bahill, 1994 and 1995), which is just a fancy way of saying that it is a mathematically hard problem with no known solution beyond brute force calculation. The implications of the system design process being NP-complete are far-reaching. Basically, it means that for any complex system design, no optimum solution can be found in a reasonable time. In fact, due to the changing nature of the cost function and the availability of components to create the system, the technology set available is not even fully known by the designer. This means it is possible (even likely) to design forever! Therefore, some limits must be set on the resources (time or money) to restrict the design process.

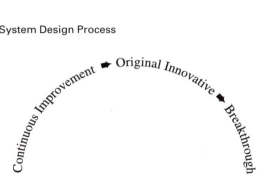

Figure 23-4   The design continuum.

In this book we have presented three types of design, which are shown in Figure 23-4, Continuous Improvement, Original Innovative, and Breakthrough. They are really a continuum.

Most design problems are Continuous Improvement, because most design is redesign. A feasible solution exists, but it is not optimal. Improvements are available and often not hard to find. The performance of the system improves quickly at first, but optimality cannot be obtained. Eventually, it is not worth the cost of the extra resources to improve the performance. See Figure 23-5.

There are many design cases where a feasible solution does not already exist, but it is not a challenge to find a solution. We call these Original Innovative designs. They are original, because no prior feasible solution exists that can be incrementally improved. This type of design requires innovation, because the first solution generated will seldom be very good and it will take a lot of search to get a good solution. When designers are given a chance to start from scratch and design a new system, they are performing original innovative design.

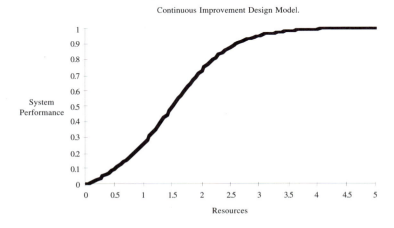

Figure 23-5   Continuous Improvement starts quickly but has diminishing marginal returns.

The final type of design is called Breakthrough design. With these designs, no known or easily obtainable feasible solution exists or has ever existed. Only a breakthrough in science or engineering will create a feasible solution. Resources are expended at an incredible rate with no improvement at all. If the project were stopped halfway through the design effort, there would be nothing to show for all the money spent. However, in some cases, a breakthrough occurs and performance improves rapidly. See Figure 23-6.

The implications for the system design process are clear. Different approaches must be used when a feasible system is at hand versus when one is not easily obtainable. The Continuous Improvement problems will have a different system design process than that for Original Innovative designs or for Breakthrough designs. None of the methods presented to approach these different design problems will guarantee optimality, but good solutions can be obtained for all.

If it is impossible to obtain optimality, then one might ask why are there so many good systems. The answer lies within the solution techniques of NP-complete problems. Even the most difficult problems in this class have algorithms to obtain good solutions (that is, solutions that are within a few percent of a theoretical optimal, when it is possible to compute) with relatively simple polynomial algorithms. The solution techniques applied to solve these problems (such as the Traveling Salesman Problem, Knapsack Problem, maximum path through a network, minimum test collection, graph 3-colorability, etc.) can also be applied (and have been applied, knowingly or not) to the system design process. This provides a mechanism to analyze the tools and techniques of design. In the next section, we will analyze the various methods of solving NP-complete problems. And in the following section, we will use the NP-complete algorithms to analyze the design case studies previously presented in this book.

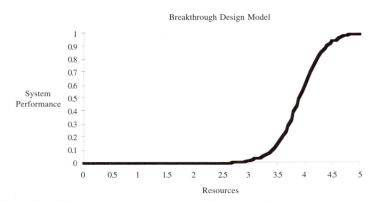

Figure 23-6   Breakthrough design starts slow and has most of the gain at the end.

Algorithms that Solve the Traveling Salesman Problem

The Traveling Salesman Problem is NP-complete (Garey and Johnson, 1980). It is easily described, but impossible to efficiently solve (Gavish and Srikanth, 1986).

This is a brief statement of this problem: Given a set of cities (coordinates in a plane), imagine a salesman trying to find the shortest path through all of the cities and returning to the first. For this problem, there is no optimal solution that will run in polynomial time. The system design problem can be mapped into the Traveling Salesman Problem (Chapman, Rozenblit, and Bahill, 1995). We will look at this problem because it has been studied thoroughly using a wide variety of techniques. There are many fast heuristics to solve the Traveling Salesman Problem; each can be proven to obtain solutions within a few percent of the optimal (Golden, Bodin, Doyle, and Stewart, 1980), (Laporte, 1992). These algorithms can provide clues to solving the system design problem. The groups are:

1. additive approaches—point insertion, incremental improvement, etc.,
2. tree search—branch and bound,
3. relaxation of requirements,
4. local optimization techniques—3-Opt and subproblems, and
5. probabilistic jumps—simulated annealing.

Additive approaches take an existing tour and add each individual point based on some simple heuristic. The nearest point, the farthest point, the least cost to insert a point between two lines, and other similar techniques have been tried. These algorithms are fast and effective. A typical algorithm runs only a few times slower than a simple sort of the data. Using this approach, solutions have been found for the Traveling Salesman Problem with a million cities, using only a few hours of computer time on a VAX 8600 (Bentley, 1992).

The key to the additive approaches is to take an initial simple feasible solution and augment it with an additional point. If there are 100 points to be satisfied, start with a few connected in an optimal way. This is often done by using a convex hull (Shin and Woo, 1986). Add points to this path one at a time, trying to keep the path as short as possible (Norback and Love, 1977). See Figure 23-7.

For a system design problem, this is equivalent to starting with a simple feasible system with a few important requirements satisfied. Additional complexity is

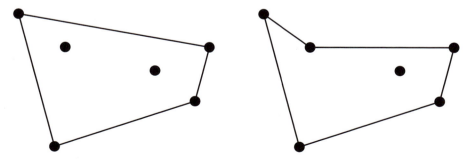

Figure 23-7   An example of an insertion of a point to a convex hull.

added to the device as new requirements are taken into account. Very little effort is expended attempting to re-optimize the entire system when the additional requirement is added. For example, the early carburetors for automobile engines were simple mechanisms. As options were added to the car, engineers used the vacuum available at the intake manifold for controls. By the early 1980s, carburetors were nightmares of complexity as additional pollution control devices were attached. Finally, the entire system was so complicated that it was junked in favor of fuel injectors and electronic controls. This happens to any system design that uses additive type algorithms. If the system is large, eventually, the additive solution is so far from optimal that the entire problem needs to be significantly redesigned or started from a blank sheet of paper.

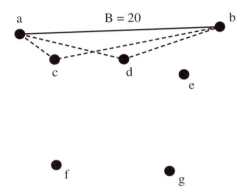

Figure 23-8   Different options in a tree search.

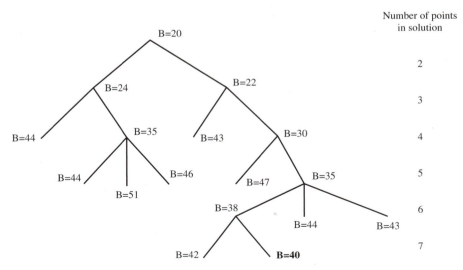

Figure 23-9   Example of a branch and bound algorithm.

Tree search algorithms place all the requirements in a tree structure and build the final design by walking through the tree. Sometimes an initial feasible solution is used, such as the minimal spanning trees (Held and Karp, 1970). Other times, a branch and bound approach is used, where bounds are set and all options within the bounds are kept active. The bound is a numerical limit that is used, to prevent traversing branches that will result in paths that are too long. The bound can be determined by a variety of techniques; then the tree is traversed down all branches that do not exceed the bounds (Fischetti and Toth, 1989). One approach is to follow the best path available to the bottom of the tree. This is called a depth first search. The other approach is to keep all branches less than a bound alive and follow one branch at a time. This is called a breadth first search. The success of these algorithms depends on the bounds.

As illustrated in Figures 23-8 and 23-9, each branch represents a different point added to the solution. The initial distance between the points "a" and "b" is 20 arbitrary units. Adding point "c" between these two gives a new distance, or bound, of 22. Adding a different point, "d," produces a path of "adb," which has a bound of 24. So if we take the shortest three point path, "acb," and add a fourth point, "d," we get a path "acdb," which has a bound of 30. This is greater than the undeveloped "adb" path with bound 24, so the "adb" path is expanded, giving bounds of 44 and 35. The branch "acdb" is the shortest four point path solution. So it is further expanded. The tree is traversed along the lowest bound, so when the bound is B=38, all branches less than 38 must be explored. The best solution for seven points was found at B=40.

Design problems that are comparable to tree structures are those where the systems engineers start with numerous options that can all be kept open. As alternatives are discovered and approved, the constraints and goals are gradually narrowed until only a few solutions are explored and developed. Exploring a few alternatives is a popular approach in industry. Theoretically, by using liberal bounds and investigating all but the most ridiculous paths, a good solution can be found. Of course, no company has the resources for this type of approach.

Integer Programming is an NP-complete algorithm that can solve problems with discrete variables. Although it can be used to solve the Traveling Salesman Problem, nothing is gained because it is also NP-complete. A relaxed simplex method can be used instead. The relaxed simplex method is a polynomial algorithm. It can solve problems with real variables, then the solution variables can be rounded off to integers. This technique is faster than the Integer Programming method. It does not guarantee optimality, but it does give excellent results. It is essentially the same as relaxing the requirements until a feasible solution is obtained, then using that solution with reduced capability. For example, an airplane has a design requirement for 400 passengers. Due to weight constraints, it may be an easier solution to limit capacity to 390 passengers, than to spend the design time searching for more weight savings. Figure 23-10 shows a solution with one point omitted. The requirement is added after the solution is obtained, but ignored during the search for a solution.

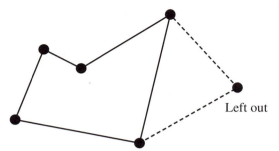

Figure 23-10   Requirements relaxation. It is sometimes easier to relax the requirements and solve the problem than to use the design time searching for an optimal solution. In this case, the requirements were relaxed and the point labeled "Left out" was ignored until after a solution was obtained.

Some local optimization procedures can be classified as redesign. When a feasible solution containing all the necessary points is already known, the goal of these algorithms is to have steady improvements in the existing tour. The most popular method is the 3-Opt method (Lin and Kerningham, 1973). Here, an initial solution is continually worked to ensure that no three points can be exchanged with three others to obtain a better answer. See Figure 23-11. Value engineering techniques used in industry are based on improving an existing design. Although not as rigorous as the 3-Opt method, these techniques are meant to eliminate unnecessary parts and combine functions onto fewer parts. The goal is the same, that is, to eliminate small nonoptimal sections from the design. This approach can be classified as continuous improvement.

Another popular local optimization technique is to break the problem into small pieces that can be optimized, and then create interfaces between these parts. This is done when a complete redesign is needed. When combined with tree search algorithms, this method can also be used for new designs. One approach for the

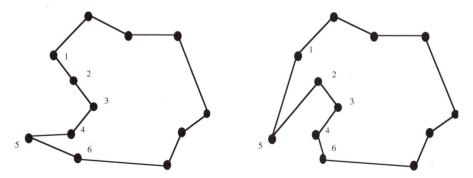

Figure 23-11   Example of 3-Opt optimization. The sequence 2-3-4 is swapped out from between 1-5 and put in between 5-6.

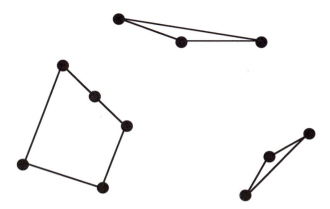

Figure 23-12   Data points divided into subproblems and optimized.

Traveling Salesman Problem is to break the problem up regionally into small portions. The small areas are optimized by brute force then all the areas are reconnected (Karp, 1977). The final result is surprisingly good. The amount of computer time expended is higher than some of the additive methods, but the results are generally more consistent. See Figures 23-12 and 23-13.

This is often how systems engineers work on well-known design problems, such as cars. Each boundary is established in advance with interface structures firmly in place. The subsystem is optimized within the constraints of the interfaces, but rarely beyond them. This approach places a larger burden on the systems engineer. If he sets the wrong boundary at the beginning of the design process, then no chance for a near optimal system is possible. For example, with guided missile design, the ten-

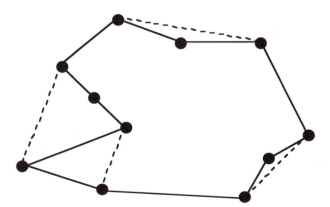

Figure 23-13   Subproblems connected example. Subproblem solutions are connected together so that all subproblems are merged into the total system. The dashed lines represent links modified from the subproblem solutions to accommodate the system solution.

dency is to push more of the actual functionality into digital circuitry and software and out of analog hardware. These decisions must be made early in a program when there is no prototype and only a simple model is available to help. If too much functionality is placed in software, then the requirements for the electronic digital computers may exceed the packaging constraints and the design time for writing the software will be too long. If few functions are placed in software, then the space and weight allocation for the analog systems may exceed the design specifications, or the analog systems may not have the accuracy needed for today's high performance rocketry.

The final approach for solving the Traveling Salesman Problem is a method to escape local minima. It relies on random jumps. The most popular algorithm for applying this method to the Traveling Salesman Problem is simulated annealing (Cheh, Goldberg, and Askin, 1991). Here, a standard branch and bound tree search is used to examine the local area for improvements. If no improvement is available, then a jump in an unlikely (that is, a nonoptimal) direction is chosen based on a prabability distribution, usually a decaying exponential. At the new location, the standard search for a local minima begins anew. See Figure 23.14.

This approach closely mimics breakthrough methods used in the development outlined in the case studies on the Light Bulb and the Superconductor. Local minima were found for both technologies. It was only by rejecting the standard path that most engineers or scientists were investigating through continuous improvement, and then by jumping to unlikely (and usually unsuccessful) new formulas that they

Local minima at 4 and global minima at 10.

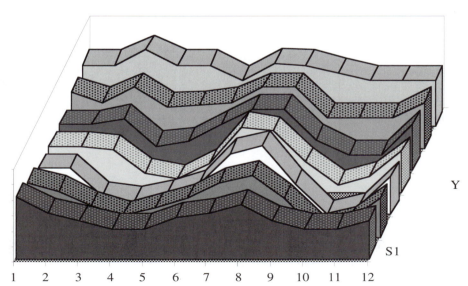

Figure 23-14   Probabilistic jump example. If an algorithm found the local minima at 4, then no direction away from 4 looks worthwhile. A probabilistic jump away from this point may land in the valley of the global minima at 10.

were fortunate enough to come upon the breakthrough necessary to meet their goals. Theoretically, if development continued forever, the optimal solution might be found with this method. Only a motivated bunch of highly skilled people should use this method, because most interim solutions are poor.

Evaluating the Designs

In this section, the case studies will be tied to the NP-complete design methodology providing a means of evaluating a design. By using the Resources versus the Design Difficulty scores calculated for each case study, a systems engineer can evaluate where in the design space a project falls. From Chapter 1, the design areas are Consumer Products, Star Wars, Seven Wonders of the Ancient World, and Moon Landing.

No individual or company should attempt to create one of the Seven Wonders of the Ancient World. This type of endeavor is strictly for nations. Pyramids and hundred mile aqueducts are not profitable and provide a poor return on investment. The solution technique for the Pyramids and the Central Arizona Project relied on a tree search approach to explore the options, combined with an additive approach to handle additional requirements. The initial plans were laid out, the options considered, and a path chosen. When problems arose, they were added to the original plans, and the construction continued. It was undesirable to undo a canal partly dug or tear up and replace the blocks of rock already laid.

Moon Landings can be accomplished, but very rarely. Apollo was a great achievement, but had no return on investment (except for national ego). One of the most complex corporate systems is the Boeing 777. But unlike the Moon Landing, before embarking on this complex and risky venture, Boeing had a number of guaranteed sales for the plane. Both projects required breaking the design into manageable subproblems. The Apollo program had to rely on some risky successes to meet their timetable, but none of the successes were due to breakthrough design efforts. The engineers relied primarily on tree searches where many options were kept open. Likewise, Boeing did not rely on breakthroughs either. There were hundreds of subproblems, most of which were simple redesign efforts. Some advanced technology was developed, but they used a tree search approach that required lots of branches.

Any project in the Moon Landing region is very difficult and costly. A small software firm attempting to create a massive new operating system, such as Windows 95™, would have to consider the project a Moon Landing. For them, the resources are massive and the design difficulty high. It would probably ruin their company to even attempt the project.

Projects in the Star Wars area are interesting. These are products we can conceptualize; and they do not appear to be outside the realm of our resources, but their complexity is very high. In this region, breakthrough designs are needed. These tend to be low budget and super high-tech. Can it be done? Yes, but the risk of failure is extremely high. Failure is, of course, relative. The engineers may be quite pleased with their creation, but the customer disgusted. Generally, failure is defined as not meeting the customer's predefined level of acceptance for the system.

The Light Bulb and the Superconductor are examples of successes in this area. Both of these products are on the border between Star Wars and Consumer Products. If successfully developed, they would be Consumer Products; but before then, they were considered intractable design problems. Failures in the Star Wars area include "cold fusion," solving the NP-complete math problem, the laser to shoot down incoming ballistic missiles, and the electric car battery to satisfy the typical consumer (at least it is a failure so far). The battery problem may be solved by breakthroughs; or possibly, given enough time, continuous incremental improvements to existing batteries may solve the problem. Since this is in the future, we are guessing at the successful solution approach.

C3P0 is a fantasy example that illustrates the need for breakthroughs. There is no way a company could put such a device on the market in the 1990s without simultaneous breakthroughs in many areas. To even attempt products in, or near this region, breakthrough approaches to design are needed. The analogy for the Traveling Salesman Problem showed probabilistic jumps. Nonoptimal moves to a new design domain must be made. Searching in the area of the current minima will not produce rewards. Others have already searched in this region and applied continuous improvement techniques, so it is reasonable to expect they would have found a solution if one existed. The teaming of highly dedicated and skilled people would also be necessary. Before attempting a complex risky project, the personnel must have previously worked together and developed a relationship (Rouse, Cannon-Bowers, and Salas, 1992), (Griffin and Hauser, 1992). The team must be unlimited in their ability to search the design space. This means chasing hundreds of dead ends, and that makes cost a problem. If the prototypes and models are too expensive, they will not succeed. Either the prototype (i.e., a physical representation of the product) or a model (an abstract representation of the product) must be created by the team for testing or validation. If hundreds of either prototypes or models can be made quickly and within budget, then there is a chance for success, although it is not certain.

For almost any design to be successful for a typical business, it must fall into the Consumer Products quadrant of the graph. Here, the key is the type of design. One of the components for rating design difficulty is design type. It is possible to need a breakthrough design on a consumer product, if the risk is acceptable. This means no feasible solution yet exists, and indicates that it will be very difficult to achieve. The distinction between breakthroughs in the Consumer Product and Star Wars areas is the other parts needed to compute the design difficulty score. If the knowledge needed for the breakthrough is available, the number of steps is acceptable, and the expected quality is moderate, then a company may attempt to create a brand new product that is not considered possible by its competitors. The *first* lightweight camcorders, auto focus cameras, lasers, and color televisions fall into this category. Success was not assured and the constraints were daunting, but the companies took the risk and created the product. The electric car battery is still in this arena. It is clearly a consumer product, if the advanced battery can be built.

Table 23-6 lists the design type for the case studies in the Consumer Products quadrant of the graph.

TABLE 23-6   Consumer Products Case
Studies Sorted by Design Type Rating.

Case Study	Design Type Score
Resistor Networks	1
House	2
SIERRA	2
Pinewood Derby	3
Second Opinion	5
American Airlines	6
Bat Chooser	6
Car Factory	7
Electric Vehicle	10

Most people design resistor networks by trial and error. This technique works all right for small problems. But it would fail miserably for large systems. With appropriate tolerancing and small networks, the complexity is minor. A problem only appears if the specified tolerancing leaves little room for a feasible solution.

Building a house in the United States requires the local optimization design approach. There are thousands of household floor designs available and easily purchased off the shelf. The site preparation and consumer preferences may modify some of the plans in a minor way, but little true design work is needed. The Traveling Salesman Problem approach, called 3-Opt, attempts to reoptimize an existing feasible solution. The simpler version of this is called 2-Opt: it only tries to swap pairs of points. This is easier and may more accurately reflect the amount of effort that goes into optimizing these designs. In the case of the house, simple modifications to a floor plan represent a move from one feasible solution to another feasible solution that is more desired by the customer.

The student exercise of designing the SIERRA railroad controller is more difficult. The entire set of constraints is laid out in advance and clearly understood before the design starts. This allows the tree search method of design. It becomes a matter of selecting the best solutions from a field of possibilities. Because the possibilities are limited (since there are only nine components available), the design space can be searched for feasibility and optimality.

Moving up in difficulty is the Pinewood Derby round robin schedule. Round robin schedules are easily understood and created. The killer constraint was that each car must race every other car at least once. This requirement made the problem infeasible. Relaxing this constraint produced a feasible design that allowed us to run the Pinewood Derby for years. Additional requirements were added later, in order to move the schedule closer to the goal of having each car race every other car. Indeed, in our final schedules given in Chapter 5, only one pair of cars failed to race each other. And this turned out to be an advantage, allowing a 12 car schedule to be used with only 10 or 11 cars.

Second Opinion® also used the additive design approach. The knowledge base was built up over several years. As a case was handled correctly by the knowledge base and inference engine, additional rules were added. Eventually, the additive method can make the product so unwieldy that it will be junked and a new design started from scratch. And that was true in the case of Second Opinion (Bahill, Bharathan, and Curlee, 1995).

For the American Airlines scheduling problem, the solution approach, using the computer algorithms to solve the schedule, was not unique. What was unique was cost-effectively using the solution approach under the pressure of ongoing, and changing, business requirements for large scale scheduling problems. None of the other major airlines spent the resources to create these scheduling algorithms. The reason was return on investment. The challenge for the developers was to take the techniques out of the textbooks and put them to work within a budget. Most of the textbook approaches would have resulted in algorithms that would be very large and slow. The American Airlines approach was to break the problem into subproblems, then to relax the requirements and shoot for fast feasible solutions. American Airlines could have used an Integer Programming algorithm to optimally solve these scheduling problems, but it is slow. Instead, American Airlines used a relaxed simplex method.

Bat Chooser represents an increase in difficulty of the design type. This product was new and the concept had never been attempted. This automatically makes the task more difficult. Feasibility is not guaranteed and thus, a different design process is needed. Each of the critical measurements needed to make a determination was carefully created independently. Several different design options were created and contrasted. This is typical of a tree search. All of the most appealing alternatives are kept open. If one seemed better, it was developed in detail until some limit was reached. At that point, other options were started. In this incremental way, the best design was eventually found. It also used some additive design elements, because the decision to measure eye-hand response time was made after the original design.

The next case study listed in the table is a harder design type: redesigning a car. A complete redesign of the entire car requires innovation and originality. Honda uses a 2-4-8 program, where they redesign small features every two years, redesign major features every four years, and completely redesign every eight years. The eight year redesign is an Original Innovative design. The design team is allowed to modify almost any part of the car in order to satisfy the customer's newest requirements. American and Japanese car designers do similar amounts of work. The basic approach of both manufacturers is to break the system into subproblems that are each optimized. The optimization of the subproblems is somewhat different from what Karp does for the Traveling Salesman Problem. The complexity is so high that optimality is not possible for the subproblems. Each subproblem uses a different design approach, based on the experience of the designers in that area. If an additive approach works best, then it is used for that subproblem area. If a tree structured approach works like the branch and bound, then that is used. The subproblems each have their own complexity and are similar to some of the smaller design projects discussed above. This is typical of large system design. No one technique is used. A top down approach breaks the system design problem into smaller problems that are then treated as complex systems that might be optimized. The system is integrated together to build a prototype; and the data collected causes reallocation of requirements similar to the 3-Opt optimization method. The two year design cycle sharply limits the subproblems that can be modified. The eight year design cycle removes the limits and greatly increases the chances for success or failure. No single approach for solving the Traveling Salesman Problem has been found for high complexity (large number of data points) problems. Multiple algorithms attack the problem repeatedly to move it toward optimality (Lawler, Lenstra, Rinnooy, and Shmoys, 1985).

The final design case study presented in the Consumer Products quadrant is GM's electric vehicle, the Impact. This car exhibited no breakthrough technologies. However, hundreds of innovations were made on the original designs. The team was allowed to start with a blank piece of paper. This is the original portion of Original Innovative design. No feasible solution existed to increment toward optimality, but the design team had to use the feasible components (that is, off the shelf technology) where possible. The systems engineers were allowed to reallocate the requirements. They shifted them from the need for power (the batteries) to the need for weight savings. The approach was still to break the problem into subproblems and optimize locally. Because the requirements had not yet been satisfied by a prior feasible solution, this was a more difficult design than the regular eight year car redesign. Thus, the optimization of each subproblem was more difficult.

A feasible design is always needed before a near optimal design can be achieved. The Impact did an excellent job solving these subproblems, by making sure the correct subproblem divisions were accomplished in advance and by employing elements of breakthrough thinking with a more traditional branch and bound. Even when the alternate subproblem concepts were nonoptimum, they were kept open longer than normal. This is comparable to exceeding the bound in a branch and bound, but following the path anyway. It is not the unstructured jump of the probabilistic jumps algorithm, but rather a blending of the two methods. For example, the styling of the vehicle was important, but the aerodynamics were even more important. The trade-offs between the two conflicting requirements necessitated examination of dozens of options. Only a few concepts were eliminated outright and most were kept open long enough to develop a good model for evaluation. This is the innovation part of Original Innovative design, and it worked well for AeroVironment's electric car design.

Table 23-7 demonstrates the design strategies used on the case studies. We are not implying that these are the only design strategies. These are merely the design strategies that have been suggested for solving difficult problems, such as the Traveling Salesman Problem. It is a coincidence that all of these case studies had elements of these Traveling Salesman strategies. As just one of many other design strategies, we will now mention model-based systems design. With this strategy, a model of the present system is constructed. Then a model of the goal state or the desired system is built. Then the engineers try to show how to move the present system to the goal state.

TABLE 23-7   Design strategy seemingly used on the case studies.

Case Study	Design Strategy
Resistor Networks	Trial and error
SIERRA	Tree search
Bat Chooser	Tree search & Additive
Pinewood Derby	Relax requirements & Additive
Second Opinion®	Additive
American Airlines	Relax requirements
Superconductors	Probabilistic jumps
Light Bulb	Probabilistic jumps
Boeing 777	Subproblems & Tree search
Apollo Moon Landing	Subproblems & Tree search
House	Local optimization
CAP	Tree search & Additive
Pyramid	Tree search & Additive
Car Factory	Subproblems
Electric Vehicle	Subproblems & Tree search
Improved Battery	Tree search
Breakthrough Battery	Probabilistic jumps?
C3PO	?
Manhattan Project	Probabilistic jumps & Tree search
Polaris Program	Subproblems
Hubble Space Telescope	Subproblems

CONCLUSIONS

The system design process is hard. Optimal designs cannot be created, but good designs can. Companies should evaluate their design efforts before they start. Using the criteria presented in Chapter 1 and the analysis in the succeeding chapters, the difficulty of the design and the amount of resources should be easy to evaluate. By comparing a new design with past successful designs, the amount of effort can be determined.

Most companies should stay within the Consumer Products region of design. They do not have the resources for either a Moon Landing or one of the Seven Wonders of the Ancient World. Star Wars projects may be attempted, but expect little success. If a design in this quadrant is tried, then a breakthrough design model must be used.

Many lessons can be learned from examining solution techniques for NP-complete problems. Although firm boundaries do not exist, the following generalities apply. Note that most of these conclusions are also common sense!

1. Use an additive approach for small design problems.
2. If many options can be examined, use a tree search.
3. All large problems must be broken into subproblems.
4. When no feasible solution seems possible, relax the requirements to achieve feasibility, then iterate towards the original requirements.

5. If a breakthrough is needed, then wide searches using many unlikely options must be tried. Expect many failures.

Combining the best options available with a knowledge based application may result in a computerized system that can actually do the design (Rozenblit and Huang, 1991).

Important aspects of design that computer models will never achieve include the ingenuity, commitment, cleverness, and vast experiences of the human participants. Often the point when the actual breakthrough design idea occurs cannot be accurately determined by the inventor. If the inventor is not able to describe how the idea came, it will make it most unlikely that any approach mimicking the human could ever be implemented by a computer. However, there are still thousands of design tasks that are incremental improvements to existing products. If no flash of brilliance is needed, then it is likely that a computer will someday be able to make changes (in materials, fit, thermal distribution, etc.) that make up the vast majority of system design tasks.

The system design process is done every day by many corporations and individuals. By evaluating a potential design effort first, then changing the process to match the design, the optimal successful solution can be found using fewer resources.

REFERENCES

BAHILL, A.T., K. BHARATHAN, and R. CURLEE, "How the testing techniques for a decision support system changed over nine years." *IEEE Transactions on Systems, Man and Cybernetics Society*, SMC-25: pp. 1533–1542 (1995).

BAHILL, A.T., M.R. CLARK, and L. STARK, "The main sequence, a tool for studying human eye movements." *Mathematical Biosciences,* vol. 24: pp. 191–204 (1975).

BAHILL, A.T., and L. STARK, "The trajectories of saccadic eye movements." *Scientific American,* vol. 240: pp. 108–117 (1979).

BENTLEY, J.J., "Fast Algorithms for Geometric Traveling Salesman Problems." *ORSA Journal on Computing,* vol. 4, no. 4: pp. 387–411 (1992).

BERN, M.W., and R.L. GRAHAM, "The Shortest Network Problem." *Scientific American,* pp. 84–89 (January 1989).

CHAPMAN, W.L., A.T. BAHILL, and A.W. WYMORE, *Engineering Modeling and Design.* Boca Raton: CRC Press Inc., 1992.

CHAPMAN, W.L., J. ROSENBLIT, and A.T. BAHILL, "The System Design Process Is NP-Complete," *Proceedings IEEE International Conference on Systems, Man, and Cybernetics,* San Antonio, vol 2: pp. 1880–1884, October 2–5, 1994.

CHAPMAN, W.L., J. ROSENBLIT, A.T. BAHILL, "Complexity of the System Design Problem," *Proceeding of The 1995 International Symposium and Workshop on Systems Engineering of Computer Based Systems,* Tucson, AZ, pp. 51–57, March 6–9, 1995.

CHEH, K., J.B. GOLDBERG, and R.G. ASKIN, "A Note on the Effect of Neighborhood Structure in Simulated Annealing." *Computers Operations Research,* vol. 18, no. 6.: pp. 537–547 (1991).

CROSS, N., *Engineering Design Methods.* New York: John Wiley and Sons, 1989.

FISCHETTI, M., and P. TOTH, "An Additive Bounding Procedure for Combinatorial Optimization Problems." *Operations Research,* vol. 37, no. 2: pp. 319–328 (1989).

GAREY, M., and D. JOHNSON, *Computers and Intractability: A Guide to the Theory of NP-Completeness.* New York: W.H. Freeman and Company, 1979.

GAVISH, B., and K. SRIKANTH, "An Optimal Solution Method for Large Scale Multiple Traveling Salesman Problems." *Operations Research,* vol. 34, no. 5: p. 698 (1986).

GERSHON, M., "The role of weights and scales in the application of multiobjective decision making," *European Journal of Operations Research,* vol. 15: pp. 244–250 (1984).

GOICOECHEA, A., D. HANSEN, and L. DUCKSTEIN, *Multiobjective Decision Analysis with Engineering and Business Applications.* New York: John Wiley and Sons, 1982.

GOLDEN, B., L. BODIN, T. DOYLE, and W. STEWART Jr., "Approximate Traveling Salesman Algorithms." *Operations Research,* vol. 28, no. 3: pp. 694–711 (1980).

Grady, J., *Systems Requirements Analysis.* New York: McGraw Hill, 1993.

GRIFFIN, A., and J. HAUSER, "Patterns of Communication among Marketing Engineering and Manufacturing—A comparison between two new product teams." *Management Science,* vol. 38, no. 3: pp. 360–373 (1992).

HELD, M., and R. KARP, "The Traveling Salesman Problem and Minimum Spanning Trees." Part I: *Operations Research,* vol. 18: pp. 1138-1162 (1970); Part II: *Mathematical Programming,* vol. 1: pp. 6–26 (1971).

HOLLINS, B., and S. PUGH, *Successful Product Design.* Boston: Butterworths, 1990.

JANSEN, K., "The Allocation Problem in Hardware Design," *Discrete Applied Mathematics,* vol. 43: pp. 37–46 (1993).

KARP, R.M., "Probabilistic Analysis of Partitioning Algorithms for the Traveling Salesman Problem." *Mathematics of Operations Research,* vol. 2: pp. 209–224 (1977).

KARP, R.M., "Reducibility Among Combinatorial Problems." *Complexity of Computer Computations,* eds. R.E. Miller and J.W. Thatcher. New York: Plenum Press, pp. 85–103 (1972).

KERZNER, H., *Project Management: a Systems Approach to Planning, Scheduling, and Controlling.* New York: Van Nostrand Reinhold, 1995.

LAPORTE, G., "The Traveling Salesman Problem: An overview of exact and approximate algorithms." *European Journal of Operations Research,* vol. 59: pp. 231–247 (1992).

LAWLER, E.L., J.K. LENSTRA, K. RINNOOY, and D.B. SHMOYS, *The Traveling Salesman Problem.* New York: John Wiley & Sons, 1985.

LIN, S., and B.W. KERNINGHAN, "An Effective Heuristic Algorithm for the Traveling Salesman Problem." *Operations Research,* vol. 11: pp. 972–989 (1973).

NORBACK, J., and R. LOVE, "Geometric Approaches to Solving the Traveling Salesman Problem." *Management Science,* vol. 23, no. 11: pp. 1208–1259 (1977).

PUGH, S., *Total Design: Integrated Methods for Successful Product Engineering.* London: Addison Wesley, 1990.

ROUSE, W.B., J.A. CANNON-BOWERS, and E. SALAS, "The Role of Mental Models in Team Performance in Complex Systems." *IEEE Transactions on Systems, Man, and Cybernetics,* vol. 22, No. 6: 1992.

ROZENBLIT, J., and B. ZIEGLER, "Design and Modeling Concepts," *International Encyclopedia of Robotics Applications and Automation.* New York: John Wiley & Sons Inc., 1988.

ROZENBLIT, J.W., and Y.M. HUANG, "Rule-Based Generation of Model Structures in Multifaceted Modeling and System Design." *ORSA Journal on Computing,* vol. 3, no. 4: pp. 330–344 (1991).

SAGE. A.P., *Systems Engineering.* New York: Wiley-Interscience, 1993.

SHIN, S.Y., and T.C. WOO, "Finding the Convex Hull of a Simple Polygon in Linear Time." *Pattern Recognition,* vol. 19, no. 6: pp. 453–458 (1986).

SZIDAROVSZKY, F., M.E. GERSHON, and L. DUCKSTEIN, *Techniques for Multiobjective Decision Making in Systems Management.* New York: Elsevier, 1986.

WALLACE, R.H., J.E. STOCKENBERG, and R.N. CHARETTE, *A Unified Methodology for Developing Systems.* New York: Intertext Publications, Inc., 1987.

WYMORE, A.W., *Model-based Systems Engineering.* Boca Raton: CRC Press, 1993.

WYMORE, A.W., *System Engineering Methodology for Interdisciplinary Teams.* New York: John Wiley, 1976.

24

WHAT IS SYSTEMS ENGINEERING? A CONSENSUS OF SENIOR SYSTEMS ENGINEERS[1]

ABSTRACT

Systems Engineering is an interdisciplinary process that ensures that the customer's needs are satisfied throughout a system's entire life cycle. This process includes:

- understanding customer needs,
- stating the problem,
- discovering system requirements,
- defining quantitative measures,
- validating requirements,
- prescribing tests,

[1]Material for this chapter was gathered from senior Systems Engineers at Sandia National Laboratories, Hughes Aircraft Company, and the following general references: Blanchard and Fabrycky, 1990; Sage, 1992; Chapman, Bahill, and Wymore, 1992; Wymore, 1993; IEEE P1220, 1994; Grady, 1994, 1995; Hughes Aircraft Company, 1994; Martin-Marietta, 1994; Shishko 1995; Martin 1996; Proceedings of the IEEE Systems, Man, and Cybernetics International Conferences; and NCOSE and INCOSE Symposia and Proceedings.

Earlier versions of this chapter were published in the *IEEE Systems, Man, and Cybernetics Newsletter,* pp. 11–12, December 1994, and the *Systems Engineering Practices & Tools,* Proceedings of the Sixth Annual International Symposium of the International Council on Systems Engineering, vol. 1, pp. 503–508, July 7–11, 1996. A UNIX troff version is available via anonymous ftp on tucson.sie.arizona.edu at pub/WhatIsSystemsEngineering. An html document is available at http://www.sie.arizona.edu/sysengr and at http://dpopenet.sandia.gov/syseng/index.html. If you want to explain the Systems Engineering process to others, please feel free to use our 66 color transparencies that are also available at these www sites.

- exploring alternative concepts,
- conducting sensitivity analyses,
- performing functional decomposition,
- system modeling,
- creating a system design,
- designing and managing interfaces,
- conducting design reviews,
- integrating the system,
- performing a total system test,
- maintaining configuration management,
- implementing risk management,
- conducting reliability analyses,
- performing total quality management,
- providing project management, and
- documenting all activity.

THE PROCESS

The System Life Cycle

The system life cycle has seven general phases:

1. discovering system requirements,
2. exploration of concepts,
3. full-scale engineering design,
4. manufacturing,
5. system integration and testing,
6. operation and maintenance, and
7. retirement, disposal, and replacement.

However, the system life cycle is different for different industries, products, and customers (Chapman, Bahill, and Wymore, 1992; Wymore, 1993; Kerzner 1995; Shishko 1995).

Understanding Customer Needs

Customers seldom know what they want or need. Systems engineers must enter the customer's environment, and find out how the customer will use the system. We must exceed, not merely meet, customer expectations. Flexible designs and rapid prototyping help identify aspects that might have been overlooked. Talking to your customer's customer and your supplier's supplier can be very useful. The words *customer* and *stakeholder* include anyone who has a right to impose requirements on the system: end users, operators, owners, bill-payers, regulatory agencies, beneficiaries, victims, etc.

Stating the Problem

This is one of the systems engineer's most important tasks. An elegant solution to the wrong problem is less than worthless. Modern management calls this writing a mission statement.

The word *optimal* should not appear in the statement of the problem, because there is no single optimal solution to a complex systems problem. Most system designs have several performance and cost criteria. Systems Engineering creates a set of alternative designs that satisfy these performance and cost criteria to varying degrees. Moving from one alternative to another will usually improve at least one criterion and worsen at least one criterion, i.e., there will be trade-offs. None of the feasible alternatives is likely to optimize all the criteria. Therefore, systems engineers must settle for less than optimality.

It might be possible to optimize some subsystems, but when they are interconnected, the overall system will not be optimal. The best possible system is not one that is made up of optimal subsystems. An all-star team might have the optimal people at all positions, but is it likely that such an all-star team could beat the world champions? For example, a Pro Bowl team is not likely to beat the Super Bowl champions.

If the system requirements demanded an optimal system, data could not be provided to prove that any resulting system was indeed optimal. In general, it can be proven that a system is at a local optimum, but it cannot be proven that it is at a global optimum.

Discovering System Requirements

There are two types of system requirements: mandatory and preference. Mandatory requirements ensure that the system satisfies the customer's operational need. Mandatory requirements, which are usually written with the words *shall* and *must*:

1. specify the necessary and sufficient conditions that a minimal system must have in order to be acceptable,
2. must be either passed or failed (there is no middle ground), and
3. must not be susceptible to trade-offs between requirements.

Typical mandatory requirements might be stated as: "The system shall not violate federal, state, or local laws." Mandatory requirements state the minimal requirements necessary to satisfy the customer's need.

After understanding the mandatory requirements, systems engineers propose alternative designs, all of which satisfy the mandatory requirements. Then the preference requirements are evaluated to determine the "best" designs. The preference requirements, which are often written with the words *should* and *want*:

1. should state conditions that would make the customer happier,
2. should use scoring functions (Chapman, Bahill, and Wymore, 1992) to evaluate the figures of merit, and
3. should be evaluated with a multicriteria decision aiding technique (Szidarovszky, Gershon, and Duckstein, 1986), because there will be trade-offs between these requirements.

Typical preference requirements might be stated as: "The system should have high performance and low cost; the performance and cost figures of merit will be weighted equally." Sometimes there is a relationship between mandatory and preference requirements, e.g., a mandatory requirement might be a lower threshold value for a preference requirement. The words *optimize, maximize* and *minimize* should not be used in stating requirements (Grady, 1993). Quality function deployment (QFD) can help identify system requirements (Bahill and Chapman, 1993; Bicknell and Bicknell, 1994).

Defining Quantitative Measures

Figures of merit, technical performance measures and metrics are all used to quantify system parameters. These terms are often used interchangeably, but we think a distinction is useful. Figures of merit are used to quantify requirements. Technical performance measures are used to mitigate risk. Metrics are used to help manage a company's processes.

Performance and cost figures of merit show how well the system satisfies its requirements, e.g., "In this test, the car accelerated from 0 to 60 mph in 6.5 seconds." Such measurements are made throughout the evolution of the system: based first on estimates by the design engineers; then on models, simulations, and prototypes; and finally on the real system. Figures of merit are used to help select among alternative designs and they are used to quantify system requirements. During concept selection, figures of merit are traded-off; that is, going from one alternative to another increases one figure of merit and decreases another.

Technical performance measures (TPM's) are used to track the progress of design and manufacturing. They are measurements that are made during the design and manufacturing process to evaluate the likelihood of satisfying the system requirements. Not all requirements have TPMs. They are usually associated only with high risk requirements, because they are expensive to maintain and track. Early prototypes will not meet TPM goals. Therefore, the TPM values are only required to be within a tolerance band. It is hoped that as the design and manufacturing process progresses, the TPM values will come closer and closer to the goals.

Metrics are often related to the process, not the product. Therefore, they do not always relate to specific system requirements. Rather some metrics relate to the company's mission statement and subsequent goals. A useful metric is the percentage of requirements that have changed after the System Requirements Review.

Validating Requirements

Validating requirements means ensuring that the set of requirements is consistent; that a real-world solution can be built that satisfies the requirements; and that it can be proven that such a system satisfies its requirements. If Systems Engineering discovers that the customer has requested a perpetual-motion machine, the project should be stopped. Each requirement should fit within budget, schedule, and other constraints. Requirements are often validated by reference to an existing system that meets most of the requirements. The requirements that are not satisfied by the existing system are validated by test, inspection, demonstration, analysis, modeling, or logical argument.

Prescribing tests

Early in the system life cycle, Systems Engineering should describe the tests that will be used to prove compliance of the final system with its requirements. However, most testing should be performed by built in self-test equipment. These self-tests should be used for initial testing, postinstallation testing, power-up diagnostics, field service, and depot repair. The recipient of each test result and the action to be taken if the system passes or fails each test must be stated.

Exploring Alternative Concepts

Alternative designs should be proposed. Multicriteria decision-aiding techniques should be used to reveal the best alternatives based on performance and cost figures of merit. This analysis should be redone whenever more data are available. For example, figures of merit should be computed initially based on estimates by the design engineers. Models should then be constructed and evaluated. Next, simulation data should be derived. Subsequently, prototypes should be measured; and finally, tests should be run on the final system. For the design of complex systems, alternative designs reduce project risk.

Conducting Sensitivity Analyses

Sensitivity analyses can be used to point out the requirements and parameters that have the biggest effects on cost, schedule, and performance. These analyses are used to help allocate resources (Karnavas, Sanchez, and Bahill, 1993).

Performing Functional Decomposition

Systems engineers perform functional decomposition on new systems:

1. to map functions to physical components, thereby ensuring that each function has an acknowledged owner,
2. to map functions to system requirements, and
3. to ensure that all necessary tasks are listed and that no unnecessary tasks are requested.

This list becomes the basis for the work breakdown structure.

When analyzing (or re-engineering) an existing system, systems engineers perform functional analysis to see what the system does in order to improve its performance (often called value engineering), and they also do functional decomposition to see what the system is supposed to do. In this manner, they can describe the present state of the system and the desired (or goal) state of the system. They can then show how to get from the present state to the goal state. Making radical changes in the system is called *re-engineering*. Making small incremental changes is called *total quality management.*

Icarus, and many flight wanna-bes after him, tried to understand how to fly by just analyzing the physical components that birds used to fly: legs, eyes, brain, and wings. Using this paradigm, man was unable to fly. The Wright brothers, in contrast, identified the following functions for the flight problem: takeoff and land, sense position and velocity, navigate, produce horizontal thrust, and produce vertical lift. Once it was understood that thrust and lift were two functions, they could be assigned to two physical components. By using a propeller to produce thrust and wings to produce lift, people could fly. The following table shows a mapping of functions to physical components.

Function	Airplane Physical Component	Bird Physical Component
Takeoff and land	Wheels, skis, or pontoons	Legs
Sense position and velocity	Vision or radar	Eyes
Navigate	Brain or computer	Brain
Produce horizontal thrust	Propeller or jet	Wings
Produce vertical lift	Wings	Wings

Birds use one physical component for the two functions: thrust and lift. Humans had to use two physical components for these two functions. As this example shows, it is perfectly acceptable to assign two or more functions to one physical component. However, it would be a mistake to assign one function to two physical components. Recently object-oriented analysis has been replacing function decomposition for re-engineering large existing systems (Jacobson, Ericsson, and Jacobson, 1995).

System Modeling

Models will be developed for most alternative designs. The model for the best alternative will be expanded and used to help manage the system throughout its entire life cycle. Many types of system models are used, such as: physical devices, equations, block diagrams, flow diagrams, object-oriented models, and computer simulations. Running these models reveals bottlenecks and fragmented activities, reduces cost, and exposes duplication of efforts.

Creating a System Design

The overall system must be partitioned into subsystems, subsystems must be partitioned into assemblies, etc. Reusability should be considered in creating subsystems. For new designs, subsystems should be created so that they can be reused in future products. For redesign, subsystems should be created to maximize the use of existing products, particularly commercially available ones. Systems engineers along with team members along with team members must also decide whether to make or buy the subsystems, first trying to use commercially available subsystems. If nothing satisfies all the requirements, then modification of an existing subsystem should be considered. If this proves unsatisfactory, then some subsystems will have to be designed in-house. Engineers must understand the other subsystems that will interact with their subsystem. Flexibility is more important than optimality. Hardware, software, and bioware must be considered. *Bioware* applies to humans and other biological organisms that are a part of the system. For example, in designing a race track, the horses or dogs are a part of the bioware. Facilities for their care and handling must be considered, as should provisions for education, human factors, and safety. These activities are referred to as System Design for new systems and Systems Analysis for existing systems.

Designing and Managing Interfaces

Interfaces between subsystems, as well as interfaces between the main system and the external world, must be designed. Subsystems should be defined along natural organizational units. When the same information travels back and forth among different subsystems, a natural activity may have been fragmented. Subsystems should be defined to minimize the amount of information to be exchanged between the subsystems. Well-designed subsystems send finished products to other subsystems. Feedback loops around individual subsystems are easier to manage than feedback loops around interconnected subsystems.

Conducting Design Reviews

Systems Engineering should ensure that the appropriate reviews are conducted and documented. The exact reviews that are appropriate depends on the size, complexity, and customer of the project. The following set is common: Mission Concept Review, System Requirements Review (SRR), System Definition Review, Preliminary Design Review (PDR), Critical Design Review (CDR), Production Readiness Review (PRR), and System Test. Full-scale engineering design begins after the Preliminary

Design Review. Manufacturing begins after the Critical Design Review. (Shishko, 1995; Bahill, Bentz & Dean, 1996).

Integrating the System

System integration means bringing subsystems together to produce the desired result and ensuring that the subsystems will interact to satisfy the customer's needs. End users and engineers need to be taught to use the system with courses, with manuals, and through training on the prototypes (Grady, 1994).

Performing a Total System Test

The system that is finally built must be tested to see if it is acceptable, and how well it satisfies the preference requirements. In order to save money, a total system test was not done before the Hubble Space Telescope was launched. As a result, taxpayers paid $850 million to fix the system error.

Maintaining Configuration Management

Configuration management (also called modification management) ensures that any changes in requirements, design, or implementation are controlled, carefully identified, and accurately recorded. All stakeholders should have an opportunity to comment on proposed changes. Decisions to adopt a change must be captured in a baseline database and reflected in system documentation. This documentation is a time-frozen design containing requirements for functions, performance, interfaces, verification, testing, cost, etc. All concerned parties must be notified of changes to ensure that they are all working on the same design. The phrase *requirements tracking* is now being used for an important subset of configuration management.

Implementing Risk Management

There are two types of risk: project failure (due to cost overruns, time overruns, or failure to meet performance specifications) and harm (usually called personnel safety). A failure modes and effects analysis and risk mitigation must be performed. Project risk can be reduced by supervising quality and timely delivery of purchased items (Kerzner, 1995).

Conducting Reliability Analyses

Major failure modes must be analyzed for probability of occurrence and severity of occurrence (Kapur and Lamberson, 1977; O'Connor, 1991).

Performing Total Quality Management

Everyone must continually look for ways to improve the quality of the system. Major tools used in this process include basic concurrent engineering, Deming's quality improvement concepts, quality function deployment (QFD), and Taguchi's quality engineering techniques (Bicknell and Bicknell, 1994; Latzko and Saunders, 1995).

Providing Project Management

Project management is the planning, organizing, directing, and controlling of company resources to meet specific goals and objectives within time, within cost, and at the desired performance level (Kerzner, 1995; Tichy and Sherman, 1993). Project management creates the work breakdown structure, which is a product-oriented tree of hardware, software, data, facilities, and services. It displays and defines the products to be developed and relates the elements of work to be accomplished to each other and to the end product. It provides structure for guiding team assignments and cost and tracking control (Martin, 1996).

Documentating All Activities

All of these Systems Engineering activities must be documented in a common repository, often called the Engineering Notebook. The stored information should be location, platform, and display independent, which means any person on any computer using any tool should be able to operate on the fundamental data. Results of trade-off analyses should be included. The reasons for making critical decisions should be stated (Chapman, Bahill, and Wymore, 1992; Wymore, 1993).

Creating Systems Engineers

The traditional method of creating systems engineers was to select well-organized engineers with lots of common sense and let them acquire 30 years of diverse engineering experience. Recently, these traditional systems engineers have written books and standards that explain what they do and how they do it. Now that the tools, concepts, and procedures have been formalized into four years of undergraduate education, we can teach Systems Engineers, and they will have performance levels 50% that of traditional Senior Systems Engineers. Ten years of systems engineering experience will improve performance to 80% and another ten years will increase it to 100%. These numbers are based on real salary data, and the fallacious assumption that salary is commensurate with performance.

REFERENCES

BAHILL, A.T., B. BENTZ, and F.F. DEAN, *Discovering Systems Requirements,* SAND96-1620 UC-706, Abuquerque, Sandia National Laboratories, July 1996.

BAHILL, A.T., and W.L. CHAPMAN, "A tutorial on quality function deployment." *Engineering Management Journal,* vol. 55, no. 3: pp.24–35 (1993).

Bicknell, K.D., and B.A. BICKNELL, *The Road Map to Repeatable Success: Using QFD to Implement Changes.* Boca Raton: CRC Press, 1994.

BLANCHARD, B.S., and W.J. FABRYCKY, *Systems Engineering and Analysis.*Prentice Hall, 1990.

CHAPMAN, W.L., A.T. BAHILL, and W. WYMORE, *Engineering Modeling and Design.* Boca Raton: CRC Press, 1992.

GRADY, J.O., *System Requirements Analysis.* McGraw Hill Inc., 1993.

GRADY, J.O., *System Integration.* Boca Raton: CRC Press, 1994.

GRADY, J.O., *System Engineering Planning and Enterprise Identity.* Boca Raton: CRC Press, 1995.

Hughes Aircraft Company. *Systems Engineering Handbook,* 1994.

Humans, Information and Technology. Proceedings, 1994 IEEE International Conference on Systems, Man, and Cybernetics, San Antonio, October 2–5, 1994.

IEEE P1220 Standard for Systems Engineering. New York: IEEE Standards Department, 1994.

JACOBSON, I., M. ERICSSON, and A. JACOBSON, *The Object Advantage: Business Process Reengineering with Object Technology,* New York: Addison-Wesley, 1995.

KAPUR, K.C., and L.R. LAMBERSON, *Reliability in Engineering Design.* New York: John Wiley & Sons, 1977.

KARNAVAS, W.J., P. SANCHEZ, and A.T. BAHILL, "Sensitivity analyses of continuous and discrete systems in the time and frequency domains." *IEEE Trans Systems Man Cybernetics,* SMC-23: pp. 488–501 (1993).

KERZNER, H., *Project Management: a Systems Approach to Planning, Scheduling, and Controlling.* New York: Van Nostrand Reinhold, 1995.

LATZKO, W.J., and D.M. SAUNDERS, *Four Days with Dr. Deming.* Reading, Mass: Addison-Wesley, 1995.

MARTIN, J., *Systems Engineering Guidebook.* Boca Raton: CRC Press, 1996.

MARTIN-MARIETTA. *Systems Engineering Methodology Handbook,* EPI 270–01, 1994.

NCOSE, *Systems Engineering Process Activities, A "How To" Guide.* Draft of a handbook by The National Council on Systems Engineering, 1994.

O'CONNOR, P.D.T., *Practical Reliability Engineering.* 3d Edition, New York: John Wiley & Sons, 1991.

SAGE, A.P., *Systems Engineering.* New York: John Wiley & Sons, 1992.

SHISHKO, R. *NASA Systems Engineering Handbook,* SP-6105, 1995.

Systems Engineering: A Competitive Edge in a Changing World. Proceedings of the Fourth Annual Symposium of the National Council on Systems Engineering (NCOSE), San Jose, August 10–12, 1994.

Systems Engineering in the Global Market Place, Proceedings of the Fifth Annual Symposium of the National Council on Systems Engineering, St. Louis: July 22–26, 1995.

SZIDAROVSZKY, F., M. GERSHON, and L. DUCKSTEIN, *Techniques for Multiobjective Decision Making in Systems Management.* Amsterdam: Elsevier Science Publishers, 1986.

TICHY, M., and S. SHERMAN, *Control Your Destiny or Someone Else Will.* New York: Currency Doubleday, 1993.

WYMORE, W., *Model-Based Systems Engineering.* Boca Raton: CRC Press, 1993.

25

METRICS FOR SYSTEMS ENGINEERING AND THE DEVELOPMENTAL ENVIRONMENT

We wanted metrics that would quantitatively assess the systems engineering of a system development. A list could be generated of the numerous tasks, tools, and techniques, both technical and managerial, that are considered "systems engineering" by different people and organizations; such a list could enhance common understanding. Unfortunately, no one list would be agreeable to all people, even systems engineers. Furthermore, while there are many different tasks performed under the label of "systems engineering," some are not appropriate for application under all circumstances. Degree of task application, the formality in which the element is carried out, and how well the activity is performed are considerations affecting systems engineering effectiveness in a particular development process.

The development environment can also greatly impact and even determine the success of system development by affecting the process itself. Additionally, the challenge and magnitude of the system design is a factor impacting system performance. Therefore, it is not possible to merely present a complete "laundry" list of systems engineering tasks, tools, and techniques, and then, simply claim that if a systems development effort performs them all, success will result. Design is an iterative process; the elements of systems engineering are applied most effectively in a logical, disciplined manner throughout the life cycle of the system. Thus, development must be evaluated in several ways to obtain a clearer picture of the relationship between the system development results and the characteristics of the process employed to get there.

There are no immutable, universal templates or algorithms for applying each systems engineering element. Therefore, application of systems engineering principles and activities must be tailored to each particular system development effort. Much like designing a complex system itself, the implementation of systems engineering tasks, tools, and techniques involves many decisions. These decisions require common sense and educated evaluation of numerous trade-offs in order to achieve the best outcomes possible. Despite the qualitative judgments involved with applying and carrying out systems engineering, a credible methodology can be utilized to measure its magnitude of application on development efforts already completed. The methodology can also be used to rate the magnitude of involvement of the other characteristics of system development, such as environment, design difficulty, and required resources. Using these results alone can be useful in illustrating what systems engineering involves for the benefit of engineering students, engineers, and program managers. However, these ratings might also be useful in empirically exploring the relationships among the system development process characteristics and the end results of an effort.

How, then, can a system development effort be evaluated as to the extent of systems engineering practices followed and their effectiveness as part of the design process? We propose the following approach. First, an evaluation methodology is developed through the creation of figures of merit and a rating scale for each of the five characteristics of a system development effort. These characteristics consist of:

1. *performance,* involving technical, cost, and schedule performance;
2. *systems engineering fundamentals,* describing 11 crucial principles and practices that should be considered for application in any development
3. *development environment,* in which 11 aspects are suggested to be conducive to supporting successful system development
4. *design difficulty,* consisting of six figures of merit addressing various aspects of technical complexity, and
5. *resources,* in terms of cost, time, and infrastructure to complete development.

Within each characteristic, the figures of merit or elements are selected to be distinct and measurable, and they must have a minimum amount of dependency between each other. Scoring criteria associated with each of the figures of merit and elements are generic, and therefore they are appropriate for any type and size of system. This allows a reasonable "apples-to-apples" comparison of the quality of the development processes for different systems.

Second, in order to demonstrate the rating methodology and provide data for analysis, six case studies are presented and evaluated in accordance with the figures of merit rating criteria. The subject of the six cases is aircraft developed in the United States within the past 15 years. This topic was chosen because;

1. aircraft are some of the most complex systems developed today,
2. a reasonably large number of companies develop aircraft and each does it differently, and
3. aircraft development is a somewhat mature process.

The third part of the approach is the compilation and analysis of the results. The individual scores of the figures of merit and elements are summed together to produce one numerical score for each of the five characteristics. This approach employs a simple multiattribute rating technique. The resulting numbers are used in an attempt to uncover relationships among the characteristics, with particular emphasis on identifying a correlation between *systems engineering fundamentals* and the *performance* scores. The meaning of a relatively higher score for *performance* is not that one system is necessarily better than the other. Rather, it is a quality or success index of the development process itself.

The selection of the characteristics and their figures of merit were developed from a variety of sources. *Performance* incorporates the traditional measures (technical, cost, and schedule performance) of assessing the success of a development program. The *systems engineering fundamentals* represent the summarization and synthesis of a detailed list of principles, tasks, and techniques compiled from various systems engineering books and papers (see references). The *development environment* figures of merit were devised based on the authors' experiences as well as organizational studies (Quinn and Rohrbaugh, 1983; Elmes and Wilemon, 1992). They were also chosen based on their abilities to be measured to a reasonable degree. We have already seen the elements and rating methodology for both *design difficulty* and *resources.*

The approach and model design just presented can be viewed as logical, and they represent a first step towards systematically investigating the relationships among the high-level system development characteristics and the results of a development effort. However, there are a variety of questions and issues concerning the validity of the approach; they are related to the qualitative nature of many of the criteria, design of the numerical rating scale, independence of the figures of merit, subjectivity of the process, bias in the case studies, and bias in mathematically combining the figures of merit scores.

First of all, the assignment of scores for the figures of merit and elements is based on rating criteria for all five system development characteristics. The topics addressed by the figures of merit for *systems engineering fundamentals* and *development environment* do not lend themselves to the formation of quantitative criteria for the most part. Instead, these criteria are mostly qualitative. Given the complexity of the topics being evaluated, the criteria must be at a very high level or else be made extremely detailed. Making them detailed reduces their usefulness for educational purposes.

The 0 to 10 point scale used in most figures of merit rating criteria was selected because it allows easy separation of ratings into three ranges: high, medium, and low. Given the qualitative nature of most criteria, subjective judgments can be easily assigned among three categories based on a reasonable amount of information provided to the evaluator. Furthermore, allowing the choice of several points within each category provides the ability to score with greater fidelity, if the degree of information detail is provided. While the case studies were researched rather extensively, the information gathered was obtained from limited sources. Therefore, there may be unintended biases, omissions, or inaccuracies that may impact the ratings for particular figures of merit.

An issue of fundamental importance is whether or not the proposed figures of merit ratings, when summed into single higher-level characteristic scores, have validity and significance as generic measures, thereby allowing meaningful comparison between systems. This issue depends on the degree of dependence between the figures of merit within a characteristic, the extent to which the figures of merit and elements completely define the factors at work within a characteristic, and the appropriateness of the relative weighting within each characteristic. While some dependencies do exist between the figures of merit, most can be considered as minimal based on a simple cause-effect analysis. Also, the characteristics can be reasonably regarded as not leaving out major high-level factors, since the figures of merit address all the major areas identified in appropriate literature.

The scoring method for the first three characteristics assumes that most figures of merit have equal weight, since the relative importance of each is not understood in a quantitative way. The hope is that insights into relative weighting may be gained by applying the approach outlined in this book to a sufficiently large number of cases. The exceptions to the equal weighting assumption are the first two figures of merit in the *systems engineering fundamentals* characteristic. They are each weighted twice their ratings, based on studies that have shown that the majority of the life-cycle cost of a system is determined in the requirements and concept development phases (Zangwill, 1992). Of all the figures of merit in the *systems engineering fundamentals* characteristic, these two are most associated with the early phases of a program. While this overall weighting structure does warrant further investigation and refinement, it is meant to be a credible starting point.

An important point to make is that we are not attempting to explore in detail the combinatorial issues surrounding the summation of the ratings. While there is a huge amount of literature dealing with mathematical and behavioral aggregation, as well as multicriteria decision making; delving into those issues in this book would be unnecessary at this point in the development of the approach. Instead, as mentioned previously, the figures of merit are believed to be reasonably independent, thereby supporting the basic validity of the approach. Furthermore, only simple graphical analysis techniques are used to analyze the generated data. Due to the low number of data points generated, sophisticated statistical methods are of minimal usefulness.

While the focus of this section is systems engineering and its impact in the system development process, there is some relation to the area of organizational effectiveness. Although the model and analysis method presented are not oriented towards any specific organizational structure, they take into account organizational factors in the *systems engineering fundamentals* and *development environment* characteristics. In fact, some of the *development environment* figures of merit correspond almost directly with organizational effectiveness measures.

Many studies have been conducted attempting to determine, measure, and evaluate the characteristics of successful organizations; and many case studies have been developed describing successful and unsuccessful products and how they were developed. Furthermore, studies of the effectiveness of concurrent engineering (a development approach that can be viewed as good systems engineering), identify most of the same types of issues addressed in the systems engineering fundamentals.

(Zangwill, 1992.) However, to the author's knowledge, none have structured the development process in the same way as presented in this section or attempted to uncover high-level relationships between characteristics of system development. Furthermore, no other studies have identified *systems engineering fundamentals* as recognizable elements that can be evaluated as a group and represented with a single numerical rating. We propose such a methodology.

The outline of the evaluation methodology showing the system development characteristics and lists of the figures of merit are presented in the following sections.

PERFORMANCE

Performance is composed of measures used to assess the degree of success of the overall development process of a system. The figures of merit consist of the following:

A. **Technical performance—initial**. This is defined as compliance with customer performance requirements and specifications, as well as overall customer satisfaction at the time of initial system deliveries.

> 7–10 points are given for a highly successful system, in which the system achieves all or nearly all key technical performance requirements at the time of initial system delivery. There is a high degree of customer satisfaction.

> 4–6 points are given for a moderately successful system, in which the system meets a majority of key technical performance requirements, rendering it useful to the customer. However, operational performance of some subsystems is less than expected. The result is a moderate degree of customer satisfaction.

> 0–3 points are given for an unsuccessful system, in which the system fails to meet significant technical performance requirements at the time of initial system delivery, rendering it unusable by the customer as originally intended. The result is low customer satisfaction.

B. **Technical performance—mature**. This is defined as compliance with customer performance requirements and specifications, as well as overall customer satisfaction, one to two years after system delivery.

> 7–10 points are given for a highly successful system, in which the system achieves all or nearly all key technical performance requirements. There is a high degree of customer satisfaction.

> 4–6 points are given for a moderately successful system, in which the system meets a majority of key technical performance requirements rendering it useful to the customer. The result is a moderate degree of customer satisfaction.

> 0–3 points are given for an unsuccessful system, in which the system fails to meet significant technical performance requirements, rendering it unusable by the customer as originally intended.

C. **Cost performance**. This deals with how close the full-scale engineering development (FSED) effort (also known by its more recent name "Engineering and Manufacturing Development" or EMD) meets the budget; production costs are not considered. This is measured using percentage cost growth (overrun) of the original FSED baseline estimate. This measure is from the point of view of the funding source.

9–10 points are given for an effort that came in below the baseline cost or up to 5% over the baseline cost.

7–8 points are given for an effort with 6 to 15% cost overrun.

5–6 points are given for an effort with 16 to 35% cost growth (overrun).

3–4 points are given for an effort with 36 to 75% cost growth (overrun).

0–2 points are given for an effort with greater than 75% cost growth (overrun).

Note: A better metric might have been Total Life Cycle Cost. But we have agreed to evaluate all our metrics for the period starting with the first efforts and ending with the delivery of the first production unit. The Total Life Cycle Cost could not be estimated until much later.

D. **Schedule performance**. This is defined as the percentage of time that the FSED effort is overdue, with the effort beginning at the start of FSED and ending at the delivery to the customer of the first production unit. This is determined by taking the length of time from the start of FSED to planned customer delivery of the first production unit (planned FSED length); taking the length of time from the start of FSED to the actual delivery of the first unit; taking the difference between the two (assuming the actual is longer than the planned length); and dividing the difference by the planned FSED length.

9–10 points are given for on-time performance or not more than 2% overdue (baseline development schedule).

7–8 points are given for 3% or more overdue but less than 10% overdue.

5–6 points are given for 10% or more overdue but less than 20% overdue.

3–4 points are given for 20% overdue or more but less than 50% overdue.

0–2 points are given for 50% or more overdue.

The ratings and scores are provided in a table at the end of each case study similar to that illustrated in Table 25-1.

TABLE 25-1   Performance Scores.

Figures of Merit	Range	Weight	Rating	Score
Technical performance—Initial	0–10	1		
Technical performance—Mature	0–10	1		
Cost performance	0–10	1		
Schedule performance	0–10	1		
Performance total				0–40

SYSTEMS ENGINEERING FUNDAMENTALS

The approach to measure the degree of systems engineering followed during development involves identifying a top-level list of key principles, activities, and tasks that should be considered during any development program of reasonable complexity. This approach is in contrast to trying to develop a detailed, all-encompassing list. As part of the rating process for each case study, the fundamental systems engineering practices are evaluated as to whether or not they were accomplished, to what extent they were completed, and how well these fundamental elements were carried out. This involves not just the issue of completeness and the expertise displayed, but also the appropriateness of application and the time frame in which systems engineering elements are applied and carried out.

The following is a list of fundamental practices or elements of good systems engineering. In the author's opinion, all are accomplished as part of effective systems engineering. However, the extent and formality of the application depends on the particulars of the system being developed. The tasks associated with these figures of merit are not necessarily performed by officially designated systems engineers:

A. **Requirements development.** This is defined as understanding customer needs, properly stating the problem, and accurately specifying the requirements that define what the system must do.

> 7–10 points are given for an accurate and thorough understanding and documentation of the customer's problems and needs, and for the documentation of system-level requirements in a single specification.

> 4–6 points are given for reasonably accurate and thorough understanding of the customer's problems and needs in a requirements document, but significant adjustments are required.

> 0–3 points are given for an inaccurate and incomplete definition of the customer's problems and needs.

B. **Incipient system design.** This consists of defining system concept models at the beginning of the effort; identifying and organizing the hierarchy of functions (functional decomposition) to be performed by the system based on the top-level performance objectives; defining the system constraints and interfaces; defining the hierarchy of physical elements (physical decomposition); and allocating detailed performance and interface requirements to the physical elements (subsystems).

> 7–10 points are given for clearly defined top-level system concept models that are decomposed into functions or elements, with well-defined interfaces and detailed requirements allocations to the decomposed items. Furthermore, these are completed before FSED.

> 4–6 points are given for marginally defined top-level system concept models that are decomposed into functions or elements, with adequately defined inter-

faces and requirements allocations to the decomposed items. Furthermore, these are completed before FSED.

0–3 points are given for inadequate top-level modeling of the system concept, insufficient or inappropriate interface definitions, and poor requirements allocation, or the failure to adequately complete activities before FSED.

C. **Evaluating alternative concepts.** This refers to evaluating the relative merit of alternative concepts and designs using a design trade-off methodology (formal or informal) that uses results of analyses, simulation model testing, and/or physical model testing.

7–10 points are given for a thorough consideration and analysis of alternative concepts and/or subsystem designs using a formal or informal design trade-off methodology utilizing results of analyses, simulation model testing, and/or physical model testing.

4–6 points are given for limited consideration and analysis of alternative concepts and subsystem designs using a formal or informal design trade-off methodology utilizing results of analyses, simulation model testing, and/or physical model testing.

0–3 points are given for little or no consideration and analysis of alternative concepts and subsystem designs.

D. **Make-or-buy decision.** This is the act of determining whether a subsystem or component of the system should be developed and built by the system developer (in-house) or purchased from an outside source. This make-or-buy decision need not consume a lot of resources. It could be made simple by company policy, secrecy, or time in history. For example, company policy might require that certain items be bought, security classification might require that certain items be made in-house, and time in history forced Thomas Edison to make his own vacuum pump—although if he were living today, he would probably buy one.

Availability, cost, and quality of the components affects the make-or-buy decision. It is also affected by business considerations, e.g., companies protect their core competencies and they might buy technology in order to expand core competencies.

7–10 points are given for make-or-buy decisions that consider a majority of a system's subsystems and components (which are not already covered by a reasonable a priori development policy), and reflect the system developer's in-house capabilities and resources.

4–6 points are given for make-or-buy decisions that consider some of the system's subsystems and components (which are not already covered by a reasonable a priori development policy), and reflect the system developer's in-house capabilities and resources.

0–3 points is given for little or no consideration of the trade-offs between developing subsystems and components in-house and purchasing them from outside sources.

E. **Validation.** This consists of the validation of established requirements to ensure they are consistent with the customer needs and that a real-world solution can be built and tested to prove that it satisfies the requirements.

7–10 points are given for conducting a methodical process involving direct interaction with the customer, which ensures the system requirements are consistent with the true needs of the customer, and determines that a real-world solution can be built and tested.

4–6 points are given for a process ensuring the requirements are consistent with the true needs of the customer through indirect methods (such as referencing marketing surveys), and for determining that a real-world solution can be built and tested.

0–3 points for not reviewing requirements with regard to actual customer desires or not attempting to justify that a real-world solution exists.

F. **Verification and integrated testing.** This figure of merit refers to the determination of design compliance with performance specifications and the determination of as-built hardware and software compliance with specification and drawing requirements. This includes identifying component-level to system-level testing in a test and evaluation master plan early in development. It also refers to actually conducting tests and inspections in a complete and logical manner; these tests should examine components and subsystems individually, then combinations of components and subsystems together, and finally, the final integrated system.

7–10 points are given for a complete job of verifying design, hardware, and software compliance with specifications and drawings; clearly identifying early in development the planned component, subsystem, and system-level testing in a comprehensive test plan; and then actually conducting the testing.

4–6 points are given for a partial job of verifying design, hardware, and software compliance with specifications and drawings; incompletely identifying early in development the planned component, subsystem, and system-level testing in a test plan or series of plans; and then eventually conducting all the needed testing.

0–3 points are given for incomplete, inadequate attempts to verify design, hardware, and software compliance with specifications and drawings, not planning for and identifying early in development the component, subsystem, and system-level testing throughout system development; and not conducting important tests.

G. **Configuration management.** This refers to establishing and maintaining the status of the design configuration and interfaces, as defined by specifications and drawings (paper or digital); controlling changes to the configuration; appropriately controlling changes between subsystems and between the system and the external world; and maintaining the traceability of the configuration as it changes.

7–10 points are given for effectively controlling interface changes within a formal system; maintaining an accurate status of the design configuration; controlling configuration changes through a formal system of review, approval, and update; and maintaining the traceability of the configuration.

4–6 points are given for controlling interface changes within a formal system with some problems; maintaining a reasonably accurate status of the design configuration; controlling configuration changes with some difficulty; and maintaining reasonable traceability of the configuration.

0–3 points are given for inadequately controlling interface changes; failing to maintain an accurate status of the design configuration; inadequately controlling configuration changes; and/or not maintaining traceability of the configuration.

H. **Manufacturing considerations.** This is defined as addressing and giving priority to appropriate manufacturing considerations early in system development with the objectives of:

1. giving the manufacturing entity adequate time to prepare for fabrication and production; and
2. letting manufacturing considerations influence the design of the system and its manufacturing processes to reduce fabrication costs.

    7–10 points are given for developing manufacturing processes concurrently with the system design, and allowing the design to be significantly influenced by manufacturing considerations to improve ease and/or cost of fabrication.

    4–6 points are given for involving manufacturing personnel early in development, but not allowing the design to be significantly influenced by them to improve ease and/or cost of fabrication.

    0–3 points are given for ignoring or placing low emphasis on manufacturing issues during system design.

I. **System integration and technical management.** This function involves bringing subsystems together to produce the desired results and ensures that the subsystems will interact to satisfy the customer needs. This involves:

1. organizing the technical effort and identifying how the development will be broken out and managed;
2. integrating activities of the development team;

3. balancing the influence of all required design specialties;

4. resolving design conflicts;

5. ensuring compatibility of all physical, functional, and program interfaces; and

6. assessing and managing technical risk.

7–10 points are given for effectively bringing subsystems together through a well-organized and integrated technical effort that balances the influence of all required design specialties.

4–6 points are given for bringing subsystems together with significant difficulty, due to inadequate subsystem verification or technical efforts that do not thoughtfully balance the influence of all required design specialties.

0–3 points are given for failing to effectively bring subsystems together.

J. **Life-cycle considerations.** This refers to giving priority to long term issues, such as supportability (primarily maintainability, reliability, and training) and life-cycle costs consistent with appropriate system requirements and objectives.

7–10 points are given for fully recognizing and addressing supportability and life-cycle cost requirements and issues early in development.

4–6 points are given for recognizing and minimally addressing supportability and life-cycle cost requirements and issues early in development.

0–3 points are given for not adequately recognizing and addressing supportability and life-cycle cost requirements and issues early in development.

K. **Program management.** This involves the planning, tracking, and coordination of activities performed by all elements of the development team, as well as the resolution of impediments to program progress. Evidence of strong program management includes an integrated master scheduling system, an efficient cost accounting system that provides management visibility into development activities in a timely manner, life-cycle cost estimates, risk analyses, and regular program reviews involving all the key stakeholders.

7–10 points are given for a strong program management function that effectively keeps the effort on track through use of an accurate integrated master scheduling system, use of a cost accounting system providing timely information, and use of regular program reviews with program stakeholders.

4–6 points are given for a program management function of medium strength that keeps the effort only moderately on track, due at least partly to problems with the management support systems and practices.

0–3 points are given for a weak program management function that does not keep the effort on track and has deficient management support systems and practices.

The ratings and scores are provided in a table at the end of each case study similar to that illustrated in Table 25-2.

TABLE 25-2   Systems Engineering Fundamentals Scores.

Figures of Merit	Range	Weight	Rating	Score
Requirements development	0–10	2		
Incipient system design	0–10	2		
Evaluating alternative concepts	0–10	1		
Make-or-buy decision	0–10	1		
Validation	0–10	1		
Verification and integrated testing	0–10	1		
Configuration management	0–10	1		
Manufacturing considerations	0–10	1		
System integration and technical management	0–10	1		
Life-cycle considerations	0–10	1		
Program management	0–10	1		
Systems engineering fundamentals				
Total				0–130

DEVELOPMENT ENVIRONMENT

The third aspect of evaluating the systems development process is the environment in which it takes place. The environment is probably an equally crucial factor for success. Even expertly performed systems engineering practices can be overcome by negative environmental factors. However, a positive environment cannot make up for inadequate or poorly performed systems engineering. *Systems engineering fundamentals* and *the development environment* work together and impact each other in complex ways.

Some of the elements of this third aspect are beyond the direct control of the systems engineer, the chief engineer, and the program manager (the major exception being the first element, "emphasis on the customer"). Some of them are under the control of those in authority above the effort or totally external to it. However, if these elements are favorable, they can enhance the effectiveness of systems engineering practices and contribute to development success. They are as follows:

A. **Emphasis on the customer.** The customer requirements are the primary design drivers, and user input during the entire development process is accepted and encouraged.

7–10 points are given for a high emphasis on receiving and positively responding to direct or indirect customer involvement throughout development.

4–6 points are given for a moderate emphasis on receiving and positively responding to direct or indirect customer involvement throughout development.

0–3 points are given for little or no emphasis on receiving or positively responding to input from the customer throughout development.

B. **Stability of requirements and configuration.** The customer requirements do not undergo a series of major changes after the start of FSED; and the system configuration does not undergo numerous alterations, whether they are driven by a change in customer requirements or correction of design deficiencies.

> 7–10 points are given for minor changes to no change in customer requirements and/or for a low number of moderate configuration changes during FSED.
>
> 4–6 points are given for moderate changes in customer requirements and/or for a low number of major configuration changes during FSED.
>
> 0–3 points are given for major changes in customer requirements and/or for a moderate to large number of major configuration changes during FSED.

C. **Funding and work-force-level stability.** This means that the development effort follows a multiyear budget that does not change significantly each year from the original plan. Furthermore, the work-force-level throughout FSED follows a long term plan.

> 7–10 points are given for no unplanned, major dips or spikes in funding amounts and work-force-levels throughout FSED.
>
> 4–6 points are given for moderate funding and work-force-level deviations from long term plans during FSED.
>
> 0–3 points are given for major and severe funding and work-force-level deviations from long term plans during FSED.

D. **Strong support.** This is defined as a development effort having strong general support within its company (referring to commercial programs); or within the government, public, and media (referring to government programs) during FSED.

> 7–10 points are given for strong support throughout concept development and FSED with no significant controversy threatening viability of the effort.
>
> 4–6 points are given for moderate support or sharply contrasting levels of support during concept development and FSED due to significant controversy that moderately threatens the viability of the effort.
>
> 0–3 points are given for little or no support resulting from a significant controversy during concept development and FSED that seriously threatens the viability of the program.

E. **Continuity of core development team.** This means that a core team of designers and managers remain throughout development; there is minimal turnover of key personnel.

> 7–10 points are given for there being only little or no turnover of key designers and managers during concept development and FSED.
>
> 4–6 points are given for there being a moderate amount of turnover of key de-

signers and managers during concept development and FSED.

0–3 points are given for essentially little or no continuity of key designers and managers during concept development and FSED.

F. **Stability of organizational structure.** This means that the system development organization does not go through major reorganizations during the development of the system.

7–10 points are given for the development group not going through a major reorganization during FSED.

4–6 points are given for the development group going through a moderate reorganization during FSED.

0–3 points are given for the development group going through a major reorganization during FSED.

G. **Cooperation among stakeholders.** This refers to the existence of positive, nonconfrontational working relationships among the team members and between the team members and the customer(s). Furthermore, there are no major hidden agendas in conflict with program and customer objectives.

7–10 points are given for very positive, nonconfrontational working relationships among program participants during FSED.

4–6 points are given for generally positive to generally negative working relationships existing among program participants during FSED.

0–3 points are given for very negative working relationships among program participants that severely impede or stop program progress during FSED.

H. **Effective communication.** This is defined as how well members of the development team (including subcontractors and customers) communicate and coordinate among themselves. It is evidenced by adequate mechanisms for communication (such as close physical proximity of the workers to each other), or the existence and use of communication mechanisms (such as telephones, fax machines, computer aided design and manufacturing systems, and computer networks). It is also influenced by the organizational structure, the management philosophy, and the cultural factors of the organization.

7-10 points are given for effective communication and coordination among the development team members and between them and the customers.

4-6 points are given for moderately effective communication and coordination among the development team members and between them and the customers.

0-3 points are given for ineffective communication and coordination among the development team members and between them and the customers, due to poor circumstances and mechanisms.

I. **Flexibility and autonomy.** This refers to the ability to implement design changes quickly, thereby not being significantly hindered by organizational or procedural roadblocks. Flexibility and autonomy are evidenced by fast and efficient design change mechanisms and by the absence of bureaucratic (government or corporate) micromanagement of development activities.

> 7–10 points are given for the ability to make decisions and implement design changes quickly without procedural roadblocks or bureaucratic micromanagement.

> 4–6 points are given for a moderate degree of procedural impediments to quick decision making and change implementation, due to inflexible and inefficient procedures and/or micromanagement of development activities by corporate or government bureaucracy.

> 0–3 points are given for significant procedural impediments to quick decision making and change implementation and/or a large amount of micromanagement of development activities by corporate or government bureaucracy.

J. **Work-force qualifications.** This means that development personnel have appropriate education and experience to successfully develop the system.

> 7–10 points are given if most development team members have education and experience in appropriate areas.

> 4–6 points are given if a moderate number of development team members are educated in appropriate areas, but lack experience.

> 0–3 points are given for a severe lack of appropriate education and expertise among the development team.

K. **Accountability for system performance.** This means that the system developer is held accountable to the customer for the resulting system's performance. Such a situation is evidenced by the existence of mechanisms such as warranties, product liability laws, and total system performance responsibility provisions. Another factor is the importance of reputation to the developer, as well as the significance of reputation to future efforts. Accountability for system performance also means that the system developer is responsible to its funding source for the way the effort is conducted; and this is evidenced by award fee and incentive fee structures for cost type government contracts, bonus programs for commercial efforts, and mechanisms for quickly replacing personnel if progress is not satisfactory.

> 7–10 points are given for strong warranties on key performance parameters and defective parts, for award and bonus fee mechanisms, for product liability laws, and/or for strong motivation to maintain company reputation.

> 4–6 points are given for warranties covering the replacement of defective parts and excluding some key performance parameters, in addition to limited award fee or bonus mechanisms and product liability laws.

TABLE 25-3   Development Environment Scores

Figures of Merit	Range	Weight	Rating	Score
Emphasis on the customer	0–10	1		
Stability of requirements and configuration	0–10	1		
Funding and work-force-level stability	0–10	1		
Strong support	0–10	1		
Continuity of core development team	0–10	1		
Stability of organizational structure	0–10	1		
Cooperation among stakeholders	0–10	1		
Effective communication	0–10	1		
Flexibility and autonomy	0–10	1		
Work-force qualifications	0–10	1		
Accountability for system performance	0–10	1		
Development environment total				0–110

0–3 points for no warranties or extremely limited warranties covering replacement of defective parts and for no other significant accountability mechanism.

The ratings and scores are provided in a table at the end of each case study similar to that illustrated in Table 25-3.

REFERENCES

ELMES, M., and D. WILEMON, Determinants of Cross-Functional Cooperation in Technology-Based Organizations. *IEEE Transactions on Engineering Management,* pp. 40–46. Spring 1993.

QUINN, R.E., and J. ROHRBAUGH, A Spatial Model of Effectiveness Criteria:Towards a Competing Values Approach to Organization Analysis. *Management Science,* vol. 29, no. 3: pp. 363–377 (1983).

ZANGWILL, W.I., Concurrent Engineering: Concepts and Implementation. *IEEE Transactions on Engineering Management,* pp.40–52, Winter, 1992.

26

THE BOEING 777
COMMERCIAL AIRPLANE

The Boeing 777 is the world's largest twin-engine commercial airplane currently being built for long distance commercial passenger and cargo travel. It is intended to fill a market and product gap between Boeing's 767-300 and the 747-400 jumbo jet, and it will compete directly against the McDonnell Douglas MD-11 trijet and the four-engine Airbus Industry A330/340 family. The 777 is unique in that it was developed in a significantly different manner than the earlier Boeing aircraft, and even its competitors' aircraft. Three characteristics of this development were:

1. multidisciplinary teams working together to concurrently design the aircraft and its production processes,
2. an unprecedented participation of the customer airlines in the development process, and

3. the design and integration work being done almost entirely on computer.

All of these innovations were intended to produce an aircraft that was free of problems and ready for full service when delivered to the customer.

DEVELOPMENT HISTORY, DESIGN, AND PERFORMANCE

Boeing officially launched the 777 development program on October 29, 1990, when its corporate board of directors gave approval to take what was then a concept development effort into full-scale engineering development (FSED) and production. Despite some problems with engine development, the effort progressed according to plan. The first flight took place according to original schedule on June 12, 1994; and flight testing to certify the three different engines available to customers expected to run through March 1996. Boeing made its first 777 delivery to United Airlines on schedule in May 1995 (see Figure 26-1).

As of late 1994, there were 147 firm orders and 108 options for the $125 million airplanes. While the primary financing has come from Boeing, the Japanese companies that are fabricating large portions of the fuselage planned to provide from 8–10% of the estimated $4–$5 billion start-up costs (O'Lone, 1990).

The 777 can be regarded as an original design. However, it can also be described as a major redesign that is evolutionary in nature; the design is based primarily on experience gained from the Boeing 757 and 767 (introduced in the early 1980s) and the latest version of the 747 (introduced in 1989). The 777 has the appearance of an enlarged 767, and several major items were taken from the 757, 767, and 747-400. For example, the nose structure of the 777 is the same as the 767. The cockpit design was derived from the 747-400. The engine attachment is a scaled version of the design used on the 757. Also, one of the three engines that will be certified with the 777, the Pratt & Whitney PW4074, is a larger derivative of the existing PW4060 used on the 767. In addition to using subsystems and components from ear-

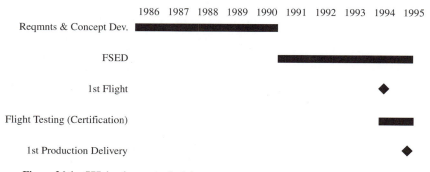

Figure 26-1   777 development schedule.

lier aircraft, the 777 utilizes a significant amount of advanced technologies both inside and out to meet challenging performance and design goals.

The primary 777 goal was to develop a large twin-engine airplane that could beat the fuel consumption performance of three-engine and the four-engine A330/A340 (Dornheim, 1991a). This accomplishment required the use of advanced materials, lightweight flight controls, and an improved aerodynamic design. For the first time on a Boeing commercial airplane, some of the primary structure is made of lightweight composites. Specifically, the horizontal and vertical tail structural boxes are made of an advanced graphite epoxy material, and composites are used in the spoilers and flaps. Overall composite content is about nine percent by weight. Boeing also used a new aluminum alloy for the upper wing skin, which is a stronger refinement of materials used on the company's three most recent airplanes. Lower weight was also achieved using fly-by-wire flight controls, thereby eliminating the need for heavy hydraulics. The use of electronic flight controls, which have been used in military aircraft since the middle 1970s, was a first for a Boeing commercial airplane. These approaches to keeping weight down were helpful, but the 777 still ended up several percent overweight (O'Lone, 1991).

In addition to reducing weight, the 777 designers intended to achieve fuel consumption goals by improving aerodynamic efficiency. According to Boeing, the 777 wing is the most aerodynamically efficient airfoil ever developed for a subsonic commercial aircraft (Boeing, ca 1994). The 777 development team also faced the major aerodynamic challenge of fitting the large engine nacelle onto the wing with the least drag penalty. To further reduce drag, Boeing designed parts of the airplane to exceptionally close tolerances for a tight fit (*Air & Space,* 1994). By using the advanced supercomputer simulation tool of computational fluid dynamics and extensive wind tunnel testing to validate the computational fluid dynamic models, the 777 designers were able to produce an overall design that met its aerodynamic performance goals.

The 777 team had another challenge developing the propulsion units. Since this large airplane is designed to fly with only two engines, each must be very large and powerful. In fact, the diameter of each of the three different candidate engines is about the same as the fuselage diameter of the 737. The three companies that developed an engine for the 777 are Pratt & Whitney, General Electric, and Rolls Royce. Of these, only Pratt & Whitney offered a unit that was derived directly from an existing engine design, thereby avoiding considerable development. Despite being a derivative design, the Pratt & Whitney unit did experience problems during development testing. Resolving these problems was crucial to Boeing, because sales of the 777s were dependent on a special early Federal Aviation Administration (FAA) certification called *extended twin-engine operations overwater (ETOPS).* This certification allows twin-engine aircraft to fly long distance flights over water. All prior twin-engine passenger jets that flew intercontinental distances over oceans have required several years of overland experience to develop a reliability history to justify ETOPS certification. Without ETOPS certification, the aircraft could not be used for many of the routes for which they were purchased. ETOPS was granted before the first scheduled passenger flight.

Another key feature that posed challenges to designers was the highly integrated and automated advanced avionics, enabling operation by a crew of only two pilots instead of the usual cockpit crew of three. The resulting Airplane Information Management System (AIMS) from Honeywell incorporated into a single system the flight management, airplane condition monitoring, central maintenance, and digital link communication functions, which in earlier aircraft were performed separately. Despite the high degree of integration, the cockpit had been designed with the growth potential to accommodate future needs for additional information (Scott, 1991).

Design flexibility has also been incorporated throughout the rest of the 777 so that it can meet a variety of customer requirements. For example, the initial version will carry up to 375 passengers a distance of over 4,560 miles (3,970 nautical miles). Boeing plans to evolve the design into configurations for carrying more than 300 passenger nearly 7,250 miles (6,300 nautical miles) and about 400 passengers over 7,000 miles. The floor was strengthened to accommodate the weight of future increases in passengers and flight amenities. Furthermore, zones of flexibility have been designed into the cabin areas as specified by the airlines. Within these zones, which have been pre-engineered to accommodate wiring, plumbing, and attachment fixtures, the galleys and lavatories can be positioned anywhere in one-inch increments. Furthermore, passenger service units and overhead stowage compartments are designed for quick removal without disturbing ceiling panels, air conditioning ducts, or support structures. A typical 777 cabin configuration change is expected to take as little as 72 hours, while such a change might take two to three weeks on existing aircraft (Boeing, ca 1994).

By any measure, the 777 is a large and complex system. It will have about 132,500 engineered, unique parts. By including rivets, bolts, and other fasteners in the count, the airplane will have more than three million (Boeing, ca 1994). Boeing's job is to ensure that those many parts work together in a manner that will satisfy its customers. The approach Boeing used in developing the 777 suggests that the airline customers will be satisfied with what they receive.

SYSTEMS ENGINEERING FUNDAMENTALS

Boeing is the world's largest developer and manufacturer of commercial passenger jet aircraft. Since the late 1950s, the company has developed the 707, 727, 737, 747, 757, and 767 series of passenger jets. Over those years, Boeing had developed and followed its version of a traditional approach to developing aircraft. That is, design engineers designed the aircraft separately and then gave the drawings and specifications to manufacturing for fabrication and to maintenance personnel for establishing maintenance procedures. This approach normally led to significant changes as the manufacturing engineers discovered design inconsistencies and unproducible component configurations. It also resulted in higher life-cycle costs, since the designs did not always emphasize ease of repair and a reduced need for maintenance. With the 777, Boeing decided on a radically new development approach that focused on the customer and placed great emphasis on ensuring that the development activities were done right the first time.

In late 1986, Boeing started identifying requirements for a large passenger airplane with the capacity between the twin-engine 767-300 and the four-engine 747-400 jumbo jet. This investigation into what Boeing then called the 767-X configuration was initiated as a result of interest expressed by airlines for a medium- to long-distance Boeing-produced aircraft in the 300–400 passenger capacity range. Boeing entered into a dialogue with interested airlines and potential subcontractors to define and refine requirements. Trade studies were conducted throughout this time, culminating in a system design concept with detailed requirements allocated to lower-level elements of the aircraft. By the end of this period, a group of national and international subcontractors were ready to develop and fabricate many of the subsystems. This four year requirements generation, requirements validation, concept development, and make-or-buy decision effort culminated with the launching of FSED.

Boeing's development and systems engineering approach is highlighted by early participation of all disciplines, as well as by unprecedented input by their customers. The basic organizational entity responsible for designing and building a portion of the aircraft is the design/build team; its membership is comprised of design engineering, manufacturing, specialty engineering, and nontechnical representatives, as well as representatives of the subcontractors and suppliers. The approach's objective is to cut development costs by reducing the amount of downstream design changes and resultant rework, which are the predominant aircraft development cost drivers (O'Lone, 1991).

On the 777 program, the teams have been organized around parts of the aircraft rather than functions. At the top are 30 integration-level teams representing the largest aircraft sections, and each has had the responsibility of maintaining the interfaces of its component parts for the other 29 sections. Various levels of subsystem and component subteams operate below. During the height of development, up to 238 of these cross-functional design/build teams worked on the effort at one time (Boeing, 1994).

Subcontractors and suppliers had unusually close working relationships with Boeing under this structure (O'Lone, 1991). For example, in cases where the subcontractor was going to build the hardware, that company's representative took the lead manufacturing role on the design/build team instead of a Boeing employee. The airline companies that placed the first orders have also taken part in the design/build process; they participated in integration-level design/build meetings, preliminary design reviews, and critical design reviews. This continual involvement by the customers and their active involvement in defining the design helped to validate the requirements that the airlines had established before the program started.

A crucial element of Boeing's development strategy was designing the 777 on an advanced computer aided design (CAD) system instead of using paper drawings. This tool, called CATIA, is a three-dimensional computer system with solid modeling capability that can produce a virtual prototype. That is, the parts can be separately drawn in three dimensions, joined together in the computer, and visually displayed on the screen. This enabled each team to create their designs and compare them with the other teams' work to check for interference between parts. With over 2,000 computer terminals linked together and available to the development team, CATIA improved the speed of determining and communicating the status of interfaces and configurations; and it greatly increased the effectiveness of configuration control activities. Although CATIA was not fully developed at the outset of the 777 program, Boeing worked with CATIA developers, Dassault and IBM. They continued to perfect and enhance the system as the 777 program advanced, achieving the virtual prototyping capability early on.

Engineers were also able to use CATIA to analyze weight, balance, and stress on the different parts, allowing for quick evaluation and refinement of alternative designs. This virtual prototyping not only eliminated the need for most paper drawings, but also the need for and cost of most physical mockups and full-scale prototypes. The most significant example is that the first 777 produced and flown was a production configuration aircraft instead of an engineering prototype.

In addition to design, analysis, and verification activities, the CATIA digital design system had a large impact on manufacturing operations. CATIA design information was combined with computer controlled machining techniques, and it has resulted in a significant improvement in dimensional accuracy (O'Lone, 1992). CATIA also caused the replacement of plaster master models with digital data, greatly improving the precision and efficiency in building manufacturing tools. Additionally, Boeing has implemented a paperless manufacturing floor, where the assembly and installation shop floor control system is computer based and enhanced by graphical instructions with links to the CATIA design database. Due to the digital design and manufacturing system, Boeing reported a 50% reduction of rework and factory floor changes compared to the 767 (Proctor, 1993).

Boeing planned a 54 month development schedule, which is somewhat greater than its traditional 48 months for a new commercial aircraft (O'Lone and Mexenna, 1989). This was to allow more time for Boeing to work out problems before aircraft delivery. In essence, Boeing took the aircraft through a break-in period to identify and correct annoying problems, instead of having the airlines experience them. This "service-ready" approach was the guiding philosophy of the development program; and it drove the Boeing team to interact closely with the customer during development, to conduct extensive integrated ground testing, to perform additional flight testing, and to address life-cycle supportability issues early. This approach was motivated by the significant difficulties experienced by airlines when they received the initial deliveries of the 747-400 in 1989.

As mentioned above, one of the strategies for achieving the service-ready goals has been extensive integrated ground testing. This has been a key element in identifying and solving development problems as early as possible in order to attain reliability goals. Boeing invested $370 million in a new test facility called the Integrated Aircraft Systems Laboratory (IASL) to accomplish this. The IASL tests individual parts, subassemblies, and integrated aircraft systems both on the static bench and under simulated flight conditions. During advanced testing, multiple hardware systems are integrated and operated "in-the-loop" with the computer simulations. In addition to conducting the ground testing of subsystems, Boeing demonstrated the performance of its fly-by-wire design and cockpit avionics on its flying avionics testbed, a modified 757, prior to the first 777 flight.

Extensive flight testing was another strategy being used to achieve "service-ready" goals. Using nine 777 aircraft, Boeing accumulated about twice as much flight test time than it normally would before delivering the first aircraft to customers (Dornheim, 1994). While Boeing has had to conduct extensive flight testing to certify performance of the 777, about 60% of the overall test time was aimed solely at meeting service-ready goals and is not required for FAA certification (Dornheim, 1994).

Placing high emphasis on life-cycle considerations early in development was another important Boeing strategy. Much of the input into design decisions affecting supportability issues came from the airlines. Most of these changes focused on improving aircraft reliability and maintainability. Specifically, lowering maintenance costs was a design goal, because maintenance labor expenses consume up to 35% of revenues at some airlines (Proctor, "Boeing," 1994b). An example of development team supportability emphasis is the Onboard Maintenance System (OMS). The OMS operates as part of the AIMS discussed earlier, and it automatically records data of interest to maintenance personnel at the aircraft's destination, thereby reducing the time to determine corrective actions. Another example is that shop maintenance personnel from four airlines evaluated proposed procedures for speed and degree of difficulty as soon as draft versions were issued. The result is that final maintenance manuals were ready for the fourth flight test aircraft instead of after initial customer deliveries, as is the norm for Boeing aircraft. Also, due to the close coordination between Boeing and the airline maintenance department, United Airlines will, for the first time, use Boeing maintenance manuals instead of redeveloping their own (Proctor, "Airlines," 1994d).

Another Boeing supportability objective was to have pilot training simulators in operation prior to delivery of the first aircraft. CAE Electronics worked closely with Boeing to develop 777 flight simulators in parallel with the aircraft, and a partial simulator was available to support training for the first flight.

As a result of the maintenance improvements, as well as the fuel efficiency advances, Boeing estimates that the 777 will cost 10% less to operate than the four-engine A340 and about 8% less than the three-engine MD-11 (Holusha, 1991).

To keep track of the many different issues, activities, participants, and costs being addressed by a large team, Boeing implemented a strong program management system; it collected the cost and technical progress data and information from the design/build groups and provided it to the managers for evaluation. The organizational structure of Boeing's concurrent engineering development approach and the communication tools available produced an environment by which the effort could be effectively tracked and managed.

DEVELOPMENT ENVIRONMENT

Boeing's concurrent engineering approach helped foster an environment conducive to appropriate and successful systems engineering practices. A prime feature was emphasis on the customer. Boeing gave actual and potential customers major voices in the development of the 777. Airlines had early and continuous involvement in the design process, and it has resulted in significant operational improvements that have increased the aircraft's appeal to them (*Aviation Week*, 1994). Through initial market surveys, Boeing learned the airlines' basic desires. Many of the airlines wanted a large airplane that used an engine design that was essentially a modified version, or derivative, of an already existing engine in use, not a totally new one. Boeing complied by giving the airlines the choice of a derivative engine from Pratt & Whitney and two new engines from General Electric and Rolls Royce.

It was through full time, on-site airline advisory teams at Boeing, though, that the initial airline customers, United Airlines, All Nippon Airways, British Airways, and Cathay Pacific, had influence over lower-level design details. Their representatives were involved in reviewing the design and developing flight and maintenance procedures. Based on airline advisory team inputs, Boeing developed a new technology cockpit derived from the advanced 747-400 cockpit instead of the 767 model. Airlines also played a pivotal role in determining the width of the fuselage. An airline representative also suggested the folding wingtips option as a solution to airport gate compatibility problems resulting from the wide wingspan. While the customers influenced some detailed design decisions, the fundamental requirements remained stable throughout development.

In addition to steadfast requirements, funding and work-force-levels followed a stable, long term plan. Boeing had totally committed itself to the four and a half year development program, and that included corporate funding to accomplish it. While Boeing was not at the mercy of its 777 customers for immediate operating funds, it did attempt to secure as many orders as possible as early as possible in hopes of recouping development costs as quickly as possible. In fact, the program was initiated with firm orders from United Airlines for 34 aircraft and options for 34 more, part of the largest single commercial order in Boeing's history (O'Lone, 1990).

While the 777 development team was large, most key designers and managers remained throughout the development. This included not only Boeing employees, but also the major subcontractors. Boeing's development approach depended partly on establishing close, long term relationships with subcontractors and suppliers so as to ensure the availability of dependable sources into production. This relationship building was also helpful in fostering cooperation among all team members. The team spirit encouraged by Boeing and the creation of multidisciplinary, multicompany teams promoted cooperation among all stakeholders.

Cooperation among all the program participants was further enhanced by the means of communication and coordination provided by Boeing. As previously discussed, CATIA gave nearly everyone in the design process instant access to the same configuration and status information. In addition, subcontractors and vendors had real-time access to select portions of the database. With all the teams and the thousands of team members using basically the same set of the latest drawings at any given time, CATIA served as a communication tool that promoted the concurrent engineering approach. While the 777 is not the first aircraft development effort adopting a "paperless" design approach, it is the first commercial aircraft program to adopt such a practice as completely as it has.

Communication was also enhanced by locating the entire Boeing 777 development team in the same general area in and around Seattle, Washington. Also residing in the Boeing program offices were full time, on-site representatives from the major subcontractors and initial airline customers.

The advanced communication environment would have had minimal impact unless the workers knew what their responsibilities were. In Boeing's design/build team structure, all workers had the means to clearly understand their responsibilities because each team had a written charter defining them. Furthermore, Boeing defined the relationships between the different levels of teams in an official document before the start of FSED. This document, a cross between a program management plan and a systems engineering management plan, had to be updated to reflect the continually changing list of design/build teams.

While Boeing is a large corporation, and the 777 development team consists of thousands of people, Boeing provided the design/build teams with the authority and autonomy to carry out their responsibilities without major interference from corporate headquarters. Furthermore, because of the speed of CATIA and its wide access, design changes were processed, evaluated, and implemented quickly; this contributed to an environment allowing a fairly high degree of design flexibility.

This level of flexibility and autonomy was also made possible by the expertise and experience of the work-force. Boeing has been designing and producing passenger jets for over 30 years, and the technical knowledge gained has been resident in the team since the 777's inception. Furthermore, Boeing employed many workers with experience gained in the 747-400 development conducted in the mid- to late-1980s. In addition, many of the key subcontractors were specialists at developing particular items, and they also had long histories of successful aerospace product lines. The 777 development team can therefore be viewed as highly capable.

Since profitability of the 777 program is dependent on the number of aircraft produced, Boeing would like to sell as many as possible. Future sales, however, are highly dependent on how well the initial aircraft performs in service. While Boeing's reputation for developing good passenger aircraft helped it gain initial customers, the company is accountable for the performance of the 777. In order to ensure that its customers are provided with the performance they ordered, Boeing warranties key performance parameters and workmanship.

SUMMARY

The 777 represents a new approach to designing and building aircraft by Boeing. It was made possible by a new development philosophy, new computer-based design and information technology, and a new cooperative attitude from the company; these were all integrated with the recognized practices and tools of aerospace design. The start of flight testing on schedule, the high degree of customer involvement throughout all phases of development, and delivery of the first production unit on time and at cost suggest a design with a significant potential for success throughout its service life. Tables 26.1 to 26.5 present our 35 figures of merit and the weight, rating, and scores we assigned for the Boeing 777.

TABLE 26-1 777 Performance Scores.

Figures of Merit	Range	Weight	Rating	Score
Technical performance—initial	0–10	1	8	8
Technical performance—mature	0–10	1	10	10
Cost performance	0–10	1	8	8
Schedule performance	0–10	1	10	10
Performance total				36

TABLE 26-2 777 Systems Engineering Fundamentals Scores.

Figures of Merit	Range	Weight	Rating	Score
Requirements development	0–10	2	10	20
Incipient system design	0–10	2	9	18
Evaluating alternative concepts	0–10	1	10	10
Make-or-buy decision	0–10	1	10	10
Validation	0–10	1	9	9
Verification and integrated testing	0–10	1	10	10
Configuration management	0–10	1	10	10
Manufacturing considerations	0–10	1	9	9
System integration and technical management	0–10	1	10	10
Life-cycle considerations	0–10	1	10	10
Program management	0–10	1	10	10
Systems engineering fundamentals total				126

TABLE 26-3 777 Development Environment Scores.

Figures of Merit	Range	Weight	Rating	Score
Emphasis on the customer	0–10	1	10	10
Stability of requirements and configuration	0–10	1	8	8
Funding and work-force-level stability	0–10	1	9	9
Strong support	0–10	1	10	10
Continuity of core development team	0–10	1	9	9
Stability of organizational structure	0–10	1	9	9
Cooperation among stakeholders	0–10	1	9	9
Effective communication	0–10	1	9	9
Flexibility and autonomy	0–10	1	7	7
Work-force qualifications	0–10	1	8	8
Accountability for system performance	0–10	1	8	8
Development environment total				96

TABLE 26-4   777 Design Difficulty Scores.

Metric	Range	Score
Design type	0–15	9
Knowledge complexity	0–10	6
Steps	0–10	9
Quality	0–10	9
Process design	0–5	4
Aggressive selling price	0–5	4
Design difficulty total	0–55	41

TABLE 26-5   777 Resources Scores.

Metric	Range	Score
Cost	0–15	12
Time	0–10	7
Infrastructure	0–10	8
Resources total	0–35	27

REFERENCES

Air & Space Magazine, p. 21, April/May, 1994.

Boeing Aircraft Company, "Boeing 777 Sets New Standards in Aircraft Design." Background information sheet. Boeing Communications Office, ca 1994.

Boeing Aircraft Company, "New Initiatives Support 777 Quality, Reliability." Background information sheet. Boeing Communications Office, March, 1994.

"CATIA Pervades 777 Program." *Aviation Week & Space Technology,* p. 40, April 11, 1994.

DORNHEIM, M.A., "777 Twinjet Will Grow to Replace 747-400." *Aviation Week & Space Technology,* pp. 43–49, June 3, 1991.

DORNHEIM, M.A., "Computerized Design System Allows Boeing to Skip Building 777 Mockup." *Aviation Week & Space Technology,* pp. 50–51, June 3, 1991.

DORNHEIM, M.A., "'Service-Ready' Goal Demands More Tests." *Aviation Week & Space Technology,* pp. 43–44, April 11, 1994.

HOLUSHA, J., "Pushing the Envelope at Boeing." *The New York Times Magazine,* pp. 5–6, November 10, 1991.

KLASS, P.J., "New Avionic Concepts Make Debut on Boeing 777." *Aviation Week & Space Technology,* pp. 60–61, June 3, 1991.

NORDWALL, B.D., "CAE About to Ship First 777 Full Flight Simulators." *Aviation Week & Space Technology,* p. 22, June 20, 1994.

NORRIS, G., "Boeing's Seventh Wonder." *IEEE Spectrum,* vol. 32, no. 10: pp. 20–23, October 1995.

O'LONE, R.G., "777 Revolutionizes Boeing Aircraft Development Process." *Aviation Week & Space Technology,* pp. 34–36, June 3, 1991.

O'LONE, R.G., "Boeing Plans 777 as First in New Transport Family." *Aviation Week & Space Technology,* pp. 18–19, October 22, 1990.

O'LONE, R.G., "Final Assembly of 777 Nears." *Aviation Week & Space Technology,* pp. 48–50, October 12, 1992.

O'LONE, R.G., and J.T. MCKENNA, "Boeing Selects Design for 777 Candidate." *Aviation Week & Space Technology,* pp. 106–107, December 18, 1989.

O'LONE, R.G., and J.T. MCKENNA, "Quality Assurance Role Was Factor in United's 777 Launch Order." *Aviation Week & Space Technology,* pp. 28–29, October 29, 1990.

PROCTOR, P., "777 Detailed Design Nearly Complete." *Aviation Week & Space Technology,* p. 35, April 19, 1993.

PROCTOR, P., "Airlines Aided Design Process." *Aviation Week & Space Technology,* p. 51, April 11, 1994.

PROCTOR, P., "Boeing Rolls Out 777 to Tentative Market." *Aviation Week & Space Technology,* pp. 36–39, April 11, 1994.

PROCTOR, P., "New Boeing Test Lab Targets Higher Reliability." *Aviation Week & Space Technology,* pp. 56–57, April 11, 1994.

PROCTOR, P., "New Twin Claims Huge Market Share." *Aviation Week & Space Technology,* pp. 48–49, April 11, 1994.

SCOTT, W.B., "777's Flight Deck Reflects Strong Operations Influence." *Aviation Week & Space Technology,* pp. 52–58, June 3, 1991.

27

LOCKHEED F-117 STEALTH FIGHTER

The F-117 Stealth Fighter is a transonic, single-pilot Air Force jet developed by Lockheed; its primary mission is penetrating enemy airspace at night undetected, destroying specifically designated high-value targets, and surviving (Miller, 1993). The design of the F-117 takes advantage of low observability technology, rendering the aircraft nearly invisible to radar systems and other detection sensors. The F-117 represents a revolution in aircraft design, and it is the first aircraft in which low observability, or stealthiness, was the main design objective (Goff, ca 1992). While the Stealth Fighter employs breakthrough technology, the development risk was minimized by the use of existing subsystems and technologies throughout the rest of the aircraft. Furthermore, it was developed in an environment conducive to generating innovative designs.

DEVELOPMENT HISTORY, DESIGN, AND PERFORMANCE

What eventually became the F-117 program began as a low-level investigation into stealth technologies, sponsored by the Defense Advanced Research Projects Agency (DARPA) in 1974. DARPA had requested that several aircraft manufacturers conduct competitive preliminary studies addressing a fighter with significantly reduced radar detectability. Technologies to counter radar detection and tracking had been investigated to a limited degree since the mid-1950s. For example, the reduction of radar cross section was a goal of the Lockheed A-12 and SR-71 development. However, it was not until the Vietnam War and the threat of radar guided surface-to-air missiles that a compelling need was recognized by military planners.

After the studies were completed, two of the contractors were invited to participate in a competitive effort to develop and test a stealth aircraft. The team from one of the contractors, Lockheed, created a revolutionary stealth design computer code and performed static low observability model demonstrations supporting the results of the code. Based on these achievements, Lockheed won the competition in April 1976 to design, develop, and test two advanced technology prototypes for flight testing in an 18 month classified advanced technology development program called Have Blue.

The program called for a variety of tests, including: radar cross-section and wind tunnel model tests of the prototype design; qualification and proof tests for various systems and subsystems; preflight testing of the assembled aircraft; and flight testing. The first flight of the unorthodox-looking Have Blue prototype was December 1, 1977, 20 months after contract award. The second prototype, which incorporated modifications over the first, was delivered seven months later; and flight testing continued until the summer of 1978.

Based on the flight tests' results, the Air Force awarded Lockheed with a fixed-price full-scale engineering development (FSED) contract and fixed-price production contract under the program name Senior Trend in November 1978 and December 1979 respectively. These contracts were for the concurrent development and production of five FSED prototypes and 15 production units based on the Have Blue prototype design. The first F-117 flight occurred on June 18, 1981, 31 months after start of FSED. It became operational in October 1983, a total of 60 months from the FSED start (see Figure 27-1). The schedule for first flight and initial operational capability by the Air Force was about a year late (about 25%), due to the crashes of two F-117s and specific development problems. The Air Force eventually bought a total of 59 F-117s, which were produced at a rate of about eight per year. The final unit was delivered in July 1990. The entire program was classified and conducted in secret until it was acknowledged to the public in November 1988.

The total cost of the Stealth Fighter development for 1978–1990 in then-year dollars was about $6.27 billion. This represents $2 billion for development and $4.27

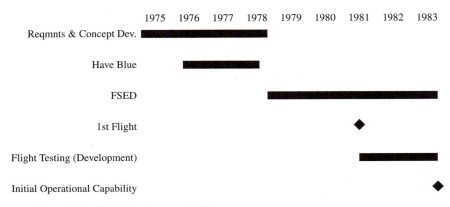

Figure 27-1 F-117 development schedule.

billion for producing 59 aircraft. Over the life of the development program, FSED costs increased by 53%, according to Air Force testimony to a U.S. senate subcommittee. A significant amount of this was due to inflation and to delays stemming from the crashes of two F-117s (Lynch, 1992).

The revolutionary nature of stealth technology requirements ensured that there would be a variety of developmental challenges. The major one was to develop a stealthy, but flyable and maneuverable, external configuration in which to integrate the aircraft subsystems. The design also had to meet minimum range and speed requirements. In all, the F-117 designers had to address seven types of observable signatures that can be used to detect an aircraft: radar, infrared, visual, contrails, engine smoke, acoustic, and electromagnetic radiation. Having to deal with all these issues significantly increased aerodynamic and subsystem integration difficulties.

Lockheed's approach to moving stealth from concept to reality was to use off-the-shelf hardware when possible, modify existing equipment where feasible, and invent new systems only when required (Miller, 1993). The objectives were to minimize system development risks and costs, enabling the design engineers to focus on reducing radar cross section without having to invent new avionics and engines (Miller, 1993). To accomplish this, subsystems and components were taken from a wide variety of aircraft existing at the time. For example, most of the cockpit avionics and the engines were derived from the McDonnell Douglas F/A-18 fighter; flight controls came from the General Dynamics F-16 fighter; the landing gear and ejection seat were from the McDonnell Douglas F-15 fighter; the inertial navigation system was adapted from the Boeing B-52 bomber; and the environmental control system components came from the Lockheed C-130 transport. Other subsystems and components were obtained from many other airplanes, going as far back as the T-33 jet trainer of the early 1950s.

While appropriate subsystems were readily available, answers to ensure stealthiness of design were not. According to Lockheed officials, one of the most difficult issues to solve involved the four small pitot tubes that extend from the aircraft nose to gather air data (Hughes, 1991). The presence of these four small tubes had a significant impact on the size of the radar signature. It took engineers three years to come up with a design solution to preserve the F-117's low observability with the pitot tubes.

Aircraft shape, though, was just one consideration of low observability. The Lockheed designers developed radar absorbent coatings for the aluminum structure and used special composite materials as weapons bay and landing gear doors, thereby reducing the aircraft's reflectivity of radar. Another challenge was to hide the hot exhaust of the engines from infrared and visual detection. This was accomplished by developing a tailpipe that would flatten and cool the exhaust, while simultaneously shrouding radar-reflecting portions of the plane. A variety of other design features were also added throughout development to enhance low observability performance.

The result of emphasizing stealthiness over aerodynamics made the F-117 unstable in flight. This dictated that the flight control system had to be a full time, computer controlled, fly-by-wire command augmentation system (Miller, 1993). The only technology with adequate technical maturity at the time was the control system used on the then-newly operational General Dynamics F-16. The only significant change required was to develop new control laws, and they were flight tested in a specially modified T-33 jet before the first F-117 flight.

Despite the use of mostly off-the-shelf avionics, integrating them was a major challenge; and it was made more difficult by the stealth requirements that mandated substantial integration of airframe avionics design. An example of an important item with integration difficulties was the Texas Instruments Infrared Acquisition and Detection System, the laser targeting subsystem for the F-117's two 2,000 pound precision guided bombs. Making the turret openings of this crucial subsystem invisible to radar was a major problem. The difficulty was finding a material for the turret coverings that would allow the laser and infrared emissions to penetrate freely while remaining invisible to enemy radar. After trying several high-priced transparent materials, the eventual solution was an innovative use of inexpensive fine wire mesh covering the opening.

As a military aircraft, the F-117, in addition to stealth design and weapons, required other special features not seen on commercial aircraft (such as an ejection seat, defensive avionics, and aerial refueling capability).

The five FSED aircraft incorporating all the design features were involved in F-117 flight testing; and they were modified throughout development to test design refinements. Flight testing was crucial to the design process, especially considering the limited simulation tools available to investigate stealth issues. The results of this flight testing contributed to design changes that would be implemented as the succeeding production aircraft was being fabricated. Some of the initial off-the-shelf subsystems used to reduce development risk were found to be inadequate in flight testing and had to be modified or replaced.

The F-117 flight test program encountered some significant problems in determining the adequacy of design solutions and the resolution of design problems. The difficulties stemmed from the fact that six different test pilots were flying three different airplanes during the initial phases of flight testing. What was adequate performance for one pilot, was in some cases inadequate for another. Furthermore, each test aircraft demonstrated its "own personality due to equipment installation tolerances"

(Lynch, 1992). Consequently, flight testing got into trouble when Lockheed tried to solve too many problems at the same time. In one case, the problem was solved by designating a single aircraft and pilot to perform the particular tests (Lynch, 1992).

Extensive ground testing of the test aircraft was performed prior to the first flight and continued throughout FSED. In addition to wind tunnel and radar cross-section testing, extensive component, subsystem, and integration testing of avionics was accomplished. Also, the essential testing to certify initial proficiency of the aircraft, somewhat equivalent to certification by the Federal Aviation Administration, was completed by the initial operational capability date of October 1983. However, flight testing continued for several years to accomplish objectives that would not fit in the Air Force's original schedule (Lynch, 1992).

The number of F-117s planned for fabrication was small, rendering the development of advanced manufacturing and assembly processes and procedures financially impractical. Consequently, much of the F-117 fabrication and assembly was done by hand. The quality appears to have been very good, with one significant exception. The first production unit crashed because the airplane's roll-rate and pitch-rate gyroscopes had been crossed when they were installed. This was an example of inadequate inspection, ground testing, and possibly deficient attention to development of manufacturing and assembly instructions. However, it does not appear to have been common throughout development.

The Air Force has been satisfied with the F-117's performance. The aircraft achieved the stealth, range, and speed requirements set at the beginning of the program. While the aircraft was developed with limited performance objectives, its design has proven to be somewhat robust. For example, in Desert Storm, the F-117 was used very successfully in a manner significantly different from its original purpose. In the Middle East, the F-117s were flying one or two operational missions per night during much of the air campaign (Kandebo, 1992). Such prolonged operations resulted in increased maintenance costs, but they were successful.

The Air Force and Lockheed continued to modify and upgrade the F-117 throughout its production and operational deployment to enhance the F-117's capability and enable the aircraft to take on new roles. The original flight computer, for example, was replaced in 1984 with a repackaged version of the space shuttle computer in order to upgrade marginal capability. Later, new avionics were installed, and the engine exhaust system was modified. New communications equipment gave the F-117 all-weather mission capabilities. The changes have been made to enhance the F-117 operability and maintainability, as well as to minimize support costs; not to correct shortcomings to initial requirements (Hughes, 1991).

SYSTEMS ENGINEERING FUNDAMENTALS

The F-117 development is characterized by the successful accomplishment of many of the fundamental systems engineering practices. Requirements definition was one of them. The written requirements placed on contract at the beginning of FSED were the result of a series of requirements and technology studies and the advanced Have Blue prototype development. Throughout this period, the Air Force refined its operational requirements based on enemy capabilities. Furthermore, the program was technology driven, and most critical performance and safety parameters were specified as requirements.

The Lockheed development team defined system and subsystem models and allocated requirements. Functional requirements were defined and work was assigned according to a detailed work breakdown structure. The team also made use of a variety of design and analysis models and simulations of somewhat limited capabilities, in order to evaluate and decide among alternative concepts and subsystem designs. The F-117 was developed with the design tools available to the aeronautics community in the mid- to late-1970s: high and low speed wind tunnels, low performance computers for running simple simulations and analysis programs, and calculators. The design team had no supercomputers, and much of the initial design calculations were done by hand.

Despite their limitations, a variety of computer simulations and physical models were essential to development. One computer program in particular, ECHO 1, guided the stealth shape design during Have Blue and the FSED program. ECHO 1 allowed aircraft designers to predict a radar return. This early computer modeling tool, however, was limited to calculations in only two dimensions. This meant that the resulting aircraft would have a faceted design, rather than a smooth, seamless one (Kandebo, 1992). Lockheed tested their calculations with a one-third scale model for radar cross-section studies, giving credence to computer simulation outputs.

As discussed previously, prototyping played a major role in F-117 development. The two advanced technology prototypes produced during the Have Blue program were 40% smaller than the eventual production aircraft; they were also simpler. However, they were successful in their role of testing certain performance projections that had been based on unvalidated models.

Physical modeling also played a role in production. Lockheed constructed a full-scale wooden mockup in 1979 before assembly line activities commenced. This was done so the exact shape and fit of each critical facet panel and component could be defined.

Another indicator of successful systems engineering practices was the definition of the integrated testing approach early in the development process. The series of integrated avionics and stealth tests on the ground, flight control testing on other aircraft, and flight testing requirements were well documented prior to the start of FSED.

The Lockheed team kept tight control over the F-117 drawings and specifications defining the configuration, including the internal and external interfaces. A simple yet flexible drawing and configuration change system was in place; it allowed fast turnaround of changes resulting from testing and other verification activities.

Lockheed needed to integrate the widely varied and interdependent work that was carried on by relatively small groups of Lockheed employees, and about 500 subcontractors and suppliers. Thus, a strong systems integration and technical management presence was provided by the Lockheed program manager and his deputies.

They kept the focus on the requirements and succeeded in integrating the subsystems into the stealth shell.

While the F-117 was a complex system to design and fabricate, its development focus was somewhat narrow and was carried out at the expense of other considerations. With this in mind, supportability, discussed here primarily in terms of maintainability, was considered in the design process of the F-117 but was not a driving requirement. Like other performance considerations, it took a back seat to stealth. Critics contend the F-117 is a prime example of what happens when support issues receive low priority (*Aviation Week*, 1990). Case in point: The F-117 presents a problem for technicians because the designers had to minimize the number of access panels and openings in the skin in order to obtain the smallest radar cross section possible. The restricted access makes the aircraft more difficult, time-consuming, and expensive to repair. Maintainability considerations, however, did have an impact on this matter. When Air Force maintenance specialists evaluated the first F-117, their feedback resulted in more panels and doors being added on subsequent units to lessen the accessibility problems (Henderson, 1991). In another recognition of supportability considerations, Lockheed simplified maintenance and reduced the frequency with which radar absorbent material coatings needed to be removed.

Except for coating maintenance, the F-117 maintenance practices are similar to those used for F-15s and F-16s. This is due largely to the fact that most of the subsystems came from existing operational aircraft. As a consequence, more than 95% of the equipment used to support the F-117 is common to that of other Air Force aircraft (*Aviation Week*, 1990). Furthermore, despite the unique requirement of coating maintenance and minimal access panels, the Air Force claims the F-117 maintenance costs during normal operations are comparable to those of other tactical aircraft (*Aviation Week*, 1990).

While the emphasis on supportability was limited, the Air Force included only limited supportability requirements. Had the Air Force levied strict requirements, the F-117 may not have looked the same or have been successfully developed at all. This was a major trade-off the Air Force was willing to make to achieve a revolutionary breakthrough in performance.

Concerning program management, Lockheed managers utilized sufficient scheduling, work, and cost tracking techniques throughout development to assess technical progress and maintain control.

DEVELOPMENT ENVIRONMENT

The F-117 was developed in an environment that emphasized the Air Force customer. The F-117 contractor team followed the golden rule: "He who has the gold, rules." Therefore, Lockheed was responsive to the Air Force, and kept its representatives informed of all technical developments. Furthermore, the F-117 contractor team reviewed the design progress with the Air Force customer at a series of major requirements and design reviews, and Air Force pilots, weapons, and maintenance crews were heavily involved during FSED.

The F-117 was also developed in a stable, protected environment that supported innovative solutions. Due to its revolutionary military nature, the effort had strong government support at the highest levels and was carried out in complete secrecy without micromanagement from Congress or the Air Force. Additionally, funding from the Air Force was stable. Furthermore, working relationships between the Air Force customer and the contractor development personnel were nonadversarial, and they operated together in a problem-solving atmosphere (Miller, 1993). These various factors were essential in enabling the program to follow very tight schedules. The classification of the program, however, did cause problems in hiring people, since extensive and lengthy security clearance checks had to be done on anyone coming into the program.

The Air Force allowed the F-117 design team to carry out much of the design process as it saw appropriate. In addition to being free from many bureaucratic considerations, the aircraft was not overly specified, enabling the development team considerable flexibility in achieving the stealth performance. In case performance had not been met, Lockheed's contract with the Air Force included warranties covering the aircraft's required range, weapon delivery accuracy, radar cross section, and workmanship defects.

In addition to the items discussed above, stability of customer requirements, continuity of core team membership, ease of team communication and coordination, and a high level of work force expertise and experience were all hallmarks of the F-117 development environment at Lockheed.

The F-117 was developed in Lockheed's Advanced Development Projects group called the "Skunk Works." The Skunk Works, which years earlier had developed the U-2, F-104, and the SR-71, was organized for the F-117 development; it was a tightly-knit team of highly talented, innovative, and motivated engineers and technicians. They included technically competent managers who were able to communicate effectively with the team and coordinate activities, enabling them to resolve design conflicts in a timely manner. This environment was conducive to generating technological breakthrough designs and then carrying those designs through small-scale production. It is nearly a paragon environment for fast prototyping of advanced aircraft designs. Most of the development environment characteristics that support effective systems engineering practices are part of the Skunk Works mode of operation.

The Skunk Works approach is encapsulated in 14 points or "rules" developed by its founder, Clarence "Kelly" Johnson. These principles can be viewed as addressing the systems engineering philosophy and practices of the F-117 development. Some of the key aspects of this streamlined approach are as follows (Miller, 1993):

1. The program manager must have complete control of the program in all aspects. It is essential that the program manager have authority to make decisions quickly regarding technical, financial, schedule, or operational matters.

2. Strong but small project offices must be provided both by the customer and the contractor. The customer program manager must have similar authority to that of the contractor.

3. The number of people having any connection with the project must be severely restricted, because more people add bureaucracy, and bureaucracy makes unnecessary work.

4. A simple drawing and drawing release system with great flexibility for making changes must be provided. This permits early work by manufacturing organizations, and schedule recovery if technical risks involve failures.

5. The number of required reports should be minimized, but important work must be recorded thoroughly. Responsible management does not require massive technical and information systems.

6. There must be a monthly cost review covering not only what has been spent and committed, but also projected costs to the conclusion of the program. Responsible management operates within the resources available.

7. The contractor must be delegated and must assume more than normal responsibility for obtaining good vendor bids for the subcontracts on the project. Commercial bid procedures are often better than military ones. The contractor must have the essential freedom to use the best talent available, but also operate within the resources provided.

8. Responsibility for basic inspection should be given to subcontractors and vendors. The contractor should not be duplicating inspection.

9. The contractor must be assigned the authority to test the final product in flight, especially in the initial stages of development. This is critical if new technology and the attendant risks are to be rationally managed.

10. The specification applying to the hardware must be defined and finalized in advance of contracting. Furthermore, the Skunk Works' practice of having a specification section clearly stating which military specification items will not be followed and the reasons for not doing so is highly recommended. Standard specifications inhibit new technology and innovation and are frequently obsolete.

11. Funding must be timely.

12. Mutual trust must exist between the customer project organization and the contractor, and there should be close cooperation and day-to-day communication. This brings misunderstanding and correspondence to a minimum. The goals of the customer and producer should be the same—get the job done well.

13. Access by outsiders to the project and its personnel must be strictly controlled by appropriate security measures.

14. Due to the small size of Skunk Works development teams, management must provide ways to financially reward people based on good performance and not on the number of people supervised. Responsible management must be rewarded, and responsible management does not permit the growth of bureaucracies.

The Lockheed team followed these tenets during development. Furthermore, the fact that the F-117 was a classified program facilitated the implementation of this systems engineering management approach.

SUMMARY

The F-117 can be considered a successful design, and its development can be viewed as somewhat successful overall. Although the program experienced cost growth and schedule delays, the stealth fighter met the primary performance requirements demanded by the customer in the contract. The F-117 design was maximized for low observability while still meeting minimum range and speed requirements. The revolutionary design was also robust enough to enable its use at Desert Storm in a manner and at a frequency not originally anticipated. The conduct of this program in a stable, streamlined environment while strongly implementing the fundamentals of systems engineering was key to its technical performance success. Tables 27-1 to 27-5 present our 35 figures of merit and the scores we assigned for the F-117.

TABLE 27-1   F-117 Performance Scores.

Figures of Merit	Range	Weight	Rating	Score
Technical performance—initial	0–10	1	8	8
Technical performance—mature	0–10	1	10	10
Cost performance	0–10	1	4	4
Schedule performance	0–10	1	4	4
Performance total				26

TABLE 27-2   F-117 Systems Engineering Fundamentals Scores.

Figures of Merit	Range	Weight	Rating	Score
Requirements development	0–10	2	9	18
Incipient system design	0–10	2	9	18
Evaluating alternative concepts	0–10	1	10	10
Make-or-buy decision	0–10	1	10	10
Validation	0–10	1	9	9
Verification and integrated testing	0–10	1	8	8
Configuration management	0–10	1	9	9
Manufacturing considerations	0–10	1	6	6
System integration and technical management	0–10	1	10	10
Life-cycle considerations	0–10	1	6	6
Program management	0–10	1	9	9
Systems engineering fundamentals total				113

TABLE 27-3   F-117 Development Environment Scores.

Figures of Merit	Range	Weight	Rating	Score
Emphasis on the customer	0–10	1	9	9
Stability of requirements and configuration	0–10	1	7	7
Funding and work-force-level stability	0–10	1	10	10
Strong support	0–10	1	10	10
Continuity of core development team	0–10	1	10	10
Stability of organizational structure	0–10	1	9	9
Cooperation among stakeholders	0–10	1	9	9
Effective communication	0–10	1	8	8
Flexibility and autonomy	0–10	1	8	8
Work force qualifications	0–10	1	9	9
Accountability for system performance	0–10	1	8	8
Development environment total				97

TABLE 27-4   F-117 Design Difficulty Scores.

Metric	Range	Score
Design type	0–15	13
Knowledge complexity	0–10	8
Steps	0–10	8
Quality	0–10	7
Process design	0–5	4
Aggressive selling Price	0–5	1
Design difficulty total	0–55	41

TABLE 27-5   F-117 Resources Scores.

Metric	Range	Score
Cost	0–15	9
Time	0–10	7
Infrastructure	0–10	8
Resources total	0–35	24

REFERENCES

"Declassified Photos Show 'Have Blue' F-117A Predecessor." *Aviation Week & Space Technology*, p. 30, April 22, 1991.

GOFF, T.J., ed., *We Own the Night*. Lockheed brochure on the history of the F-117A. Creative Publications, ca 1992.

HENDERSON, B.W., "Design and Planning Make High-Tech F-22 Easy to Maintain and Support." *Aviation Week & Space Technology*, p. 50, July 15, 1991.

HUGHES, D., and J.M. LENOROVITZ, "F-117A's Performance Boosts Wide Range of Improvements." *Aviation Week & Space Technology*, pp. 20–23, June 24, 1991.

KANDEBO, S.W., "Air Force Details Costs, Schedules for Upgrading F-117 Aircraft Systems." *Aviation Week & Space Technology*, p. 58, July 6, 1992.

LYNCH, D.J., "How the Skunk Works Fielded Stealth." *Air Force Magazine,* pp. 22–28, November, 1992.

MILLER, J., *Lockheed's Skunk Works: The First Fifty Years, The Official History.* Arlington, Texas: Aerofax, Inc., 1993.

"Pentagon Reveals F-117A Costs, Photos; Upgrades Are Under Way at Palmdale." *Aviation Week & Space Technology*, pp. 19–20, April 9, 1990.

28

NORTHROP B-2
STEALTH BOMBER

The Northrop B-2 is the United States Air Force's newest intercontinental strategic bomber. This highly complex aircraft uses revolutionary stealth technologies; it was designed to penetrate the air defenses of the former Soviet Union and survive in order to deliver nuclear weapons. With the end of the Cold War, the B-2 is expected to be capable of attacking heavily defended targets with precision guided conventional weapons in addition to its primary nuclear mission. The challenging and costly integration of this wing-shaped aircraft was made possible not only by breakthroughs in stealth technology, but also by new advanced manufacturing processes, a powerful computer tool for assisting in the design of large hardware systems, and the disciplined application of systems engineering principles.

DEVELOPMENT HISTORY, DESIGN, AND PERFORMANCE

From 1978 to 1980, the Air Force conducted concept development of what was initially called the Advanced Technology Bomber (ATB), the same time the F-117 Stealth Fighter was undergoing full-scale engineering development (FSED). In 1981, two contractors, Northrop and Lockheed, competed in a source selection to develop the ATB. While Lockheed's proposal included a detailed point design that was almost at preliminary design review stage, Northrop's design was much more conceptual and flexible with much less detail (Edward, personal communication). According to a government engineer involved in the source selection, the decision was close. However, at the conclusion of the competition in November 1981, the Air Force selected Northrop, one of the largest military aircraft companies in the United States, to further develop the design and take it into FSED.

Despite the radical new design and manufacturing techniques employed in the aircraft, the Air Force and Northrop followed the high risk concept (overlapping prototype and production) in an attempt to compress the time from development to initial operation. However, before fully embarking on FSED, the Air Force had Northrop go through a pre-FSED risk reduction phase to address critical technology and producibility issues (Edward, personal communication). This phase ended in May 1984 with the presentation of the preliminary design review.

Although the B-2 program started out on a very tight schedule, it was relaxed somewhat after the B-1 bomber program was reinstated in 1982. With a revised schedule, the first flight of the planned flight test program was scheduled for 1987. However, it did not occur until July 1989, about five years after the FSED start. The first production aircraft was delivered to the Air Force for operational deployment in December 1993, nearly two years late (see Figure 28-1). This represents an FSED schedule slip of about 25%. The delay was caused primarily by a major redesign in

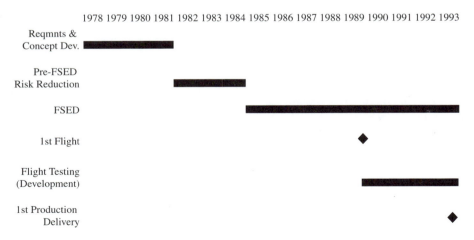

Figure 28-1   B-2 development schedule.

1984 and difficulties associated with developing numerous new design and production technologies (Dornheim, 1988).

The government had paid $17.5 billion in base-year 1981 dollars ($24.7 billion in then-year dollars) for pre-FSED and FSED activities and the fabrication of six airplanes, five of which would be delivered for operational use after completion of operational flight testing. Another $11.8 billion in base-year 1981 dollars ($19.2 billion in then-year dollars) was being spent for 15 more, with the last one delivered in 1997 (CPR, 1993). In addition to Air Force funding, Northrop made close to $2 billion in capital investment. The cost on the cost-plus development contract has about doubled over the original estimate (Gala, personal communication). However, much of the cost growth was due to economic factors related to the extension of the program and was not due solely to unanticipated problems and changes (CPR, 1993).

When the B-2 FSED contract was awarded to Northrop, the Air Force was planning to purchase a total of 132 development and production units. As a result, Northrop and its major subcontractors and suppliers structured their facilities, tooling, and personnel planning to support a large, long term capital intensive program (Scott, November 11, 1991). In 1990, however, the Department of Defense reduced the planned production quantity to 75, based on the receding threat from the Soviet Union and the aircraft's high cost. Then in 1993, with mounting criticism of the program's costs, Congress capped B-2 production at 20 (see Table 28-1). However, based on only 20 B-2s, the unit cost, which included development expenditures, was projected to be over $1 billion per aircraft in base-year 1981 dollars. However, had the original 132 production quantity remained, the unit cost was expected to be about $330 million in base-year 1981 dollars ($525 million in then-year dollars). In 1994, the last unit entered production, and the contractors started closing down parts of the production line. Despite its production cap, Congress voted funds for government fiscal year 1995 to keep the B-2 production line viable for another year while it decided whether or not to purchase more.

The high cost of the B-2, made significantly higher by government imposed quantity reductions and schedule stretches, is due to its revolutionary design. The bomber is essentially a flying wing fabricated out of advanced composites and materials to render its cross section nearly invisible to radar. The design is also meant to reduce infrared, electromagnetic, and acoustic detection. The only aircraft with a similar aerodynamic shape was the Northrop YB-49 test aircraft from the late 1940s. The B-2 represents the fourth generation of stealth technology, drawing upon the advances in low observability design, materials, and coatings attained on the SR-71, the Advanced Cruise Missile, and the F-117A Stealth Fighter programs (Scott, 1990). Like these earlier programs, the B-2's early development occurred in complete secrecy.

TABLE 28-1   B-2 Production Quantity Changes.

Year	1981	1990	1993
Planned production quantity	132	75	20

   The primary design challenge for the B-2 program was to attain the desired degree of stealthiness with aerodynamics that would allow needed range, speed, and payload to be realized. To help achieve the radar cross-section requirements, 900 new materials and processes were developed (Scott, 1990). Included were the processes to make the composite wings, the largest single piece composite structures ever built. Furthermore, the B-2's shape was generated with the help of a three-dimensional stealth analysis code run on powerful computers. The resulting aerodynamic design was unique and untried, but 24,000 hours of wind tunnel testing and years of simulator tests before the first flight confirmed the aircraft would be stable (Scott, May 8, 1989).

   The other key challenge was systems integration. The B-2 was intended to be flown and all its numerous, complex elements operated by a crew of two pilots; this required a high degree of integration and interaction among all onboard subsystems. Within the B-2's airframe is packed a wide array of subsystems, including both off-the-shelf and new technology items. In addition to four General Electric engines and avionics from a variety of companies, the B-2 has: a quadruple redundant electronic flight control system, a weapons delivery system, an electronic warfare system, an aerial refueling capability, and ejection seats for the crew. The B-2 also incorporates an advanced radar that is a significant technological step in developing active sensors that are compatible with low observable aircraft (Scott, March 11, 1991). Provisions were made in the B-2 for a third crew member in case avionics automation did not provide enough workload relief for the two person crew.

   The B-2 development team encountered a range of difficulties. For one, there were a variety of problems in developing a large number of new materials and processes. Also, the crew ejection seat development and integration were a significant problem, and it helped delay the initial flight test. Weight increased higher than planned, and it impacted the projected payload versus range performance. Delays in fabricating the first aircraft were caused by problems such as wiring bundles either not being installed or being installed incorrectly. Some of these errors were not discovered until complete electrical checkouts were ready to begin (*Aviation Week*, 1988).

   Some other troubles were stress discontinuities in the cockpit windscreen and cracking of composite wing leading edge sections. The most publicized event, however, occurred during flight testing in 1991; the B-2 failed to meet the radar signature requirement for a few particular cross sections at a narrow frequency band. The B-2 has hundreds of cross sections of interest that are subjected to thousands of test measurements covering the full, wide spectrum of radar frequency. In the domain where the performance deficiency occurred, the B-2 is already substantially better than the F-117 (Rice, 1991). The Air Force considered the failure minor and not impacting operational effectiveness (Morrocco, 1994). Furthermore, in order to avoid any major design changes that could have been implemented to possibly correct the problem, the Air Force relaxed the requirement.

   A major design change did, however, take place earlier in the program. The initial B-2 design proposed by Northrop was intended for high-altitude operations only. However, the Air Force had concerns about future vulnerability as threats and missions changed, and it therefore added a low-altitude mission capability require-ment after source selection. This made the B-2 an all-altitude aircraft and gave it more future operational flexibility for nuclear or conventional weapons missions. The redesign resulted in a greater fatigue life, more aerodynamic efficiency, and lower weight (Dornheim, 1988).

The prospect of flying at low altitudes also increased concerns about bird strikes, resulting in changes in wing leading edge shape and materials. In addition, the engine installation was altered to protect against bird ingestion. While these changes improved the flexibility of the B-2, the redesign in the middle of develop-ment was a major contributor to the two year slip in program schedule, costing about $1 billion (Dornheim, 1988).

Many of the B-2 program's early resources were devoted to developing manu-facturing technologies needed to build a bomber with the tight tolerances necessary for a large stealth aircraft. This necessitated implementing a sophisticated three-dimensional computer aided design and manufacturing (CAD/CAM) program, as well as new tool designs and manufacturing capabilities (Scott, 1990).

This new CAD/CAM system was the prime element of Northrop's advanced development approach. It enabled the aircraft to be defined almost entirely on com-puter, nearly eliminating paper drawings. This system was also part of a streamlined design-to-production tooling process that was supposed to improve the parts fit of the first units. As a consequence, no full-size mockups or advanced technology pro-totypes were built, since the database served as the master model. The B-2 was the first program to implement a computer-based development system to such a large ex-tent. However, its introduction and development were difficult, as evidenced by the discovery of errors.

As a result of the problems in the CAD/CAM system, there were significantly more ill-fitting skin panels during assembly of the first B-2 than expected. Subse-quent aircraft, though, had better fitting parts as the design and manufacturing data-base was refined and updated (Scott, June 5, 1989).

In addition to design and manufacturing process advances, Northrop also changed how the production workers operated by introducing the Integrated Man-agement Planning and Control for Assembly system in 1991. It was designed to vir-tually eliminate paper on the manufacturing floor. Computer terminals at each aircraft work center provided current and accurate diagrams and instructions for all tasks (Scott, November 4, 1991).

After the drastic reductions in production quantities, some manufacturing and cost-efficiency improvements supporting large scale production were not imple-mented; this was because the low production rates of about 1.5 B-2s per year, down from the projected four aircraft per month, did not justify the cost. Therefore, the production B-2s, like the FSED aircraft, are essentially "handmade" (Gala, personal communication).

The B-2 airframe has a service life requirement of 10,000 flying hours, which represent about 20 years in typical service. However, if the 40 year old B-52 is any guide, the B-2 will probably be utilized as long or longer. The Air Force recognized this and had the aircraft designed to survive twice the service life. Furthermore, to demonstrate durability performance, a B-2 airframe was subjected to the equivalent of 40 years of normal flying, bending, twisting, vibrating, and flexing. Only minor modifications to the design were required as a result of this successful series of tests (Scott, November 4, 1992).

Despite the high cost, the Air Force operational user, the Air Combat Command, is quite satisfied with the B-2. The B-2 has a range of about 6,600 nautical miles unrefueled and over 10,000 nautical miles with one in-flight refueling, enabling it to reach nearly any place on the earth. The aircraft meets the original mission requirements, even though a few of the specification requirements on contract did not (Gala, personal communcation).

SYSTEMS ENGINEERING FUNDAMENTALS

A high degree of planning went into developing the B-2. The foundation of this planning was a strong set of requirements at the beginning of the program. As the customer, the Air Force was responsible for defining what the B-2 was supposed to be able to do. The top level requirements were developed in response to the Air Force Mission Needs Statement, a document that indicates an actual or projected operational deficiency. This was the basis of the System Operational Requirements Document (SORD). Using this document and the input from the user at the time, the Strategic Air Command, the Air Force developing organization defined a set of performance requirements in a draft system specification that was given to the two competing contractors. This system specification focused on performance and stayed away from functional requirements, giving the contractors greater flexibility in defining a design solution. The B-2 program was one of the first large Air Force programs driven primarily by performance requirement specifications (Edwards, personal communication). A consequence of this was a smaller number of engineering change proposals during development than normal.

To help develop detailed requirements, Northrop and the Air Force used a variety of modeling and simulation programs covering threat assessments, performance objectives, and affordability (Modeling and Simulation Users Survey, 1994). The detailed requirements were documented, but this was done mostly by Northrop, not the government.

Since Northrop did not have many details of the F-117 to use as a guide, the company used the results of the threat simulations and drew upon its prior work in the area of low observability, primarily its three-dimensional radar cross-section code, to form its top-level design concept. The concept was put into a work breakdown structure, as is normally required at the beginning of an Air Force systems development effort. This decomposition approach, which addressed both functional and product issues, helped guide the definition of interfaces and the allocation of requirements for the incipient system design. Northrop provided its initial version of this decomposition as part of its proposal to the government, and it updated it as necessary throughout development. Furthermore, the company established reliability requirement allocations early in the program (Edward, 1995). These allocations were essential in helping identify candidate alternatives.

As part of source selection, the Air Force evaluated and chose between two design concepts. Even before then, however, Northrop had gone through a process of evaluating alternatives itself. Using computer models, Northrop assessed a variety of design approaches by running a series of iterations and by evaluating the performance and cost trade-offs. The refined concept is what was proposed to the Air Force. In addition, alternative subsystem design approaches and parameters were evaluated using computer simulations and analyses throughout the B-2 development.

Along with performing design trade-offs, Northrop also had to decide where the parts or software items would be produced. Since Northrop was primarily an experienced aircraft integrator, it did not possess all the design and manufacturing capabilities necessary to perform the effort by itself. For example, it was not in the business of developing and building engines. Therefore, it was predisposed to purchase many items outside of the company and its Boeing and LTV partners. Furthermore, as a classified program, there were limitations as to where components and subsystems could be obtained. While the B-2 make-or-buy decision process was constrained, it was carried out as required by the government, which resulted in a large number of subcontractors and suppliers.

When it came to validating B-2 requirements, both the Air Force and Northrop had major roles. The Air Force followed its formal procedure for validating requirements, as discussed previously. Northrop's validation activities to determine if a real-world solution existed centered on a variety of threat and low observable simulations that were continually refined throughout development. An aircraft with the survivability characteristics of the B-2 had never been built before. The F-117, a good guidepost, was much smaller and it had less low observable performance than that sought for the B-2. Whether or not the B-2 design could be made to perform at a level completely satisfactory to the customer was an issue, which mandated the evolutionary requirements definition and evaluation throughout both the requirements development and concept development phases.

To ensure the B-2 design conformed to performance requirements, Northrop's team and the Air Force conducted a large amount of testing. As part of Northrop's verification strategy, the company developed sophisticated laboratories to perform component and subsystem testing early in the development process. Nearly a million hours of test time accumulated through environmental stress screening, ground avionics testing, and flights of a C-135 avionics testbed. Extensive wind tunnel, avionics, flight controls, computer systems, qualification, and acceptance testing greatly reduced the number of program unknowns, despite the extensive use of new materials, technologies, and manufacturing processes (Scott, 1990). The final result of these efforts was early elimination of many reliability problems that normally arise during flight testing and initial operational service (Scott, October 12, 1992).

The B-2's extensive four year development flight test program involved six air-craft, five of which were planned for eventual delivery as operational units. These B-2s were instrumented for testing during manufacturing and assembly. Focus of the testing ranged from envelope expansion to avionics, comparable to a commercial aircraft flight test program. However, the program also included military specific tests involving defensive avionics, advanced radar, electromagnetic compatibility, and low observables. About one-fourth of flight testing was devoted to low observables performance verification.

From the beginning, Northrop also planned a very extensive ground durability and structural test series of the B-2 airframe that was conducted parallel to flight testing. Two complete B-2 airframes without engines and electronics systems were built for the sole purpose of conducting these tests. The durability test unit demonstrated two full service lifetimes of vibration and flexing with no major structural damage, and the static test unit demonstrated structural integrity at 150% of design limits (Scott, December 14/21, 1992).

With the great complexity of the B-2, keeping track of and controlling the interfaces and design configuration was of critical importance. Since the B-2 design was in a three-dimensional digital database, both engineering and manufacturing worked with the same drawing database. Furthermore, Northrop had formal procedures for controlling changes. As a result, Northrop performed effective configuration status accounting and control. Interface control, however, was somewhat more difficult. The digital database did not have the ability to automatically identify interference between components. However, it did serve as a forcing function to help highlight the need for interface control and served as the basis for those activities (Edwards, 1995).

As discussed previously, the early involvement by manufacturing personnel in the B-2 was critical, since a large number of the advanced features of the design were process dependent. For many of these items, practical manufacturing methods did not exist at the beginning of the program. Methods were developed and were used to produce the development hardware. Later in development and production, some of the methods and processes in the program were refined to reduce cost. In fact, the Air Force funded manufacturing improvements to decrease machining time for some parts and produce others in less expensive materials (Scott, March 11, 1991).

In addition to focusing on manufacturing process development early in the effort, there was the critical need to manage the complex integration of the subsystems and components into the airframe. This was done through a methodical approach with sufficient up-front planning. Before performing detailed integration, Northrop first had to complete the Air Force's mandated pre-FSED risk reduction to address 10 critical issues. They included low observables performance, the fabrication and use of large composite sections, and engine inlet compatibility. None of the items were show-stoppers, and all were addressed to the Air Force's satisfaction (Edward, 1995).

FSED was then allowed to proceed, and systems integration activities were conducted primarily by Northrop with its subcontractor team members. Northrop's personnel were organized along strict functional lines, but they worked together to address interdisciplinary issues in a loose structure centered on zones of the aircraft. This zone management worked during development and mainly involved engineering and supportability personnel, but not nontechnical workers. The zone leader was essentially the crew boss and helped coordinate the activities of the group. This interaction mechanism was significantly enhanced by the existence of the three-dimensional CAD/CAM database. The digital database served as the master model and forced good coordination between the members working in a zone. Despite the use of this informal structure that evolved during the early period of the program, B-2 development was still driven functionally. Furthermore, the people formally empowered to carry out development and integration activities were program and functional engineering managers, not the zone managers (Edwards, 1995).

Northrop's development approach included a series of design reviews, as required by the Air Force. The contractor generated a program management plan, but it was the Air Force that produced the initial systems engineering management plan. Also, the company did not have a separate systems engineering organization. The Air Force B-2 System Program Office (SPO) had one, and it included a team performing independent performance analyses. The SPO encouraged Northrop to create its own systems engineering office, but it did not, choosing to keep the activities distributed in the functional organizations (Edward, 1995).

Life-cycle considerations were taken very seriously during B-2 development. In fact, there was heavy supportability emphasis during requirements definition, and representatives from the Air Force's organization that were responsible for maintaining aircraft, Air Force Logistics Command, were deeply involved from the very beginning. The Air Force imposed strict reliability and maintainability requirements on the contract, and Northrop was required to present its plan for dealing with the issues in the Reliability Program Plan and the Integrated Logistics Support Plan. Also, the Air Force placed a high level of emphasis on supportability testing, which primarily involved ensuring that the maintenance manuals agreed with the aircraft configuration and actual procedures (Scott, Novermber 18, 1991). This approach gave logistics testing and flight testing near-equal priorities (*Aviation Week*, 1991).

Some outcomes of this focus on supportability were that:

1. a flight simulator was ready to use before the first flight,
2. the B-2 was the first new Air Force aircraft to enter service with maintenance manuals available upon delivery of the first unit, and
3. the projected maintenance man-hours per flight hour was expected to be considerably less than the requirement (Scott, October 12, 1992).

Keeping proper emphasis on life-cycle issues was one job of Northrop's program managers. To do this, the company appears to have maintained a reasonably strong program management function in a classified environment to keep track of progress on the tremendously complex aircraft. Computer-based schedules were used, and an effective cost reporting system was in place.

Program management also held a series of regular program reviews. Early in the program, they were quarterly and located at the different contractor locations. Later, they became less frequent and more issue-related as the detailed design took shape. The program managers did not, however, use these meetings to usurp the responsibility of the design managers to maintain oversight over the details of their technical areas (Edward, 1995). This reflects the cooperative environment inside the secret development world of the B-2.

DEVELOPMENT ENVIRONMENT

As a large military program, the B-2 was developed with the close involvement of government representatives. These Air Force military service and civil personnel from the B-2 SPO and the Air Force Plant Representative Offices oversaw all aspects of development; and the Air Force's user and maintainer organizations interacted heavily with the contractor team from the beginning. Also, the B-2 program represented a large piece of Northrop income, and the cost-plus development contract included an award fee that gave the contractor incentive to be responsive to the Air Force. Therefore, Northrop and its subcontractors could not help emphasizing the Air Force customer.

The contractors looked to the Air Force primarily for performance requirements that would not change. Early in the B-2 program, however, there was a major change with significant consequences. As previously mentioned, soon after source selection, the Air Force added the requirement that the B-2 must have all-altitude capability to ensure future flexibility, instead of having only high-altitude capability as Northrop proposed. Then in 1983 during pre-FSED, extensive structural analysis by contractor and Air Force engineers indicated loads were significantly higher than originally believed. This initiated a redesign to the trailing edge. Early in 1984, fatigue and structural problems associated with the low-altitude mission profiles were discovered as the result of analysis. This resulted in moving the cockpit 30 inches. These design changes were made before FSED and hardware fabrication, but they did have significant cost and schedule impacts.

As in other large, complex aircraft programs, B-2 changes were introduced on the production line, thereby creating different production configurations. The B-2s were separated into three blocks representing configuration sets. Block 10 and Block 20 had a total of 18 B-2s, and Block 30 had two. The Block 30 configuration reflected features and performance the program originally sought, and the 18 other aircraft would be retrofit with the capability at the completion of unit 20.

The majority of B-2 development occurred while the program's existence was classified. This situation shielded the effort from congressional and public scrutiny and contributed to an environment of funding and political stability, as well as work-force-level stability. This enabled the developers to concentrate on designing the aircraft instead of constantly justifying the program. The Air Force did not have problems obtaining funding for the B-2 until late in development, after the program was publicly acknowledged in 1988. While Congress was very supportive when the

B-2 was a classified program, political pressures had changed some lawmakers' positions. As the Cold War ended, pressures to reduce military expenditures prompted major quantity reductions of the B-2. Furthermore, the rising unit cost of a shrinking B-2 production program had been widely reported and criticized in the media. In the early 1990s, the impact of this reduced political support was stretched-out production and the gradual reduction of the work-force-level. Although production funding had been severely restricted, development funding was never significantly impacted.

A factor that may have played into Congress's reluctance to cancel the program was the large amount of production tooling that was implemented up front to produce the FSED and production aircraft. Instead of completely hand fabricating the initial units, production tooling was developed, fabricated, and implemented in accordance with the concurrent engineering approach. This made for high manufacturing infrastructure costs early on. However, it also may have convinced some in Congress that the large sunk cost investment in the standing manufacturing capability was too great to scrap the production line without gaining any aircraft from them.

Along with stable FSED funding, the B-2 also possessed a high degree of continuity among key managers and engineers from early development to production. Contributing to this stable environment, the Air Force B-2 SPO maintained unusual continuity in its leadership, keeping the same military program director in place from 1983 to 1991.

The constancy of the core development team mirrored a stable contractor organizational structure throughout development. As mentioned previously, Northrop's leadership of the B-2 contractor team had a strong functional orientation that was reflective of the way the company has been traditionally organized. While the structure appeared to work reasonably well, the Air Force program directors were looking to change to an integrated product development (IPD) approach; this would formally establish interdisciplinary integrated product teams and force business and technical issues to be worked together. IPD was implemented in 1991, when the majority of development was complete. Northrop, however, had resisted fully adopting IPD. With the program starting to close down, the Air Force decided not to enforce full compliance (Edward, 1995).

While one aim of IPD was to improve the level of interaction and cooperation across functions and organizations, a spirit of cooperation was already evident within the B-2 team early in development, according to two government engineers involved since source selection. In their opinion, the relations among the Air Force, Northrop, and the subcontractors were very good. They claim there was free and open dialogue, and that the team viewed everyone as true partners. They also commented that the contractors were not afraid to identify problems, and they took a proactive approach to propose solutions (Edward, 1995).

The degree of team communication and coordination, therefore, appeared to be reasonably high despite the fact that the team was widely scattered throughout the country. Furthermore, very tight security requirements made making phone calls and mailing packages difficult, and there was no computer link between sites initially. Much of the interaction came as a result of many on-site meetings throughout the country. In addition, the three-dimensional CAD/CAM digital database was very useful, and it provided the basis of effective technical interaction at many of these meetings.

Once the B-2 became publicly acknowledged, security procedures were relaxed, and this allowed old communication means to be reestablished and new ones to be implemented. An important new link established in 1992 was the Logistics Support Management Information System, a computer network connecting Northrop with subcontractors, suppliers, and the Air Force's supportability centers and users (Scott, October 12, 1992).

The widely scattered team members recognized what their responsibilities were. Northrop was the prime integrating contractor with overall responsibility to the Air Force to make the system work. This included the engine, which the Air Force was responsible for developing and buying directly from General Electric. The various subcontractors were responsible for their respective subsystems, and they understood to whom they reported at Northrop. The zone management structure described earlier, though not a formal organization with documented relationships, worked reasonably well due to the cooperation of the team members.

The ability of any group to perform work on the B-2 was greatly impacted by the security requirements. One of the biggest problems in conducting the program was getting people security clearances in a reasonable amount of time, since it could sometimes take a year. However, once that hurdle was crossed, the B-2 program offered a high degree of flexibility and autonomy in conducting the design work. This was despite the fact that the Air Force had an SPO of several hundred people overseeing the effort. They were not a major hindrance because the Air Force implemented streamlined management techniques. Instead of imposing detailed functional specifications, they imposed top-level performance specifications. Many military standards were either heavily tailored or presented as guidelines. In addition, members of the Air Force SPO worked well with the contractors in general, and they added value by being the interfaces in areas that required government input. As one example, the systems analysts from the B-2 SPO worked closely with the contractors to help identify and solve technical issues, and they were viewed as contributing members and not as threats (Edward, 1995).

An effort with the national importance, technical challenge, and budget of the B-2 warranted that the organizations involved allocate their best people to it. Northrop did this by appointing its top aircraft designer to lead the technical effort. Further motivation for Northrop was that as the prime contractor, it had total system performance responsibility, thereby making it contractually accountable to the Air Force. Furthermore, as a cost-plus contract with award fee, profit during development was dependent on how well Northrop performed on a yearly basis. Perhaps most importantly, the Department of Defense required extensive performance and workmanship warranties be placed on Northrop to enforce accountability.

SUMMARY

The B-2 is a very complex and expensive system; its extended development was conducted in accordance with systems engineering fundamentals in the relative stability of the world of classified military programs. Northrop's paperless development approach using a three-dimensional CAD/CAM system contributed to that stability, and it pioneered, despite shortcomings, the new direction of aerospace development. This breakthrough design combined both existing and advanced technologies in a highly integrated, yet supportable, stealth package with the capability to perform intercontinental nuclear and conventional weapons missions for the Air Force well into the twenty-first century. Tables 28-2 to 28-6 show our 35 figures of merit and the scores we assigned for the B-2.

TABLE 28-2   B-2 Performance Scores.

Figures of Merit	Range	Weight	Rating	Score
Technical performance—initial	0–10	1	8	8
Technical performance—mature	0–10	1	9	9
Cost performance	0–10	1	3	3
Schedule performance	0–10	1	4	4
Performance total				24

TABLE 28-3   B-2 Systems Engineering Fundamentals Scores.

Figures of Merit	Range	Weight	Rating	Score
Requirements development	0–10	2	8	16
Incipient system design	0–10	2	8	16
Evaluating alternative concepts	0–10	1	10	10
Make-or-buy decision	0–10	1	9	9
Validation	0–10	1	9	9
Verification and integrated testing	0–10	1	10	10
Configuration management	0–10	1	7	7
Manufacturing considerations	0–10	1	9	9
System integration and technical management	0–10	1	7	7
Life-cycle considerations	0–10	1	10	10
Program management	0–10	1	7	7
Systems engineering fundamentals total				110

TABLE 28-4 B-2 Development Environment Scores.

Figures of Merit	Range	Weight	Rating	Score
Emphasis on the customer	0–10	1	9	9
Stability of requirements and configuration	0–10	1	3	3
Funding and work-force-level stability	0–10	1	9	9
Strong support	0–10	1	6	6
Continuity of core development team	0–10	1	8	8
Stability of organizational structure	0–10	1	9	9
Cooperation among stakeholders	0–10	1	9	9
Effective communication	0–10	1	7	7
Flexibility and autonomy	0–10	1	7	7
Work force qualifications	0–10	1	8	8
Accountability for system performance	0–10	1	7	7
Development environment total				82

TABLE 28-5 B-2 Design Difficulty Scores.

Metric	Range	Score
Design type	0–15	13
Knowledge complexity	0–10	8
Steps	0–10	9
Quality	0–10	8
Process design	0–5	5
Aggressive selling price	0–5	1
Design difficulty total	0–55	44

TABLE 28-6 B-2 Resources Scores.

Metric	Range	Score
Cost	0–15	12
Time	0–10	8
Infrastructure	0–10	8
Resources total	0–35	28

REFERENCES

BOND, D.F., "USAF Resists Change in B-2 Configuration." *Aviation Week & Space Technology*, pp. 69–70, November 4, 1991.

DORNHEIM, M.A., "Air Force Cites 1984 Redesign as Major Reason for Schedule Lag." *Aviation Week & Space Technology*, p. 20, November 7, 1988.

EDWARDS, D., personal communication. Telephone interview on January 30, 1995. Edwards is former Chief of Flight Systems Engineering for the B-2 System Program Office. Participated in B-2 source selection in Fall 1980. Joined the program office in late 1981 and left in 1987.

"Flight Testing, Lab Simulation Prompt Changes That Improve B-2 Capability." *Aviation Week & Space Technology*, p. 51, February 4, 1991.

GALA J., personal communication. Telephone interview on January 30, 1995. Gala is Deputy Director of Engineering for B-2 System Program Office.

"Northrop Assured of B-2 Profit Even if Program Held to 15 Aircraft." *Aviation Week & Space Technology*, pp. 81–82, November 11, 1991.

MORROCCO, J.D., "Low Observable Discrepancy Delays Second B-2 Delivery." *Aviation Week & Space Technology*, p. 20, April 18, 1994.

RICE, D.B., "Viewpoint: The B-2 Stealth Question." *Aviation Week & Space Technology*, p. 7, September 23, 1991.

SCOTT, W.B., "Air Force, Northrop Open B-2 Production Facility to Journalists." *Aviation Week & Space Technology*, pp. 21–23, June 25, 1990.

SCOTT, W.B., "Air Force Weighs Several Options for Improving B-2 Stealth Qualities." *Aviation Week & Space Technology*, p. 80, November 11, 1991.

SCOTT, W.B., "B-2 Contractors Cut Manufacturing Time." *Aviation Week & Space Technology*, pp. 68–69, November 4, 1991.

SCOTT, W.B., "B-2 Radar Designed to Match Bomber's Stealth Characteristics." *Aviation Week & Space Technology*, pp. 55–56, March 11, 1991.

SCOTT, W.B., "B-2 Reliability Focus Pays Early Dividends." *Aviation Week & Space Technology*, pp. 52–53 October 12, 1992.

SCOTT, W.B., "B-2 Test Program Remains on Track to Meet Aero-structural Milestones." *Aviation Week & Space Technology*, pp. 63–64, November 18, 1991.

SCOTT, W.B., "Cheney and Senior Defense Aides Take Firsthand Look at B-2 Production Facilities." *Aviation Week & Space Technology*, p. 23, June 5, 1989.

SCOTT, W.B., "Initial Flight of B-2 to Verify Aerodynamics." *Aviation Week & Space Technology*, p. 31, May 8, 1989.

SCOTT, W.B., "Ultimate Load Testing Will Break B-2 Airframe." *Aviation Week & Space Technology*, p. 64, December 14/21, 1992.

"Technical, Manufacturing Problems Will Delay First Flight of B-2 Bomber." *Aviation Week & Space Technology*, p. 25, April 18, 1988.

"Test Failure." *Aviation Week & Space Technology,* p. 19, September 16, 1991.

U.S. Department of Defense. B-2 System Program Office. *Cost Performance Report (CPR)*, December 31, 1993.

U.S. Department of Defense. B-2 System Program Office. *Modeling and Simulation Users Survey*. Wright-Patterson AFB, Ohio: ca 1994.

WILSON, M., personal communication. Telephone interview on January 30, 1995. Wilson was Chief of Structures until 1993 for B-2 System Program Office.

29

MCDONNELL DOUGLAS C-17
MILITARY TRANSPORT

The McDonnell Douglas C-17 is the latest Air Force aircraft developed to meet air-lift requirements for the Air Force, Army, and Marine Corps. The C-17 is intended to carry large cargo over intercontinental distances and deliver it on short, unpaved run-ways. The aircraft is also expected to require only minimal ground support, need only a small parking space, be able to airdrop troops and equipment, and operate with a crew of only two pilots and a loadmaster. The need for such a versatile aircraft was highlighted by the failed Iran hostage rescue attempt in 1980, which exposed the lack of sufficient mobility to respond quickly to emergencies in remote locations (McCloud, 1993). Furthermore, the C-17 is needed to replace the 30 year old C-141 Starlifter fleet that is planned for retirement before the year 2000. Although most of

187

the subsystems of this original design utilize proven, off-the-shelf technology, this complex aircraft has faced a number of integration, performance, and management problems during its long development to a successful system.

DEVELOPMENT HISTORY, DESIGN, AND PERFORMANCE

The Air Force issued a request for proposals (RFP) to aircraft development contractors for a new airlifter in late 1980. In August 1981, Douglas Aircraft—Government Segment, a company in the McDonnell Douglas Corporation, was selected as prime contractor in a competitive source selection for what was then called the C-X program. However, contract award and the start of work were put on hold since the Air Force had just been authorized by Congress to build more C-5 and KC-10 cargo aircraft, thereby diminishing the immediacy of the C-17 effort. A year later, the Air Force awarded the $6.6 billion fixed-price full-scale engineering and development (FSED) contract that included options for six initial production units as part of a concurrent development and production strategy. However, Douglas was funded at a low level, only about $30 million a year, for three years for advanced technology development and pre-FSED activities. Not until late 1985 did the government finally fund Douglas to begin FSED. With this delayed start date, the Air Force expected production to begin by 1988, expected the first flight to occur in August 1990, and expected 12 operational aircraft in early 1992.

In January 1988, the first production contract option was exercised according to schedule. However, the first flight did not occur until September 15, 1991, over a year late. The first production C-17 was delivered to the Air Force for operational testing in September 1992. Developmental flight testing was completed in December 1994, and the C-17 was declared operational in January 1995; this was three years after the originally projected date and 14 years after Douglas won the source selection (see Figure 29-1). This represents an FSED schedule delay of about 35% when compared to its projected length when it began in 1985.

Along with the stretch in schedule came an increase in costs. The fixed-price development effort has an overrun of $571 million on $3.5 billion stated in base-year 1981 dollars (DAES, 1994). This represents an overrun of approximately 16%. Since the C-17 was developed on a fixed-price contract, McDonnell Douglas was liable for the overrun.

The unit price of the C-17, which takes into consideration the cost of development, depends to a large degree on the quantity the Air Force purchases. Normally, the larger the quantity, the lower the unit price. The planned number of C-17s to be acquired, though, had been drastically reduced since the program started. Originally, the Air Force planned to purchase 210 aircraft. However, due to delays, technical difficulties, and perceived capability reductions, Congress reduced the buy to 120 in 1990. Congress then decided to limit production to 40 units in 1993 (see Table 29-1), while alternatives to the C-17 were investigated. An additional 80 aircraft were to be purchased if Douglas resolved performance, cost, and schedule problems by the end

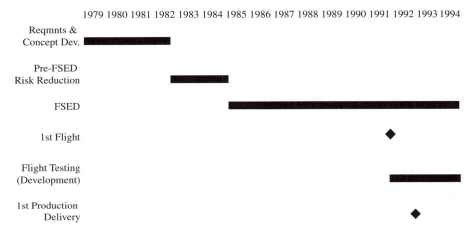

Figure 29-1   C-17 development schedule.

of 1995. Based on the purchase of 120 aircraft, the unit cost was projected to be about $300 million (then-year dollars) or $144.5 million (base-year 1981 dollars), which included development costs, but not initial spares, modifications, and outyear operations and maintenance support. However, if production were limited to 40 aircraft, the unit cost of the C-17 was estimated to be $408 million per aircraft (then-year dollars) or $219 million (base-year 1981 dollars) (DAES, 1994). In November 1995, the Pentagon awarded McDonnell Douglas an $18 billion order for 80 additional C-17s.

As the high costs suggest, the C-17 has a lot of functional capability. It is a large aircraft with the length of the Air Force's medium airlifter (C-141) and the fuselage width of its heavy airlifter (C-5). It is propelled by four Pratt & Whitney engines that are essentially the same as those used on the Boeing 757 since 1984. It contains many of the same features found on large commercial airliners, such as advanced, highly integrated avionics and fly-by-wire flight controls. Being a military aircraft, it also includes noncommercial features, such as an air refueling capability to increase range, defensive avionics, the ability to take off from and land at small austere airfields, the capability to back up and park unassisted, and a complex cargo handling system that enables offloading by a single person. The C-17 was designed to carry palletized cargo and heavy, oversized items (such as a large battle tank or three attack helicopters), in a single load. In addition to its cargo transport role, the C-17 must also be able to perform medical evacuation and paratrooper airdrops. In

TABLE 29-1   C-17 Projected Production Quantity Changes.

	1985	1990	1993	1995
Projected production quantity	210	120	40	120

essence, the C-17 represents the merging of capabilities of the existing small and large Air Force airlifters that perform a wide range of missions.

Even though the C-17 is an expensive and very complex aircraft, its development was originally conceived as a low-risk venture, in which technology proven on other aircraft would be integrated in the new airframe design. But integration of the features on a single aircraft of the size and intended versatility of the C-17 turned out to be a much greater undertaking than Douglas officials had anticipated (Smith, April 12, 1993).

The C-17 was designed to be highly automated to enable operation of all flying and avionics system duties without a third person. This was made possible by 44 interconnected computers controlling and integrating all the aircraft's subsystems. Understandably, avionics integration has been the leading technical challenge, with primary emphasis on the mission computers (Gilmartin, 1990). There are three identical mission computers in the C-17, and there had been some difficulty getting them into synchronous operation due primarily to software problems. Because of these and other technical and schedule difficulties, Honeywell, the subcontractor in charge of designing and developing the avionics suite, was dropped in 1989; and General Electric was brought on board with a different, more complex design (Scott, 1991).

The C-17 program is replete with other examples of design challenges and difficulties. One of them concerns the wings. The wings were not initially considered a major design challenge, but they became a large, expensive problem. The wings should not have failed when loaded to 150% of their nominal vaue. However, the full-size structural test vehicle failed the wing load test at 128% in October 1992. The failure was discovered to be the result of an inadequate design caused by: a computational error by the Douglas engineers, optimistic assumptions, and high and uneven distribution of the test pads on the wing (Lynch, 1993). The structural test vehicle, with a temporary modification to the wing, failed the test again in September 1993, this time at 144%. A new, permanent design, judged to be operationally safe and technically sound by an independent consulting team, was developed and successfully tested in January 1994, and it was incorporated into the production line.

Other major design challenges have been to keep weight growth to a minimum and to get the commercially derived engines to meet fuel consumption requirements. In 1994, the weight was about three percent above the original allocation, and the Pratt & Whitney engine fuel efficiency was 2.8% below original projections (DAES, 1994). Both of these deficiencies have impacted payload/range performance.

In addition to a considerable number of design problems, difficulties with Douglas's manufacturing operations have contributed greatly to cost increases and schedule delays. In the first years of the C-17 program, Douglas's production system was very inefficient. Inaccurate or outdated engineering drawings led to thousands of man-hours spent on doing rework and repair out of position on the assembly line, thereby adding costs and delaying deliveries (Lynch, March 1994). These problems were compounded by a variety of quality related issues, such as faulty rivet machines, flawed composite flight control surfaces, and out-of-round fuselage cross-sections. Douglas, however, did not make significant improvements to its production operations until the early 1990s. Furthermore, manufacturing improvements initiated in 1994 as part of the broad government-McDonnell Douglas settlement, resulted in faster and smoother work, and reportedly cut rework and repair costs almost in half (Grier, 1995).

The C-17 does not meet all of the Air Force's original performance requirements as demonstrated in extensive flight testing using production aircraft. Among them is the payload/range performance, whose shortfall can be attributed to aircraft weight increase, engine fuel efficiency shortfall, and increased aerodynamic drag. This requirement has gone through great changes since the beginning of the program. Interestingly, the C-17's shortfall in this area does not reflect a high degree of customer dissatisfaction.

The initial Air Force requirements, as contained in the request for proposal in 1980, called for the new transport to carry a maximum of 130,000 pounds of cargo for an undefined unrefueled range, later suggested at 2,400 nautical miles. The document also expressed the Air Force's goal of carrying a maximum cargo load of 160,000 pounds. In its proposal, Douglas claimed that its aircraft would carry up to 167,000 pounds of cargo for an unrefueled range of 2,400 nautical miles. Douglas won the competition and agreed to an official increase in the specification payload requirement to its higher proposed value of 167,000 pounds.

As the C-17 development progressed, it became apparent to Douglas and the Air Force that some of the requirements, including payload/range, would not likely be met. This appears to have caused the Air Force to reevaluate the performance requirements on the C-17 contract to see if they were appropriate. The 1989 review of requirements to determine if the C-17 was overspecified resulted in the relaxation of the specification requirement to 160,000 pounds for the 2,400 nautical mile mission. However, the production C-17s tested in the early 1990s did not meet the revised requirement, either.

In 1993, the Air Force reviewed the C-17 requirements again in light of the end of the Cold War. Based on reduced wartime airlift requirements for Europe, it established a new requirement of 157,000 pounds for 2,400 nautical miles; and it established a new requirement of 110,000 pounds for a 3,200 nautical mile mission. These changes were part of a broad contractual settlement in which Douglas agreed to drop monetary claims against the government, invest more money in the C-17 program, and improve its management. A summary of the payload/range requirements change is shown in Table 29-2.

Other original specification requirements and goals were relaxed as part of the 1989 review, with minimal impact to capability. These included changing the launch response time from 5 minutes to 15 minutes (the same requirement on the C-141), as well as relaxing about three dozen less-significant contract specifications (Morrocco, 1991). The Air Force operational users reviewed performance requirements again in 1993 and changed many to objectives (Morrocco, 1994a).

The Air Force had the contractual authority to require full compliance with the performance requirements. However, keeping to the original specifications would have forced a switch to even more powerful engines, thereby eliminating its

TABLE 29-2   C-17 Requirements/Specification Changes.

Subject	Original RFP 1980 (lb.)	Original Spec 1982 (lb.)	FSED Start 1985	Revised Spec 1989 (lb.)	Revised 1993 (lb.)
Maximum payload	160,000	172,200		172,200	169,000
Maximum payload mission (2,400 nm)	130,000	167,027		160,000	157,000
Heavy logistics mission (2,400 nm)	120,000	——		——	——
Heavy logistics mission (2,700 nm)	——	150,000		150,000	145,000
Heavy logistics mission (3,200 nm)	——	130,000		130,000	110,000
Intertheater logistics mission (distance TBD)	100,000	——		——	——
Intertheater logistics mission (2,800 nm).	——	124,039		120,000	114,000
High performance logistics mission	70,000	81,140		74,987	74,987
Ferry range	5,000 nm	4,915 nm		4,600 nm	4,300 nm

nm stands for nautical miles. (System Specification for C-17 Airlift System, 1990; DAES, 1994; Morrocco, 1991; Morrocco, 1994a.)

commonality with commercial airline engines and adding to future maintenance costs (North, 1993). Furthermore, this modification would have delayed the program even more, thereby threatening the continuation of the program and the means to fulfill projected airlift needs.

In addition to issues surrounding payload/range requirements, there were questions about reliability and maintainability performance. Both are areas with long term implications for the Air Force. The C-17 was failing by a substantial margin to meet three system specification requirements for reliability in developmental and initial operational flight testing. They were Mean Time between Removal, Mean Time between Maintenance—Inherent, and Mean Time between Maintenance—Corrective. Not meeting Mean Time between Removal could increase the quantity of spares required, and not meeting Mean Time between Maintenance could affect resources to support the system. During the last half of 1994, however, the reliability of the C-17 demonstrated in operational flight testing dramatically improved and was meeting or exceeding system specification growth curve requirements (RM&A, 1994). Meanwhile, demonstrated maintainability performance, measured in Maintenance Man-hours per Flying Hour and Mean Man-hours to Repair, continued to be better than the growth curve requirements; and the C-17 was meeting its Mission Capable Rate and largely surpassing its Mission Completion Success Probability requirements (RM&A, 1994). Douglas and the Air Force expected improvements to continue, leading up to the July 1995 Reliability, Maintainability, and Availability

Evaluation (RM&AE), a critical hurdle that helped determine whether the 80 additional C-17s were to be built or if modified commercial aircraft were to be purchased to supplement the 40 C-17s already ordered.

Even before the RM&AE, the C-17 had demonstrated the ability to meet most, if not all, the performance requirements. Attaining them will provide the Air Force a significantly enhanced airlift capability over what it currently has. The Air Force customer expects the C-17 will be adequate for its operational needs and considers it the most cost-effective solution to meeting military airlift requirements (Morrocco, April 25, 1994). This position was further enhanced by the "spectacular performance" demonstrated by the C-17 during the RM&AE (Grier, 1995).

As described earlier, mission flexibility was designed into the aircraft, and it is a key element in the Air Force's criteria for satisfaction with the C-17. The design incorporates lessons learned from the operational experience of the current Air Force airlifters, the Lockheed C-141, C-5, and C-130. This has resulted in a design with great cargo handling versatility. Cargo handling items that are optional on other aircraft are standard equipment on the C-17. Although this versatility increased weight and consequently decreased potential payload/range capability, the Air Force accepted this trade-off to ensure the mission flexibility was always available to each aircraft (Dornheim, 1993).

The Air Force also expects the C-17 to be in operation a long time. According to the C-17 Prime Item Development Specification, "The C-17 airframe service life shall be 30,000 flight hours. Utilization shall be based on the mission profiles contained in the C-17 System Specification. The airframe shall be designed for twice the service life." It continues, "The C-17 shall have a useful life of not less than 30 years under any combination of operating service and storage life, when operational service life has not been exceeded." As current Air Force aircraft in service attest, particularly the B-52, C-141, and C-130, 30 years is a realistic length of time to expect aircraft to operate. Obtaining a C-17 design to achieve that long life and flexibility has been a long and difficult process.

SYSTEMS ENGINEERING FUNDAMENTALS

McDonnell Douglas is one of the world's largest developers of military and commercial aircraft. Over the past 30 years, its companies have built a wide range of successful jets, including the DC-8, DC-9, and DC-10 passenger transports, the F-15 and F/A-18 fighters, and the KC-10 cargo transport and aerial refueling aircraft. During this time, McDonnell Douglas had followed a traditional approach to aircraft development. This method, supported by a functionally oriented organizational structure, was characterized by a high priority placed on design engineering activities with minimal influence of manufacturing design concerns.

Since the C-17 is a military aircraft, the Air Force was closely involved in most aspects of Douglas's development activities. As the customer, the Air Force defined its requirements for what would become the C-17 in a formal process that normally culminated in the issuance of a Mission Need Statement (MNS) and then a document defining operational requirements. The MNS certified that an operational need existed and defined it. The requirements generated from the Air Force airlift study in 1980 formed the basis of the top-level mission requirements in a MNS for what was at that time, designated the C-XX aircraft. Operational performance requirements were defined afterwards by the Air Force in a System Operational Requirements Document (SORD), and these were used to define system requirements in conjunction with Douglas. The requirements were formally documented in a system specification and a prime item development specification. As previously discussed, Douglas allowed a more stringent specification to be imposed than what the Air Force originally suggested. This was probably done by Douglas as a way to help win the contract source selection. However, it had long term negative impacts for the program.

Douglas had modeled its C-17 system concept using previous transport and research aircraft as guides. The next step was to follow a structured approach to decompose the elements of the complex system into a work breakdown structure (WBS), as is normally required at the beginning of an Air Force systems development program. This approach, which addressed both functional and product issues, helped define interfaces and allocate requirements. Douglas provided its initial version of this decomposition as part of its proposal to the government, and it updated the WBS as necessary throughout development.

The Air Force selected among several basic designs from several contractors when it held source selection. Furthermore, during the C-17 concept development phase, Douglas evaluated alternative concepts and designs to come up with one it believed would meet the Air Force's requirements. Douglas continued performing trade-off studies throughout the pre-FSED effort and into production, as it attempted to define, improve, or correct the configuration.

Along with performing design trade-offs, Douglas also had to decide where the parts or software items would be produced. The large number of subcontractors and suppliers on the C-17 contract indicates that the least expensive approach for Douglas was not to do everything in-house. The company has been primarily an aircraft integrator and airframe manufacturer, and it has obtained engines and avionics from outside companies. Douglas's make-or-buy decision process on the C-17, a normal commercial practice in large aerospace firms, was also required by the Air Force contract.

When it came to validating C-17 requirements, both the Air Force and Douglas had major roles. The Air Force followed its formal procedure for validating requirements, and it culminated in the approval of the C-XX SORD. On the C-17 program, the Air Force also evaluated the requirements two other times to determine if they were still reflective of the mission. These validation reviews occurred over a 13 year development period, and they resulted in changes that reflected changing needs. However, such reviews probably would not have occurred if the C-17 had not encountered technical, cost, and schedule difficulties.

As for Douglas, it performed its primary validation activities during concept development, before source selection, to determine if its concept design was feasible. Douglas reviewed the structural capability of the existing transports, integrated aerodynamic features it developed in the late 1970s to enable short takeoff and landing, conducted wind tunnel tests of resulting models, and performed other analyses to help determine if a real world system could be built.

Once the C-17 requirements and design concept were validated, Douglas had to verify that the equipment it was developing conformed to requirements. To do this, Douglas used extensive physical mockups of the fuselage and cargo sections to demonstrate equipment placement and cargo handling capability; two structural ground test articles for static and durability tests; and a cockpit and avionics bay mockup, called the flight hardware simulator, for integrated avionics testing on the ground. Also, prior to first flight, each test aircraft underwent the On Ground Aircraft System Test, which is a hardware-in-the-loop test that simulates aircraft flight on the ground and exercises the aircraft's system components together instead of individually. Additionally, Douglas produced and flew one FSED prototype flight test unit before completing construction of four FSED flight test units that were to be later delivered for operational use. This was all performed in accordance with the Air Force's required formal test and evaluation master plan and formal test procedures.

C-17 flight testing was originally expected to be run much like a fast-paced commercial transport program, in which Douglas would take the lead. However, the Air Force later decided to manage it. Commercial aircraft test programs typically require 10–14 months, while Air Force test programs generally involve a slower paced approach in order to evaluate safety requirements and previous test data (Smith, April 26, 1993). Furthermore, military aircraft must conduct additional tests to demonstrate maneuvers and capabilities that are unknown in the commercial world (Lynch, 1993). In the case of the C-17, technical problems discovered during flight testing also extended the effort. Consequently, the development flight test program that began in 1991 was finally completed three years later.

Because the C-17 has been a highly concurrent development and production program, Douglas delivered aircraft to the Air Force while still evaluating and modifying the design. Therefore, there was no stable, approved baseline configuration to which the aircraft were being built. As a result, the first 28 C-17s were of widely varying configurations (Smith, March 22, 1993). Although Douglas had a system for interface and configuration status accounting and control much like that of other large aerospace contractors, it was not effective in tracking so many different configurations. For three months in 1994, the Air Force C-17 System Program Office (SPO) and Douglas formed a special action team to define a stable configuration for the Air Force to declare operational. The team was also chartered to develop a disciplined process to track the status and configuration of each aircraft (PPR, 1994). The team defined an operational baseline and formed the Integrated Configuration Management Database that provided instantaneous status information to interested program participants.

Some of the configuration changes has been prompted by difficulties experienced on the production floor. While the Douglas manufacturing organization conducted the C-17 production planning, it did not have a large amount of influence with the design engineers. Therefore, the components and assemblies of the C-17 were not designed with ease of manufacturability as a primary design driver. This is partly reflected in the high rework and repair rate, especially on the first C-17s. Forty percent of the labor hours on the first two C-17s went to repair, rework, and nonstandard work (Smith, April 12, 1993). As it overran the development contract, Douglas had great financial incentives to recoup the losses during production. Therefore, Douglas started developing and evaluating part redesigns aimed at reducing the cost of the remaining production units.

While being an expensive aircraft, the C-17 does not significantly advance the state of the art in individual technology areas. It does, however, involve the sophisticated integration of a lot of technologies in a type of aircraft Douglas had not worked on before. Unfortunately, the company failed to conduct adequate early risk assessments on some of these systems (Morrocco, 1991). Douglas essentially underestimated the extent and complexity of the development effort, and the result has been constant design changes to correct problems and minimize the attendant schedule slips.

Some of Douglas's difficulties can be traced to competing priorities for limited company resources. By the time Congress authorized FSED funding in 1985, McDonnell Douglas was starting to run other major aircraft development programs. In 1987, the company was involved simultaneously in developing the Navy T-45 trainer and the MD-90 and MD-11 commercial transports, as well as the C-17. These four concurrent programs overburdened the resources and talent of a company that had not produced a new aircraft design in over a decade (Morrocco, 1993). The C-17 program had been drained of the company talent and management attention that had originally been assigned to it before Douglas had won the source selection in 1981. The inadequate allocation of qualified engineering and manufacturing personnel contributed to the design difficulties and led to inefficiency on the manufacturing floor.

To improve its manner of developing aircraft, McDonnell Douglas decided to move its company from a traditional, functionally oriented development approach to a team-based approach that would improve the interaction between the engineering, manufacturing, and support disciplines. In 1989, McDonnell Douglas attempted to implement its Total Quality Management System (TQMS) corporatewide, including Douglas. However, it was poorly carried out and disrupted the entire company, thereby slowing C-17 program progress and failing to improve the program's situation.

McDonnell Douglas needed help to resolve the extensive C-17 technical and management problems that continued to face the contractor in the early 1990s. Thus, the Pentagon forced McDonnell Douglas and the Air Force to fully and effectively implement an integrated product development teaming approach in 1993 for the completion of C-17 development and production of the remaining units. This involved extending the teaming concept already in place at Douglas to physically locating interdisciplinary team members together and formally including Air Force personnel. In response, Douglas and the Air Force C-17 SPO established a network of nine integrated product teams, with each of these teams overseeing subordinate teams (Lynch, March, 1994). This arrangement was formally documented in an integrated product team plan. In addition, Douglas was required to implement a paperless design system through use of an advanced computer aided design network, much like that implemented by Boeing during 777 development.

Although Douglas had significant technical and management problems, the company did follow most of the Air Force's required sequence of design reviews and fulfilled most of its required documentation submittals.

Some of these submittals documented how Douglas was going to address a broad range of life-cycle considerations, as required by the Air Force. Reliability and maintainability requirements were called out in the system specification with the objective of ensuring mission accomplishment and controlling maintenance costs; plans addressing these areas were required. However, an aggressive reliability growth program was not implemented until 1994 (DAES, 1994). The Air Force also called for ease of item accessibility to reduce the time and difficulty of repairing and replacing C-17 components, and there was maximum use of built-in test features to reduce maintenance and troubleshooting times. Training was given importance, and Douglas developed a flight hardware simulator to train flight crews. The results of these efforts were incorporated into a life-cycle cost model, which was used by Air Force planners.

The importance of life-cycle considerations on the C-17 program is illustrated by the decision to forgo additional efficiency improvements to the engine design in order to maintain its commonality with its commercial counterpart. By doing this, the Air Force expected to save on spare parts costs and possible reliability and maintainability cost increases (North, 1993).

While supportability concerns have been addressed on the C-17 effort, they have not always prevailed. One design result that may have a negative long term impact is the proliferation of computer languages in C-17 software. Six different computer languages are used throughout the aircraft, and many subsystems contain more than one language. This diversity is likely to result in excessive software maintenance costs in the long run (Bond, 1992). This approach, however, was consciously chosen to accommodate shorter term schedule and cost considerations. The Air Force plans to eventually have all the software converted to Ada.

In summary, although not all the outcomes have been commendable, supportability issues did receive a high level of attention throughout C-17 development.

Douglas program management had a difficult time keeping track of the program during most of the C-17's development. In the past, the output of the Douglas cost schedule and control system often lagged 60 days behind factory floor work (Lynch, November 1994). An independent Department of Defense panel concluded as late as 1993 that Douglas's business systems were struggling to provide the management visibility and control needed to properly support the program (Lynch, March 1994). Managers therefore did not have the timely management data to help identify problems. Furthermore, the program did not have the Douglas management focus and resources during much of the program to quickly resolve the problems once discovered. With the implementation of the integrated product teaming approach in 1993 came an improved ability to track and manage the program for both Douglas and the Air Force. This included a new, computer based cost and schedule accounting system, in which the reports are generated and provided to Douglas management and the government within seven days after the close of the monthly accounting period. A key feature of the new C-17 management operations is that there is only one set of plans, teams, and schedules, and therefore no longer separate government and contractor versions. The improvement in program management effectiveness in the mid-1990s, due in part to the management changes implemented, also followed attendant improvements in the development environment.

DEVELOPMENT ENVIRONMENT

As is evident from the discussions up until now, the C-17 program did not progress smoothly. Mirroring the discord, and in some cases contributing to the problems, had been a difficult development environment for both Douglas and the Air Force.

The C-17 was conducted in the manner of a typical Air Force system development program. That is, the Air Force customer was involved in overseeing all aspects of the effort through representatives in the SPO and on-site presence of the Air Force Plant Representative Office. As was typical at the time, the Air Force also specified in great detail what it expected the system to do. Furthermore, the Air Force expected to be kept informed of development progress. Therefore, Douglas could not escape emphasizing the customer. This arrangement, in place during all of development, allowed much input by the Air Force. However, Douglas would not do everything the Air Force wanted done to correct problems, due to the overrun on the fixed-price contract.

While the Air Force was obliged to provide guidance on requirements, Douglas was fully responsible for design and fabrication. The Air Force specification requirements had remained stable throughout most of development until 1989, when the Air Force relaxed some of them. Up until that time, though, Douglas constantly modified the detail requirements and configuration throughout FSED and production in response to problems encountered as the program produced hardware and software.

A design change that had a major impact on the program was the addition of a fly-by-wire electronic flight control system. With Air Force concurrence, Douglas officials decided in 1987, two years after the start of FSED, that the aircraft needed the electronic system to realize its full capability and meet operational requirements (Scott, 1991). The change of this magnitude in the middle of FSED, with its attendant systems impacts, contributed significantly to the cost overrun and schedule delays.

Another change with significant consequences was the use of more powerful versions of the engine than used originally. This upgrade was implemented late in development to improve payload capability due to aircraft weight growth. Thrust for each of the four engines increased to 41,700 pounds from the previous rating of 37,000 pounds. The resulting increase in exhaust temperature unexpectedly led to the need for a higher-temperature and heavier material for the wing's externally blown flaps, since the old material could not survive the new environment. This added weight and increased cost.

Due to the highly integrated nature of the C-17, Douglas had to deal with the rippling effects of other design modifications and alterations. Even during production in 1994, the program continued to be adversely affected by issues such as design and materials changes (PPR, 1994).

Stability has also largely eluded C-17 funding and work-force-levels. The start of FSED was delayed for nearly four years, preventing Douglas from ramping up manpower in preparation. When FSED funding finally came through in late 1985, Douglas had to hire a large number of people in a short period of time. After this, the work-force-level was reasonably stable as Congress supplied funding during the first three years of FSED in accordance with the long term budget plan. In 1989, prompted by slippage in the program schedule, cost increases, and performance problems, Congress started to cut the program's yearly budget and alter the production profile. As a result, Douglas started experiencing constant and increasing labor turnover. This had the effect of severely reducing FSED production personnel in 1992 and 1993, then requiring a sudden ramping up again in 1994.

In addition to cutting funds and reducing production quantities throughout the early 1990s, Congress had threatened to cancel the program altogether. The program was placed on probation at the end of 1993, as part of a settlement between the Department of Defense and McDonnell Douglas. In this settlement, the contractor was given two years to prove it could meet revised schedule, cost, and specification requirements and successfully complete flight testing. McDonnell Douglas also agreed to spend an additional $456 million on facilities and testing, and drop $1.7 billion in claims against the government. If technical, schedule, and cost performance were improved significantly by the end of the probation period, the Air Force would be allowed to buy more than the 40 C-17s already delivered or on order (Lynch, March 1994). If not, Congress supposedly would have funded off-the-shelf alternatives, such as buying more of the large C-5s or a military version of the 747 cargo freighter. Much of the C-17 development and production had been conducted in a volatile political environment with widely varying degrees of support.

Douglas had problems keeping a core C-17 development team together even before the political turmoil. The four year delay of FSED in the early 1980s prompted some of the key C-17 technical and management personnel involved with the earlier design work to find jobs in other McDonnell Douglas programs that needed the expertise. Stability was also impacted during production in the early 1990s by constant labor turnover; this was due to union seniority rules that gave workers laid off from Douglas's commercial production programs the right to claim jobs on the C-17 line (Lynch, 1993). Furthermore, in 1989, implementation of the TQMS displaced most workers, and some of the key C-17 personnel did not return. For example, at the executive level, 194 positions were filled in the restructured organization chart, but a year later, fewer than 50 of those executives remained in the same positions (Smith, April 12, 1993).

The Douglas top-to-bottom TQMS transformation was imposed suddenly and without advance notice. The company's organizational structure, composed of functional groupings, was virtually eliminated, and the process of defining and filling the new management positions took up to six months to complete. According to some employees, once the positions were filled, many managers were frequently moved from one position to another. Furthermore, some did not have the necessary technical qualifications for the job (Smith, April 12, 1993). Unfortunately, this transformation did not achieve its intended effect, and the C-17 program continued to founder.

In 1993, in response to continued technical and management problems, the Department of Defense directed the C-17 SPO and Douglas to implement a new master plan for the C-17 program under the auspices of an Integrated Master Plan. This action established integrated product teams as part of integrated product development (SAR, 1993).

If integrated product development had been adopted earlier in the program, it could have enabled the Douglas engineering and manufacturing workers to work better together than they did under the traditional functional organization. Douglas's relationships with subcontractors and suppliers, while businesslike, could also have been enhanced through product teams. As difficulties befell the program, Douglas's interactions with its subcontractors were negatively affected. This was especially true of Honeywell, the avionics developer and integrator, which was replaced in the middle of development.

The Air Force SPO interacted heavily with Douglas, as was required of its oversight role. Traditionally, government program representatives and contractors have had a mildly adversarial relationship. In the case of the C-17, a strongly negative atmosphere pervaded as the many problems became apparent; and both sides blamed each other for them, creating gridlock and seriously impeding progress (Lynch, March, 1994). The agreement to relax performance requirements and avert Douglas legal action mentioned previously, in addition to the appointment of a new Douglas program manager who reported directly to the Chairman of McDonnell Douglas, was intended to diffuse the poisonous relations and allow the program to continue.

Throughout development and into production, the C-17 program members depended on the standard means of communication, such as telephones, mail, meetings, and later faxes and limited computer networks. Most of the Douglas workers were based in Long Beach, California, and they were located in buildings within several miles of each other, usually with other members of their functional specialty. Most of the company's major subcontractors and suppliers have been located across the country, as well as its Air Force customers. Douglas had conducted technical working meetings, as well as program reviews, and design reviews at a variety of locations to provide the team members the opportunity to work together to develop the aircraft. It had also maintained representatives at subcontractor plants to enhance communication, and some of the subcontractors had representatives at Douglas for the same purpose.

As mentioned earlier, Douglas and the Air Force implemented an advanced computer aided design and manufacturing system at the tail end of FSED in 1994. As an enhancement to team communication, it allowed much quicker transfer of the design to program participants and enhanced the speed and coordination of configuration updates.

Due to the large presence of Air Force representatives and extensive reporting requirements, Douglas's flexibility and autonomy for conducting the C-17 effort was less than what would normally be available on a commercial transport effort. For example, a former Douglas official claimed the management control system imposed by the Air Force required excessively detailed expenditure breakdowns and was expensive to implement. Furthermore, it focused excessively on program detail and led some managers to lose sight of the big picture (Smith, April 12, 1993). Also, the Air Force decided to run the test program instead of having Douglas do it, as originally planned. This slowed flight test progress down, especially when a three flight per week limitation was imposed. Finally, the large amount of effort required to respond to Air Force and congressional inquiries diverted the attention of members of the technical and management team from their primary work.

Most of Douglas's workers initially assigned to the C-17 effort were technically qualified for their work. However, as discussed earlier, many engineers, managers, and production floor workers with valuable technical expertise left the C-17 program to take jobs with other companies during the four year lag between being selected as prime contractor and full development funding. Then, when FSED funding was authorized in December 1985, a sharp surge in commercial aircraft orders, as well as ongoing military programs, made it difficult for Douglas to find employees with the required skill levels (Smith, 1993). The presence of a large number of inexperienced workers contributed to the production floor inefficiencies.

Douglas was, and continues to be, responsible for cost and schedule performance as well as the output of its workers. Furthermore, it is responsible for the performance of the C-17s it delivers to the Air Force. To enforce this accountability, large Department of Defense contracts are required by law to contain warranties providing the government recourse if the delivered item is inadequate. The C-17 warranty is very extensive and includes provisions to ensure that the C-17s delivered:

1. are free from material and workmanship defects at delivery,
2. shall meet or exceed the system-level specification on reliability, maintainability, and availability requirements,
3. shall have had all subsystems, accessories, equipment, and parts installed according to specification, and
4. shall have airframes that do not develop structural defects.

If an item fails to meet any of the above, the contractor must correct the failure at no additional cost to the government (C-17 Warranty Briefing, ca 1994). Given the difficulties experienced on the C-17 program, such assurances are important to the Air Force in establishing confidence in the future viability of the aircraft.

SUMMARY

As a large, Air Force-sponsored, systems development program, the basic systems engineering fundamentals were attempted to one degree or another during the development of the C-17. However, as previously indicated, some of the activities were not performed well. In addition, the environment in which the systems development was carried out primarily by Douglas was clearly turbulent in many areas, and it significantly contributed to the program's shortcomings. The end results of the C-17's technical and management problems were a significant schedule delay and a significant cost overrun, but only minimal performance degradation. In spite of the difficult development, the C-17 design is a very capable aircraft and its operational performance is satisfactory to the customer. Tables 29.3 to 29.7 show our 35 figures of merit and the scores we assigned for the C-17.

TABLE 29-3   C-17 Performance Scores.

Figures of Merit	Range	Weight	Rating	Score
Technical performance—initial	0–10	1	3	3
Technical performance—mature	0–10	1	9	9
Cost performance	0–10	1	6	6
Schedule performance	0–10	1	5	5
Performance total				23

TABLE 29-4   C-17 Systems Engineering Fundamentals Scores.

Figures of Merit	Range	Weight	Rating	Score
Requirements development	0–10	2	8	16
Incipient system design	0–10	2	7	14
Evaluating alternative concepts	0–10	1	8	8
Make-or-buy decision	0–10	1	9	9
Validation	0–10	1	8	8
Verification and integrated testing	0–10	1	8	8
Configuration management	0–10	1	3	3
Manufacturing considerations	0–10	1	6	6
System integration and technical management	0–10	1	4	4
Life-cycle considerations	0–10	1	8	8
Program management	0–10	1	3	3
Systems engineering fundamentals total				87

TABLE 29-5   C-17 Development Environment scores.

Figures Of Merit	Range	Weight	Rating	Score
Emphasis on the customer	0–10	1	7	7
Stability of requirements and configuration	0–10	1	2	2
Funding and work-force-level stability	0–10	1	2	2
Strong support	0–10	1	2	2
Continuity of core development team	0–10	1	2	2
Stability of organizational structure	0–10	1	1	1
Cooperation among stakeholders	0–10	1	3	3
Effective communication	0–10	1	5	5
Flexibility and autonomy	0–10	1	5	5
Work force qualifications	0–10	1	5	5
Accountability for system performance	0–10	1	8	8
Development environment total				42

TABLE 29-6   C-17 Design Difficulty Scores.

Metric	Range	Score
Design type	0–15	9
Knowledge complexity	0–10	6
Steps	0–10	9
Quality	0–10	6
Process design	0–5	4
Aggressive selling price	0–5	2
Design difficulty total	0–55	36

TABLE 29-7   C-17 Resources Scores.

Metric	Range	Score
Cost	0–15	10
Time	0–10	8
Infrastructure	0–10	8
Resources total	0–35	26

REFERENCES

BOND, D.F., "C-17 Program Faces Problems in Manufacturing, Software." *Aviation Week & Space Technology,* p. 31, May 18, 1992.

BOND, D.F., "USAF Plans to Combine C-17 Production, Smoothen Workload at Douglas Aircraft." *Aviation Week & Space Technology,* pp. 24–27, July 9, 1990.

C-17 System Program Office. C-17 Aircraft Vehicle Integration IPT. *White Paper on the C-17 RM&A Readiness Review, 3–16, November 1994,* by Lt. Col. William Miller, EPMR Topics Memorandum, November 21, 1994.

Defense Acquisition Executive Summary (DAES) Report, C-17. pp. 3-2, 5-3-2, 6-2-1, July 25, 1994.

DORNHEIM, M.A., "C-17 Test Pilots Report Flight Control Problem." *Aviation Week & Space Technology*, p. 51, October 12, 1992.

DORNHEIM, M.A., "Versatility, Automation Key to C-17 Cargo Operations." *Aviation Week & Space Technology,* pp. 48–49, May 10, 1993.

FLORA, W., "USAF Projects Slip in C-17 Operations to Fiscal 1992." *Aviation Week & Space Technology,* p. 267, September 3, 1984.

GILMARTIN, P.A., "Air Force, Douglas Press C-17 Assembly to Retain First Flight in 1991." *Aviation Week & Space Technology,* pp. 17–18, January 15, 1990.

GILMARTIN, P.A., "Congress Increases C-17 Scrutiny in Wake of Reported Cost Overruns." *Aviation Week & Space Technology,* pp. 25–26, September 2, 1991.

GILMARTIN, P.A., "Senate Arms Panel Wants Pentagon to Reexamine C-17's Capability." *Aviation Week & Space Technology,* p. 22, August 5, 1991.

GRIER, P., "The C-17 Makes Its Point," *Air Force Magazine,* pp. 38–41, October 1995.

KOZICHAROW, E., "DoD Seeks C-17 Full-Scale Development." *Aviation Week & Space Technology,* pp. 19–20, March 19, 1984.

LYNCH, D.J., "Airlift's Year of Decision." *Air Force Magazine,* pp. 24–30, November 1994.

LYNCH, D.J., "The C-17 Fights the Headwinds." *Air Force Magazine,* pp. 34–40, July 1993.

LYNCH, D.J., "The C-17 on Probation." *Air Force Magazine,* pp. 30–34, March 1994.

MCCLOUD, J., "McDonnell Douglas Saves Over $1,000,000 Per Plane with Reengineering Effort." *Industrial Engineering,* pp. 27–30, October 1993.

"McDonnell Agrees to C-17 Probation." *New York Times*, p. D14, January 7, 1994.

"McDonnell Caves." *Aviation Week & Space Technology,* p. 21, January 10, 1994.

McDonnell Douglas. Financial Planning and Control, *Program Progress Report (PPR), C-17, January 1994 through 30 June 1994.* McDonnell Douglas Integrated Schedules (TA-BCB). July 20, 1994.

"McDonnell's Jet Problems." *New York Times,* March 11, 1991.

MORROCCO, J.D., "Congressional Support Eroding for C-17 Program." *Aviation Week & Space Technology,* pp. 30–31, March 15, 1993.

MORROCCO, J.D., "Easing C-17 Specs No Threat to AMC." *Aviation Week & Space Technology,* pp. 26–27, January 3, 1994.

MORROCCO, J.D., "Fogelman Cites Need for 70-80 C-17s." *Aviation Week & Space Technology,* pp. 18–20, April 25, 1994.

MORROCCO, J.D., "MAC Satisfied C-17 Meets Requirements, But Fears Further Production Delays." *Aviation Week & Space Technology,* pp. 52–53, September 9, 1991.

NORTH, D.M., "C-17 Should Fulfill USAF Airlift Mission." *Aviation Week & Space Technology,* pp. 42–47, May 10, 1993.

"Perilous Times for the C-17." *Aviation Week & Space Technology*, p. 9, December 3, 1990.

Prime Item Development Specification for C-17A Air Vehicle, Specification Number MDCS002(I)C, August 1, 1990.

ROPELEWSKI, R.R., "C-17 Wind Tunnel Tests Near Completion." *Aviation Week & Space Technology,* pp. 258–263, September 3, 1984.

SCOTT, W.A., "C-17 First Flight Triggers Douglas/Air Force Test Program." *Aviation Week & Space Technology,* pp. 21–22, September 23, 1991.

Selected Acquisition Report (SAR) (RCS: DD-COMP(Q&A)823), Program: C-17, December 31, 1993.

"Several Thousand Layoffs Feared if Congress Cuts C-17 Appropriations for Fiscal 1992." *Aviation Week & Space Technology*, pp. 22–23, September 23, 1991.

SMITH, B.A., "First C-17 Flight Marks Key Program Milestone." *Aviation Week & Space Technology*, pp. 18–20, September 23, 1991.

SMITH, B.A., "Flight Test Pace for C-17 Under Review." *Aviation Week & Space Technology,* pp. 20–21, April 26, 1993.

SMITH, B.A., "Management Miscues, Delays Snarl C-17 Program." *Aviation Week & Space Technology,* pp. 30–31, April 12, 1993.

SMITH, B.A., "USAF Backs Plans to Bring C-17 Wings Up to Spec." *Aviation Week & Space Technology,* pp. 28–29, March 22, 1993.

System Specification for C-17 Airlift System, Specification Number MDC S001C, FSCM, September 1, 1990.

U.S. Department of Defense. C-17 System Program Office. *C-17 Warranty Briefing,* Wright-Patterson AFB, Ohio: ca 1994.

30

LEARJET MODEL 60
BUSINESS JET

The Model 60 from Learjet, is a midsized, twin-engine, transonic business jet designed for transporting up to eight passengers and luggage on flights of up to 2,750
nautical miles. Learjet developed the Model 60 in response to marketing research
findings that customers existed for a larger and longer range version of the successful
Model 55. Although the company failed to recognize the proper requirements initially, the design group eventually developed an aircraft that met customer desires by
carrying out, often informally, many of the fundamentals of systems engineering.

DEVELOPMENT HISTORY, DESIGN, AND PERFORMANCE

Model 60 development began in July 1990. In just a few months, the program moved from concept definition to full-scale engineering development (FSED). The first flight of the engineering prototype took place 11 months later. Development ended in January 1993 with the first delivery of a production unit to a customer (see Figure 30-1). This two and a half year development program that included four aircraft was six months behind original schedule (20%) and cost about $90 million, which is double its initial estimate for the smaller scope program. The delay and cost growth were due primarily to the requirements changes generated by the marketing department. However, when considering the cost estimate update after the new requirements were imposed early in FSED, the cost overrun was only about 20% (Etherington, 1994).

Learjet has been designing and building business jets for about 30 years. The company usually designs and builds the airframe, and then integrates engines and avionics developed and built by other companies. The Model 60, which is the largest and longest range aircraft Learjet builds, is a direct derivative of the Model 55 that was introduced in 1981. The Model 55 underwent several performance upgrades throughout 1983 and 1984. Then the Model 55B was introduced in 1985, incorporating a digital flight deck and increased takeoff weight. The Model 55C was introduced later, and it incorporated the earlier aerodynamic and performance improvements, as well as a few others. The Model 60 retains the Model 55 series enhancements, but adds new elements to the same basic airframe (North, 1993). The Model 60 development is classified as a redesign effort.

The primary changes reflected in the Model 60 are more powerful engines, modified aerodynamics, a 3.5 feet fuselage extension, and a larger fuel tank. The results were greater range, improved aerodynamic efficiency, and increased payload.

The Model 60 development program was originally intended to involve merely a 28 inch stretch to the Model 55 (Etherington, 1994). Just after the program was initiated, the Federal Aviation Administration (FAA) issued a change in takeoff requirements that required Learjet to use a more powerful engine on the Model 60 than the one used on the Model 55. The engine selected, the Garrett-4, was an off-the-shelf

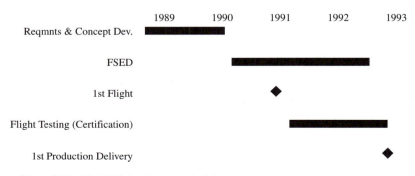

Figure 30-1   Model 60 development schedule.

design being used on a competing business jet, the Citation 7. The Garrett-4 would easily fit the Model 60 using the existing nacelle and pylon design. Therefore, this was considered a minor change in requirements with only a minimal impact to cost and schedule (Etherington, 1994).

Several months later, the Model 60 design team presented the preliminary design during the first program review. This meeting was the sales department's first look at plans for the new aircraft. After the presentations, the vice president of the sales department stated that the aircraft would not sell; the design did not match the desires of the customers they had recently surveyed. The sales department then provided new requirements, primarily increasing range to a transcontinental distance and increasing luggage space (Etherington, 1994).

These changes had major impacts on the design and the program. The new range requirement drove the need for even more powerful engine, greater fuel capacity, and improved aerodynamic efficiency. To accommodate increased luggage space, the fuselage was stretched about a foot more than the originally planned 28 inches.

Instead of having to persuade an engine company to develop a new engine, Learjet engineers found an existing design that met its performance requirements. The PW305 engine from Pratt & Whitney Canada was completing development and was slated for use on the British Aerospace 1000 business jet. Two of the engines could provide 10,450 pounds of thrust, well above the 9,200 pounds of thrust needed. However, to fit on the Model 60, the PW305 required a change in pylon design (Etherington, 1994).

To implement a new pylon design without increasing drag unacceptably was a greater challenge than expected (Etherington, 1994). The change also led to modifications to the wing leading edge. Learjet undertook a major effort using the TRANAIR computational fluid dynamics code to explore design modification options and using high speed wind tunnel tests to confirm drag predictions (Phillips, 1991). The new engine also required the development of full authority digital electronic control software that would optimize power and efficiency and monitor all engine functions.

The integrated avionics suite selected by Learjet was the Collins Pro Line System 4. This system, designed to minimize pilot workload and panel scanning, was essentially off-the-shelf hardware requiring minimal hardware and software modifications.

The Model 60 airframe was designed to last for a time comparable to that found on other business jets. The significant design margin is evidenced by one aircraft being subjected to 50,000 continuous cabin pressure cycles of pressures from sea level to 51,000 feet. This is equivalent to 100 years of typical business jet use (Learjet, ca 1994).

Considering sales projections from its sales department, Learjet established its production tooling requirements for 150 units. By the first delivery in January 1993, Learjet had 33 firm orders (about a one and a half year backlog) and was expecting to be producing Model 60s at a rate of 18–33 units per year to at least the year 2000 if projected sales materialized. As of July 1994, Learjet had sold about 50 Model 60 aircraft. The unit production sales price of one of the aircraft in mid-1994 was approximately $9.5 million (Etherington, 1994).

The Model 60 development was a company funded effort performed by a small team of Learjet employees located at the company's Wichita, Kansas, headquarters. About 200 people, including subcontractors, were involved in the design and prototype fabrication, and they used many of the design, analysis, and manufacturing tools used by the aerospace industry in the late 1980s and early 1990s.

SYSTEMS ENGINEERING FUNDAMENTALS

In the development of the Model 60, the Learjet team followed many of the fundamental systems engineering principles and techniques. However, much of the process was conducted with minimal formality. Given the relatively low complexity of this redesign effort, such an informal approach was adequate and appropriate.

Some formality in the development process was evident in certain controlled documents. Specifically, the design requirements were documented in a system specification by the engineering department after receiving the top-level customer desires from the marketing department. The other formal documents consisted primarily of a test master plan, test plans and procedures, a configuration management plan, and a quality plan. Interface control documents were also maintained and controlled. However, no systems engineering management plan or equivalent was developed by Learjet, and neither were subsystem specifications. Subsystem specifications probably existed with the subcontractors, who had developed their items independent of Learjet, but they were not generated as part of the Model 60 development.

Given the redesign nature of the development effort and the minimal complexity, the Learjet team did not formulate a new top-level model of the aircraft and its subsystems; nor did it establish a work breakdown structure. However, it did allocate requirements and define new interfaces as a result of the performance requirements and subsystems that were different from those of the Learjet Model 55C (Etherington, 1994).

Other systems engineering tasks of the design process were also somewhat informal. While modeling and analysis tools were used to assess and refine the design, primarily in the area of aerodynamics, the team never performed a formal trade-off analysis of options. Furthermore a risk analysis was never performed (Etherington, 1994). Instead of beginning from a clean slate, the existing Model 55C was deemed the starting point of development, with the expectation that the end result would be merely a modification. The approaches to meet the performance requirements, with the possible exception of the aerodynamic refinements, were rather straightforward given the initial design constraints.

Consistent with its stated company approach, Learjet built the Model 60 airframe in-house and obtained most of the subsystems from elsewhere. This is reasonable since Learjet is not a large aerospace company, and it does not possess the resources in people, facilities, and experience to fabricate everything itself economically On this fact alone, Learjet would be expected to conduct no more than minimal make-or-buy evaluations, since the make-or-buy decisions were clear-cut on most items. Furthermore, since the Model 60 uses a majority of the same subsystems and components as the Model 55, most of the parts and suppliers were already set. Despite only limited evaluations, the Model 60 make-or-buy decision performance based on Learjet's policy was reasonable.

Since the Model 60 is a direct redesign, there was not a significant issue in the beginning about being able to technically develop it. The program, however, never performed a validation audit of its requirements (Etherington, 1994). Instead, Learjet appears to have relied primarily on the market surveys early in the program that indicated that potential customers were interested in increased range and payload. The Model 60 team also performed extensive simulation testing and analysis to validate the aerodynamics requirements of the aircraft.

Learjet followed verification and integrated testing in a manner required for FAA certification. Therefore, most of the verification and integrated testing requirements were known at the beginning of the effort. The program created and flew one engineering prototype before completing three deliverable preproduction units that were flown in the flight certification test program. Based partly on the results of the engineering prototype flight test, additional refinements were made to the design to improve range, handling, and center of gravity limits (*Aviation Week,* 1991). These changes were retrofitted into the engineering prototype and incorporated into the four preproduction prototype aircraft. No major problems hampered the completion of development from that point to production, and no major manufacturing or quality problems developed. The only issue of note was the need for minor modifications to the environmental control system. Besides the varying options ordered by different customers, the basic aircraft configuration has remained highly stable from the four preproduction prototypes through production (Etherington, 1994). Furthermore, the four preproduction units were delivered to customers after the successful completion of the 18 month flight test program and FAA certification.

The off-the-shelf integrated avionics suite simplified the integration task for Learjet by reducing the interfaces Learjet had to develop. The avionics supplier, Collins, was responsible to Learjet for ensuring that the flight management system computer, the navigation and guidance units, the weather radar, and the cockpit displays all worked together when installed in the airframe. Purchasing the entire avionics suite from one source reduced the need for extensive ground avionics integration testing by Learjet. Also, with the engine already having been developed and flight tested by Pratt & Whitney Canada on a different test aircraft, the first engines arrived at Learjet as developed and tested units. Therefore, Learjet's developmental testing responsibility was primarily system-level using engineering and production prototype flight units to demonstrate integrated performance as part of FAA certification requirements.

The changes in requirements, interfaces, and configuration that occurred throughout FSED were all controlled adequately by Learjet. While the program did not have a full-blown configuration management system, it did have a formal change control system with a change control board (Etherington, 1994).

Since Learjet is a small, manufacturing oriented company, the production organization was involved early in the program to help in planning for production. Since the Learjet was a redesign of a successful aircraft, there was not a strong motivation to review and possibly revise the manufacturing processes for the Model 60 to improve ease of manufacturing and reduce cost. Learjet, however, used some computer aided design (CAD) partially integrated with advanced numerically controlled milling machine tools for manufacturing airframe components. The fabrication of the Model 60 did not, however, require the development of advanced, unique manufacturing processes.

Even though Learjet was not involved in developing the avionics suite and propulsion units, the Model 60 team had to manage the avionics integration into the airframe, as well as the interfaces between the engines and airframe. The most critical interfaces between subsystems that Learjet had to directly control were those between the avionics and the engines. This was done with extensive involvement by the engine and avionics subcontractors.

The management of the systems integration, as well as the entire technical effort, was done in a manner consistent with a small, cohesive technical team. Consequently, the only formal reviews held were the preliminary design review and software walk-throughs on the digital engine control software. These were in addition to the weekly engineering meetings involving primarily Learjet team members. There were limited forums for formal review of the design, but they do not appear to have been needed, since the customers were not involved in development.

Life-cycle considerations did not require a major amount of attention from the design team. The ground support equipment, maintenance procedures, and the training were the same as for the Model 55, except for support elements dealing with the new engine. Furthermore, the Learjet design team appears to have sought to maintain mission reliability at the level of the Model 55, already very high, rather than to push for marginal improvements. However, the Model 60 does incorporate a key supportability feature to enhance maintenance operations, which is a built-in diagnostic system in the engines to record performance data.

In order to plan and track the progress of the Model 60 development effort, the program manager used Gantt chart scheduling and a computerized cost accounting system. While not particularly sophisticated tools, they were adequate for the relatively low complexity level of the effort. The program manager, however, did not convene regular program reviews, which was indicative of the informal nature of conducting the development.

DEVELOPMENT ENVIRONMENT

After the requirements changes early in FSED, the development environment was stable due to consistent funding, stable requirements, low personnel turnover, and reasonably high configuration stability. The Model 60 development was fully funded by Learjet and FSED was initiated even before firm orders were received. The company funded the effort at a rate of about $30 million per year. Learjet had made a strong commitment to develop the aircraft and did not constrain funding flow, reduce the work force, or threaten to cancel the effort as the cost estimates increased due to the changes in scope.

Designers used a three-dimensional wire-frame computer aided design (CAD) program called UG II for designing the portions of the Model 60 that were different from the Model 55. In addition to using a computational fluid dynamics program with a NASA Cray computer and wind tunnels to verify the computational fluid dynamics results, the design team utilized the NASTRAN finite element program for mechanical analysis and AutoCAD for minor wiring diagram changes. A cabin mockup was built to show cabin modifications, and one engineering prototype flight unit was fabricated and flown.

The Model 60 was developed in a close-knit project team environment. The relatively small airframe and integration engineering team were physically located together, and the manufacturing personnel were on the same grounds. Close cooperation existed between the Learjet personnel and those from the major subcontractors. However, Learjet did not oversee the development of the major subsystems, especially since they were already developed by the time the program began. Furthermore the development team did not have any direct involvement with the customers, most of whom were corporations. That task was left to the sales department, and it appears that interaction between the top-level requirements developers and the design team was limited.

The limited complexity of the program, the small size of the development team, and the physical proximity of the Learjet members with each other enabled adequate communication within the technical team, thereby precluding the need for more formal systems engineering activities and techniques. Furthermore, the maturity of the major subsystems lessened the degree of Learjet's oversight activities over the subcontractors and minimized potential communication problems.

The Model 60 was designed to attain specific performance on a variety of parameters, the primary one being range. The warranty, however, does not address it or other performance parameters specifically. Instead, the warranty covers the failure of parts built by Learjet that occur within five years after delivery and the failure of parts manufactured by subcontractors and vendors that occur within two years after delivery.

SUMMARY

The Model 60 aircraft design attained the range and capacity performance desired by the business jet market and specified by the Learjet sales department. In achieving this success, the development team performed many of the fundamental practices of systems engineering informally in this low-risk redesign effort. While the development environment was reasonably stable in most areas, the requirements development process in the beginning of the program was not conducted effectively. The consequences of the changes in key requirements after program initiation were increased scope, delay in schedule, and cost overrun. Despite these shortcomings of the development effort, the Model 60 met its key performance requirements and satisfied its customers.

Tables 30-1 to 30-5 present our 35 figures of merit and the scores we assigned to the Model 60.

TABLE 30-1   **Model 60 Performance Scores.**

Figures of Merit	Range	Weight	Rating	Score
Technical performance—initial	0–10	1	9	9
Technical performance—mature	0–10	1	10	10
Cost performance	0–10	1	2	2
Schedule performance	0–10	1	4	4
Performance total				25

TABLE 30-2   **Model 60 Systems Engineering Fundamentals Scores.**

Figures of Merit	Range	Weight	Rating	Score
Requirements development	0–10	2	1	2
Incipient system design	0–10	2	7	14
Evaluating alternative concepts	0–10	1	6	6
Make-or-buy decision	0–10	1	8	8
Validation	0–10	1	5	5
Verification and integrated testing	0–10	1	8	8
Configuration management	0–10	1	7	7
Manufacturing considerations	0–10	1	5	5
System integration and technical management	0–10	1	7	7
Life-cycle considerations	0–10	1	7	7
Program management	0–10	1	6	6
Systems engineering fundamentals total				75

TABLE 30-3   **Model 60 Development Environment Scores.**

Figures of Merit	Range	Weight	Rating	Score
Emphasis on the customer	0–10	1	6	6
Stability of requirements and configuration	0–10	1	3	3
Funding and work-force-level stability	0–10	1	8	8
Strong support	0–10	1	8	8
Continuity of core development team	0–10	1	10	10
Stability of organizational structure	0–10	1	9	9
Cooperation among stakeholders	0–10	1	8	8
Effective communication	0–10	1	5	5
Flexibility and autonomy	0–10	1	8	8
Work force qualifications	0–10	1	8	8
Accountability for system performance	0–10	1	6	6
Development environment total				79

TABLE 30-4   Model 60 Design Difficulty Scores.

Metric	Range	Score
Design type	0–15	3
Knowledge complexity	0–10	4
Steps	0–10	6
Quality	0–10	5
Process design	0–5	3
Aggressive selling price	0–5	4
Design difficulty total	0–55	25

TABLE 30-5   Model 60 Resources Scores.

Metric	Range	Score
Cost	0–15	9
Time	0–10	5
Infrastructure	0–10	6
Resources total	0–35	20

REFERENCES

ETHERINGTON, D., Questionnaire completed by Mr. Dick Etherington, Director of Technical Engineering and Configuration Development, Learjet, Inc., July 1994.

Learjet. *Model 60 Brochure*, ca 1994.

"Learjet Plans Return to Market Leadership, Modifies Model 60 Jet." *Aviation Week & Space Technology,* p. 59, July 29, 1991.

NORTH, D.M., "Learjet 60 Stakes Claim in Corporate Market." *Aviation Week & Space Technology,* pp. 38–43, June 28, 1993.

PHILLIPS, E.H., "Learjet Model 60 Initial Flight Testing to Focus on PW305 Engine Performance." *Aviation Week & Space Technology,* p. 82, June 24, 1991.

31

MCDONNELL DOUGLAS MD-11 COMMERCIAL AIRPLANE

The MD-11 is a large, long-range, three-engine commercial airplane developed in the late 1980s and early 1990s by the Douglas Aircraft Company of the McDonnell Douglas Corporation for commercial passenger and cargo travel. The MD-11 was intended to fit into a market segment between the large capacity Boeing 747 and the medium capacity Boeing 767 and the Airbus Industry A300 and A330. The MD-11's direct competitors are the four-engine Airbus A340 and the new twin-engine Boeing 777. Douglas initially approached the MD-11 development as a relatively simple, low-risk modification of the DC-10. The effort, however, quickly became significantly more complicated as unanticipated systems issues appeared. As a consequence, the program was a difficult experience. However, despite problems during development and initial customer operation, the MD-11 was eventually developed into a successful product.

DEVELOPMENT HISTORY, DESIGN, AND PERFORMANCE

McDonnell Douglas launched the MD-11 full-scale engineering development and production (FSED) program on December 30, 1986, with firm orders from 12 airlines for 52 aircraft and options for 40 more. The first flight took place three years later on January 10, 1990. The flight test program involved five aircraft for 10 months, allowing the first customer delivery in late 1990 (see Figure 31-1). Up until flight testing, the development program was nearly a year behind original schedule due to a variety of problems at Douglas. These included overly optimistic schedules, delays in receiving parts, sweeping management and production changes attempted in the middle of development, and various technical difficulties (*Aviation Week*, 1989). However, the company reduced the schedule delay during flight testing, and the first customer delivery of a certified aircraft was nine months (23%) late.

The $722 million development effort was funded entirely by McDonnell Douglas, and it experienced an overrun of about 30% over the original baseline cost (Larson, 1995). By late 1994, 122 MD-11s had been delivered, 51 units were in various stages of fabrication, and 88 were on option or reserve order. This is in excess of the program's breakeven point for MD-11 deliveries, thereby making the MD-11 a profitable venture (Larson, 1995). The 1994 selling price for each of the initial, shorter range versions of the MD-11 with standard training and maintenance manuals is about $116 million.

The MD-11 is a stretched and updated version of the DC-10, and it therefore can be categorized as a redesign. The initial version was designed to carry nearly 300 passengers a distance of almost 7,000 miles. The basic airframe is the same as the DC-10, but the fuselage is 18 feet 6 inches longer, aerodynamics are improved, more powerful engines are used, and a new highly integrated digital avionics system is incorporated. The MD-11 design philosophy was to use a high level of automation to take care of routine flying tasks, as well as emergency procedures, thereby enabling two pilots to handle the workload without a flight engineer. As a consequence, the cockpit has 60% fewer switches, gauges, and lights than the DC-10 (*Aviation Week,* June 4, 1990).

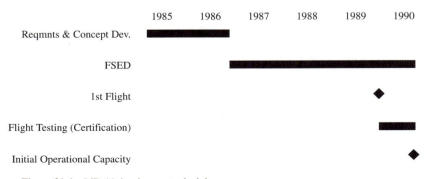

Figure 31-1   MD-11 development schedule.

The fact that the MD-11 was a derivative, or redesign, of the DC-10 helped reduce development risk. However, major technical challenges still existed that Douglas did not anticipate. Of primary significance was the sophisticated new digital avionics system that impacted every subsystem on the aircraft (Smith, January 29, 1990). This dual flight management system allows automatic operation of the aircraft fuel, air, electrical, and hydraulic systems; it also incorporates the automatic flight system. Each of these subsystems is controlled by a pair of dedicated computers. The subcontractor, Honeywell, was responsible for supplying and integrating all the avionics for the program, a role normally filled by the aircraft contractor. Even though Douglas personnel oversaw the complex avionics integration effort instead of performing it, Douglas still had to integrate the avionics with the rest of the aircraft. This required developing new interface devices for the analog DC-10 components that were carried over into the MD-11 design, as well as for new subsystems. From Douglas's point of view, its avionics challenge was therefore mainly that of software integration, since that was the major area with which they had little knowledge or experience (Smith, January 29, 1990). The software problems turned out to be more difficult to deal with than expected.

The MD-11 development team also faced a significant challenge to improve aerodynamic performance. The design target was to reduce drag by 8 percent compared with the DC-10 (*Aviation Week*, October 22, 1990). To achieve this, the designers included improved aerodynamic features such as winglets, a redesigned wing trailing edge, a smaller horizontal tail with integral fuel tanks, and an extended tail cone. A considerable amount of wind tunnel testing was conducted to verify and refine the design. At the time of the first aircraft deliveries, drag reduction was short of the goal. Nominal aerodynamic performance, however, was reached in 1991 and retrofitted into the completed aircraft.

While Douglas anticipated some difficulties with improving aerodynamic design, it did not expect many hardware problems. One such problem that did arise impacted key performance. The fuel consumption performance for the engines from Pratt & Whitney and General Electric, both of which are upgraded versions of established propulsion units used on other aircraft, were below design requirements by amounts from 4.5-6% for the initial units delivered to Douglas (Smith, August 6, 1990). Although the engine subcontractors improved fuel consumption efficiency throughout development and production, the original allocated performance goal was never achieved (Larson, 1995).

Compounding the engine shortfalls was another problem common to most aircraft programs, weight growth. The earliest MD-11s weighed about 4,000 pounds, one and a half percent overweight. The extra weight was a result of changes in preliminary load figures, higher than expected weights for the interior configuration, some new MD-11 components from subcontractors, and configuration changes requested by customers (Smith, January 29, 1990). The result of the overweight condition coupled with the lower engine efficiencies and the less than expected improvements in aerodynamics, was that the initial MD-11s did not meet the promised payload/range performance. This was of critical importance since many of the customers were drawn to the advertised MD-11 payload/range capability that enabled them to fly profitable nonstop international flights. Furthermore, Douglas was contractually liable for payload/range capacity. Although Douglas eventually resolved most of the shortfall, primarily through aerodynamic improvements and weight reductions, the initial aircraft delivered were not in compliance and had to be modified once fixes were identified. At four years into production, the MD-11s coming off the production line met all performance guarantees (Larson, 1995).

Given the high level of commonality between the MD-11 and the DC-10, and the fact that the DC-10 production line was ending at the same time the MD-11 fabrication was to begin, manufacturing planned to refurbish most of the DC-10 tooling to original condition for MD-11 use. The rest of the needed tooling, about 20% of the total, were either modifications or new purchases (*Aviation Week*, 1987).

With the commonality between the MD-11 and DC-10 designs and production lines, it is not surprising that the MD-11 experienced the same type of manufacturing problems, primarily inefficiency on the production floor. This situation was indicated by a high degree of rework and repair and was due to quality related problems. Another measure of inefficiency is the percentage of drawing rereleases from the initial drawings for an aircraft on the production floor. These drawing changes are a result of design updates due to errors, as well as customization features requested by the customer, and a 40% rate was not uncommon at Douglas. Such errors are expensive. The administrative cost of processing these drawing rereleases, or engineering orders, is about $4000 per drawing, and the initial MD-11s built had approximately 100 to 350 engineering orders against each (Larson, 1995).

In order to improve the way it did business and reduce manufacturing costs, McDonnell Douglas tried to implement a product teaming approach that it called the Total Quality Management System (TQMS) throughout the entire corporation in 1989, including Douglas. This effort restructured Douglas's entire way of developing aircraft, thereby replacing the traditional functional and hierarchical management approach. This transformation, however, was not carried out effectively. Furthermore, anticipated improvements had not yet become tangible as high error rates were still seen on the newest MD-11s coming off the production line (Larson, 1995).

While the MD-11 design had its problems, it did possess a certain flexibility and robustness. From the outset of the program, there were four versions of the MD-11 planned. These consisted of the standard MD-11, the longer range MD-11ER with a standard DC-10 length fuselage, the MD-11 combination passenger/freight airplane, and the MD-11F all-cargo aircraft. Later, a stretched version of the MD-11, the MD-12X, was also considered. And finally, Douglas is looking at a possible twin-engine version of the MD-11.

This flexibility is due partly to the structural margin included in the basic airframe design. Douglas Aircraft Company airplanes have the best structural integrity of the large airliners (Larson, 1995). They have traditionally been overdesigned for safety reasons as part of a conservative design approach. The company, therefore, has not been inclined to embrace new, lightweight structural materials as much as its competitors. For example, the MD-11 has a somewhat low overall composite content by weight of 3.7% compared to about 9% for the Boeing 777. The added structural weight appears to contribute to longer airframe life. The projected design life of the MD-11 airframe is 60,000 flight hours, or 20,000 flights. (Airplane wear is a function of cycles, not flight time.) The aircraft can fly for longer periods, but the Federal Aviation Administration (FAA) requires more inspections after 60,000 hours. Having greater structural integrity can extend useful operating life beyond the projected life, and this makes a Douglas airplane design better for modification and re-engineering. According to a Douglas Aircraft employee, as a result of this structural robustness, Douglas aircraft generally have a greater resale value than its competitors' aircraft of the same age (Larson, 1995).

While airlines and air freight carriers may consider long term design flexibility and resale value as an element in customer satisfaction, operating performance is the fundamental determinant. One example of this deals with the MD-11's controllability. According to a Douglas engineering manager, the DC-10 has a reputation for being an excellent pilot's airplane (Larson, 1995). Therefore, the MD-11's controllability was judged against the DC-10. The FAA and Douglas pilots who flew the MD-11 during certification flights agree that the aircraft's handling qualities and control harmony are equal to or better than those of the DC-10 (Scott, 1990).

While payload/range performance has always been superior to the DC-10, the initial MD-11s were not meeting the requirement. Over a period of two years, Douglas developed improvements and had them retrofit into the delivered aircraft. In the meantime, though, the airlines had less capable aircraft to operate.

The performance of the initial MD-11s was marginal in other areas as well. One example dealt with the experience by one of the first MD-11 customers, Swissair. The airline experienced numerous minor, but frequent and annoying, mechanical problems during the initial months of operation; these involved the fuel system and passenger comfort and entertainment systems. In spite of the many problems, Swissair claims it experienced fewer overall early phase-in problems with the MD-11 than with other aircraft for which it was an initial, or launch, customer (Lenorovitz, 1991).

American Airlines, another early customer, was greatly displeased with the MD-11's initial performance. Like Swissair, American had to undergo a difficult period of aircraft introduction. After Douglas spent a considerable amount of resources correcting problems, the airline became satisfied with the MD-11. Now that the primary problems have been worked out by Douglas, the aircraft in operation and those coming off the production line exceed stated performance requirements in almost all categories (Larson, 1995).

The MD-11 has a total of 434,970 parts, not including nuts and bolts. With a system this large and complex, some problems can be expected for the first units regardless of how well the development is carried out. However, many if not most of the MD-11 problems could have been prevented had Douglas not underestimated the integration challenge.

SYSTEMS ENGINEERING FUNDAMENTALS

Over the past 30 years, Douglas Aircraft Company, which is one of the world's largest developers and manufacturers of commercial passenger jet aircraft, has produced a series of successful commercial airplanes, including the DC-8, DC-9, DC-10, and MD-80. During this time, it had developed its own version of a traditional approach to aircraft development. It was essentially a sequential process by which engineers drove the aircraft design with minimal influence by nonengineering organizations. Manufacturing was involved during the design phase in order to plan for fabrication, but it was not in a role to significantly influence the design itself. Furthermore, the Douglas approach was identified by a breakout of the technical and nontechnical specialties under separate and highly functionally oriented organizations. This approach, with its attendant weaknesses, was in place at the beginning of the MD-11 development effort.

During the development of the MD-11, the company possessed aerospace and systems development tools standard for the mid-1980s, such as computer aided design and drafting, mechanical analysis programs, computer simulations, and wind tunnels. It was therefore adequately equipped to conduct a redesign effort.

The primary market potential for the MD-11 was as a replacement for the DC-10s and Lockheed L-1011s flying transcontinental and international routes. Since top McDonnell Douglas and Douglas Aircraft Company management viewed the MD-11 as a relatively straightforward modification of an existing design, there was little emphasis on developing a new set of system requirements. As a result, no integrated requirements document was developed at the beginning of the program. Instead, Douglas used the existing DC-10 specification and the standard commercial aircraft design specification, DS-1100 (Larson, 1995). Douglas's approach to supplementing these old requirements documents was to use marketing surveys to refine higher level requirements. However, concerning detail design issues, the development team made assumptions as to what the airlines would want (Larson, 1995). There was one exception: Douglas involved pilots from 37 airlines in the development of the MD-11 cockpit.

The detail requirements, although incompletely defined by the MD-11 designers and inadequately flowed down to lower-tier suppliers, were allocated to closely match the DC-10 system model. Furthermore, while many of the subsystems did not change much, the interfaces between many of them did. This was due in large part to the new integrated avionics system that tied together many of the aircraft's functions.

Douglas had delegated integrated avionics development responsibilities to its subcontractor, Honeywell, and the engine development was the responsibility of Pratt & Whitney and General Electric. Furthermore, the company sought to maintain a high degree of design and manufacturing process commonality with the DC-10 in order to reduce the MD-11 development risks and costs. Nevertheless, alternative subsystems in areas directly under Douglas's design control were considered to a limited extent throughout the aircraft. Two of the key areas where Douglas performed considerable trade-off analysis were aerodynamics and structural weight, both in order to improve fuel efficiency and achieve the payload/range performance requirements.

Analysis had also gone into determining whether to develop and build a subsystem or component in house, or buy it from outside the company. There are, however, several major components that Douglas did not even consider fabricating itself. Its role is primarily that of airframe manufacturer and integrator, and therefore it purchases engines and avionics from companies specialized in those areas. Regarding the airframe and the rest of the aircraft, the large number of subcontractors and suppliers, both national and international, attest to a high level of consideration going into the make-or-buy decision process.

Validating the MD-11 requirements was another activity performed by Douglas, although not formally. Since the MD-11 was a redesign that did not require the development of new technologies, it was obvious to Douglas that the system could be built. Furthermore, through the use of computer simulations and wind tunnel testing, Douglas was confident that the aircraft it was designing would meet the customers' top-level requirements as understood from the marketing surveys and discussions with the airlines that had placed firm orders. However, it did not accomplish formal requirements audits.

As systems integrator with a large number of subcontractors and suppliers, Douglas was focused more on verifying performance at the system level rather than at the component and subsystem level. However, during FSED, it participated in and paid close attention to the tests performed by subcontractors. This was especially true for the engine tests.

In house, Douglas used a variety of tools to assist in verification activities. It built and tested wind tunnel models to refine the aerodynamic design. A DC-10 fuselage was turned into an MD-11 development mockup, and it was used for checking the mechanical fit of interior components and potential cabin configurations. No engineering prototypes were built, though. The first units produced were relatively mature configurations, and they were subjected to a full range of inspections and tests. Furthermore, they were delivered to customers after modifications at the end of flight testing.

Although avionics integration was performed primarily by the subcontractor, Honeywell, Douglas representatives participated in and conducted some of the testing. Due to the critical importance of the avionics to the entire aircraft, a large amount of avionics ground testing and software checks had been planned. Some of these tests were performed on a flight deck simulator that was run by actual aircraft computers. These activities were accomplished well in advance of the first flight test, with some of them in the Douglas avionics test center.

Although considerable ground avionics component checkout by Douglas occurred during development, the production verification approach was very different. During production, Douglas installed avionics units without bench testing and returned any faulty ones to the manufacturer. This placed the avionics component verification burden on Honeywell, and it allowed Douglas to eliminate its avionics test center (*Aviation Week*, 1987).

The MD-11 was subjected to a comprehensive series of integrated flight tests in accordance with a comprehensive test and evaluation master plan leading to certification by the FAA. In preparation of testing, 350 miles of test wiring and more than 1000 remote sensors were installed during assembly of the first aircraft so that 8000 different temperature, pressure, acceleration, and stress measurements could be recorded (Kubel, 1991). When completed, this MD-11 was subjected to ground vibration tests to demonstrate that the airframe had sufficient structural damping characteristics. It passed with no problems.

Five of the first production MD-11s were used for FAA flight certification testing. While originally planning for only three aircraft, Douglas added two more to minimize a slip in the overall program schedule. Two of the units were focused mainly on avionics testing, while the other three were primarily dedicated to aerodynamic, engine, functional, and reliability testing.

Douglas performed interface and design configuration status accounting and control with varying degrees of success. Most of the initial MD-11 design was placed on two-dimensional computer aided design and drafting (CAD-D) tools, and much of it was transferred directly from the DC-10 paper drawings. Three-dimensional wireframe CAD-D was employed on about 40% of the configuration, but it was used primarily to assist in making the two-dimensional drawings. To control changes to the design configuration and interfaces, Douglas had an administrative system of review, approval, and implementation.

Despite residing in a computer system, the functional drawings were not integrated. With separate mechanical, electrical, structural, and fuel drawings for the same area, and different sets of people responsible for these different drawings, and these different sets of people in most cases reporting to different managers, the act of effectively assessing the impacts of changes was difficult. As a result of this arrangement and the integrated avionics system interfacing with most of the aircraft's subsystems, there were many interface problems (Larson, 1995).

Despite the shortcomings of the tools and methods for identifying interface problems and controlling changes, such issues were eventually resolved. To assist in the process, Douglas developed an order of precedence for interface dispute resolution. The areas of most importance to least importance on a priority scale were: pilot control, fuel system, environmental ducts, electrical system, and interiors/insulation blankets (Larson, 1995).

The interdisciplinary nature of a complex system like the MD-11 suggests an early design involvement by a variety of specialties along with engineering. Perhaps foremost of these specialties is manufacturing. However, early manufacturing involvement did not occur to the extent it should have. As a redesign effort, Douglas did not intend to significantly change manufacturing processes for the MD-11. Furthermore, as mentioned earlier, a majority of the MD-11 manufacturing tooling and processes were taken directly from the DC-10 production line with the assumption that this would keep the up-front program costs low. Therefore, there were no pressures placed on engineering and manufacturing personnel to redesign parts for the purpose of lowering production cost.

As the MD-11 weight problems and cost overrun became apparent in the middle of development, Douglas began to implement producibility efforts involving manufacturing that have been continued into production. These efforts, called design for manufacturing and assembly, were focused on weight reduction, production cost reductions through the simplification of parts, and production cost reductions through the change of assembly order. This push to reduce manufacturing costs was also driven by competitive pressures to reduce the sales price of the MD-11 (Larson, 1995).

During MD-11 development, there was no systems engineering management plan or equivalent, nor had there been a separate systems engineering group. In the original organization, the engineering design department was responsible for systems engineering. The MD-11 chief design engineer, who was also the program manager, was head of this department. He worked with the heads of the functional specialties in the engineering organization under him, and he had a staff of deputies that he individually assigned to work technical problems. The deputies were responsible for identifying and bringing issues to him for resolution. However, these issue oriented engineers did not have formal authority over the nonengineering technical specialists, the subcontractors, or even some of the engineers. Furthermore, there was a tendency on the part of the deputies of not wanting to escalate issues since they wanted to try to resolve them themselves (Larson, 1995). This behavior prevented issues from being communicated adequately throughout the team and resolved in a more timely manner.

In addition to the deputy design engineers, an independent team, called the system compliance engineering group, was chartered to roam throughout the program, find issues, and help fix them. The problem with this overall arrangement was that nobody was clearly in charge of interdisciplinary issues except the chief design engineer. The lower-level responsibilities were separated primarily by functional specialty, and nobody was responsible for the cross-functional activities of a specific area of the aircraft. This situation contributed to the interface difficulties of the program.

Major subcontractors played critical, and sometime leading, roles in MD-11 development. While the key subcontractors had on-site representatives at Douglas, their technical work was done back at their facilities. Furthermore, since Douglas had no permanent, on-site technical personnel at the subcontractors' locations, they were on the road a considerable amount of time visiting the subcontractor plants.

The delegation of critical responsibilities to subcontractors freed Douglas of some work, but resulted in difficulties in addition to large amounts of travel. Since too many details were vague or not specified in the specifications and subcontracts, Douglas had only limited control over what activities it could get the subcontractors to perform. This became more of an issue as the design changed and the schedule slipped, due to the underestimation of the development effort by Douglas. While relations between Douglas and its subcontractors can be considered normal overall, some scope of work conflicts did result in legal action and delays. Because of this, a Douglas engineering manager believes Douglas should have done more in-house integration (Larson, 1995). Despite the difficulties, Douglas eventually succeeded in integrating the subsystems and the airframe.

Recognizing the problems inherent in the functionally oriented way the entire corporation did business, McDonnell Douglas tried to implement the TQMS mentioned earlier. The MD-11 organization was part of this transformation, and it occurred in the middle of the aircraft's development. This attempt was painful to the company due to its poor execution. The change took much longer to implement than planned, and the disruption contributed to the slip in schedule. The MD-11 effort, however, did eventually move into a more product oriented structure with interdisciplinary product team members physically located together. By the time this structure was fully implemented and functioning, development was complete.

According to a Douglas engineering manager, a cross-functional teaming arrangement like integrated product teams would have helped MD-11 development if it had been in place at the beginning of the program (Larson, 1995). Such a structure would have improved the efficiency of technical management and systems integration.

Despite technical management problems, life-cycle issues were addressed by the MD-11 development team throughout development. These issues included reliability, maintainability, and training. Such supportability issues, though, were not a major challenge. The aircraft was designed to be fully compatible with existing ground support equipment and to require about the same level of maintenance as the DC-10 (Lenorovitz, 1991). Training was also very similar. Additionally, the detailed approach to achieve the DC-10-level safety related reliability goals was contained in a reliability plan, and it was verified by flight testing. Therefore, operating costs were projected to be as good as, if not better than, the DC-10.

Life-cycle issues, like all other MD-11 issues, were ultimately the responsibility of the program manager. As mentioned earlier, the program manager also filled the role of chief design engineer, and he was given full responsibility to execute the program. He possessed full authority over engineering, but he had to appeal to a vice president if he could not resolve issues with his manufacturing counterpart. The program manager set the program milestones and assessed design and program status at periodic technical and management reviews. Development risk assessment was also under his purview, but it was not effectively carried out in the beginning of development.

Helping him keep track of the effort was the master schedules group, which had the capability to assess schedule impacts to the overall program when problems appeared. The program manager's activities were also supported by a computerized cost accounting system that, although not very timely, provided an adequate level of visibility into cost performance. Such tools were critical to providing control in a less than ideal development environment.

DEVELOPMENT ENVIRONMENT

The MD-11 was developed with the customer in mind, but direct interaction between Douglas designers and potential airline customers was minimal. Marketing surveys were the key means of obtaining information on top-level airline requirements and desires throughout the first phases of development. Although airlines that had placed firm orders were able to order custom features, most of the MD-11's design details were left to the Douglas engineers to determine without customer review or comment. The one exception was the MD-11 flight deck design that evolved directly from a collaboration between Douglas and pilots from potential customer airlines.

If airlines had been invited to review the MD-11 design at periodic design and program reviews, they would have seen the detailed technical requirements and design change considerably during development and production. Only a few of these alterations originated with the customers, since the airlines had not changed their minds as to what they fundamentally wanted from the MD-11. The changes were the result of the aircraft not being well specified up front by Douglas. Furthermore, due to the need to alleviate performance shortfalls, Douglas was continually introducing design fixes during development and production.

Program funding and work-force-level, while not terribly volatile, were not completely stable, either. During concept development, Douglas started hiring many people to prepare for FSED and production. However, once the program ramped up at full speed, the program was placed on hold as management tried to choose the design configuration and whether the program should go ahead or not. Also, even though McDonnell Douglas had approved the three year budget of just over $500 million at the beginning of the program, the effort faced reduced funding during portions of FSED due to cash flow problems caused by the overrun. Both situations resulted in the temporary reduction of work force.

Despite the funding reductions, the MD-11 received support from corporate management throughout development. The MD-11 program was initially sold to the McDonnell Douglas corporate management as a low-risk derivative of the DC-10 that would only require small changes, resulting in a relatively short design and development cycle. Since McDonnell Douglas did not want to invest much of its capital in commercial aircraft, preferring the lower risk of government funded cost-plus development programs, approval was predicated on the price being relatively low. The program cost estimate that Douglas gave to corporate management was low, because it was based on assumptions of small changes that later turned out to be wrong (Larson, 1995). While McDonnell Douglas was not pleased with the schedule slip and cost overrun, the program was still supported due to the projected profitability of the product line.

Along with corporate support, continuity of the key development team members was maintained to a moderately high degree. Despite the functional structure, specific engineers were assigned to the effort on a long term basis. Furthermore, many key designers and managers during concept development remained on the program when it entered FSED and production. The continuity of the development team and the stability of the organizational structure, though, were seriously impacted temporarily by the 1989 TQMS implementation.

During this transformation, the MD-11 program completely reorganized. Positions changed and everybody had to reapply for new positions (Larson, 1995). Despite the chaos, most of the key designers and managers who had been on the program from the beginning eventually made it back under the new, integrated product teaming structure.

Douglas employees covered a broad range of expertise and backgrounds, and they did not always cooperate as well as they could have. This was true of the relationship between the Douglas engineering and manufacturing organizations. Douglas is a production oriented company in which the greatest amount of power is resident in the manufacturing organization. Like many other companies, Douglas had a cultural wall between the two disciplines. In the Douglas culture, the manufacturing group is never happy with what the engineering group gives them and they viewed design engineering negatively as an overhead function that did not generate company revenues (Larson, 1995). Even though the working-level relationships between engineering and manufacturing were positive, the company atmosphere did not promote closer working relationships. The implementation of the TQMS was partly meant to remove the barriers between them, but it did not have immediate success.

The relationship between Douglas and the subcontractors can generally be described as businesslike, but not particularly close. As mentioned previously, technical problems and poor specification development by Douglas increased the amount and the scope of effort required from some of the subcontractors, resulting in conflicts involving legal actions. Although the TQMS was partly aimed at increasing cooperation between Douglas and its subcontractors, those relationships, at least initially, were not significantly impacted by the change in organizational structure and operating philosophy. But, it did create confusion as the Douglas points of contact continually changed.

Relations between Douglas and the airlines were good at the beginning, but again, not particularly close, since interaction with the customer was limited. When problems with the initial MD-11s surfaced, the relations with some MD-11 recipients turned negative. The large effort by Douglas to solve the problems was crucial to regaining the confidence of the customer airlines.

The means of interaction between all members of the MD-11 development team were primarily telephones, face-to-face meetings, and mail. While adequate, it was not an efficient arrangement for transferring large amounts of technical information. Also, meetings to coordinate activities and resolve problems with the subcontractors were expensive and required greater time to allow for travel, since the MD-11 participants were widely distributed geographically. While most Douglas workers were located within several miles of each other in Long Beach, California, everyone else was dispersed. Honeywell is in Phoenix, Arizona, Pratt & Whitney and General Electric are on the East Coast, and the many other subcontractors and vendors were located throughout the United States and even the world. To facilitate communication, the key subcontractors had on-site representatives at Douglas facilities, and Douglas personnel spent a large amount of time at the major subcontractor plants.

Douglas is a big company in a large corporation, and it had its share of bureaucratic procedures and approval chains with which to comply during MD-11 development, as with most other systems contractors. Furthermore, Douglas's configuration change control activities were not structured for quick and efficient changes. Despite these difficulties, Douglas did have the flexibility to tailor business relationships without significant government involvement, as is the case in government sponsored projects.

Workers followed the established procedures of Douglas Aircraft Company, and the top-level managers were given the responsibility and authority to carry out the development effort without micromanagement from the corporation. Not until the schedule slip and overrun started to materialize did corporate managers become more involved. This involvement was not all negative, since technical experts from outside Douglas were provided to assist in solving the problems causing the delay (Larson, 1995).

As for the numerous subcontractors and suppliers, they were managed traditionally. That is, Douglas maintained oversight through on-site visits and correspondence, and the subcontractors were given the flexibility to do what they needed to do without burdensome procedures to follow.

As one of the biggest producers of large commercial jet aircraft in the world, Douglas had a considerable amount of manufacturing expertise and experience inherent in its 4000 to 6000 person work force during the height of MD-11 development and production. At the beginning of the MD-11 effort, the company was solely a production house producing the MD-80 and DC-10, and it had not developed a new aircraft in years. Therefore, it did not possess a large pool of design engineering and development expertise (Larson, 1995). As a consequence, a large number of engineers were hired to conduct the program. Although the engineering design team was technically capable, they of course lacked the experience of working together.

Given that the amount of profit obtained from the MD-11 is due significantly to the number of aircraft sold, given that the number of sales is tied to how well the MD-11 operates in service and satisfies the customers, and given that the future Douglas aircraft will be judged partly on the reputation of the MD-11, the company had a lot of incentive to ensure the MD-11 performed to customer expectations. The basic warranty offered to all MD-11 customers was supposed to ensure this. In addition to workmanship and parts quality provisions, Douglas guaranteed payload/range performance that would enable certain non-stop, international flights. While performance was not attained by the initial MD-11s delivered, Douglas developed modifications and retrofit the delivered aircraft.

SUMMARY

The MD-11, intended as a low-risk redesign, turned out to be a complex systems integration effort. The development team failed to anticipate the integration challenges, and it was not structured to handle them efficiently. The nine month delivery delay of an original three year schedule and a 30% overrun are significant for a redesign that did not require breakthrough technology. Despite the problems with the development process, the eventual attainment of performance requirements, the potential for further improvements, and the number of orders ensuring program profitability to McDonnell Douglas suggest the MD-11 is a reasonably successful design. Tables 31-1 to 31-5 present our 35 figures of merit and the scores we assigned for the MD-11.

TABLE 31-1   MD-11 Performance Scores.

Figures of Merit	Range	Weight	Rating	Score
Technical performance—initial	0–10	1	3	3
Technical performance—mature	0–10	1	10	10
Cost performance	0–10	1	5	5
Schedule performance	0–10	1	4	4
Performance total				22

TABLE 31-2   MD-11 Systems Engineering Fundamentals Scores.

Figures of Merit	Range	Weight	Rating	Score
Requirements development	0–10	2	2	4
Incipient system design	0–10	2	5	10
Evaluating alternative concepts	0–10	1	6	6
Make-or-buy decision	0–10	1	8	8
Validation	0–10	1	6	6
Verification and integrated testing	0–10	1	7	7
Configuration management	0–10	1	4	4
Manufacturing considerations	0–10	1	6	6
System integration and technical management	0–10	1	5	5
Life-cycle considerations	0–10	1	7	7
Program management	0–10	1	3	3
Systems engineering fundamentals total				66

TABLE 31-3   MD-11 Development Environment Scores.

Figures of Merit	Range	Weight	Rating	Score
Emphasis on the customer	0–10	1	6	6
Stability of requirements and configuration	0–10	1	4	4
Funding and work-force-level stability	0–10	1	6	6
Strong support	0–10	1	6	6
Continuity of core development team	0–10	1	5	5
Stability of organizational structure	0–10	1	2	2
Cooperation among stakeholders	0–10	1	5	5
Effective communication	0–10	1	5	5
Flexibility and autonomy	0–10	1	6	6
Work force qualifications	0–10	1	5	5
Accountability for system performance	0–10	1	8	8
Development environment total				58

TABLE 31-4   MD-11 Design Difficulty Scores.

Metric	Range	Score
Design type	0–15	4
Knowledge complexity	0–10	5
Steps	0–10	9
Quality	0–10	6
Process design	0–5	4
Aggressive selling price	0–5	4
Design difficulty total	0–55	32

TABLE 31-5   MD-11 Resources Scores.

Elements	Range	Score
Cost	0–15	10
Time	0–10	6
Infrastructure	0–10	7
Resources total	0–35	23

REFERENCES

"Douglas Begins Building Long-Lead MD-11 Components." *Aviation Week & Space Technology*, pp. 50–51, April 6, 1987.

"Douglas New Systems Automation Policy to Ensure Minimal MD-11 Pilot Workload." *Aviation Week & Space Technology*, p. 20, June 4, 1990.

"Douglas Prepares Initial MD-11 for First Flight." *Aviation Week & Space Technology*, p. 19, October 23, 1989.

KUBEL, B., *MD-11 Flight Test.* Long Beach, CA: Douglas Aircraft Company Teleproductions, April 29, 1991. Video.

LARSON, M.N., Telephone interviews with Mark N. Larson, Business Unit Manager—Design Quality, McDonnell Douglas Long Beach. October 1994, November 10, 1994, and March 6, 1995.

LENOROVITZ, J.M., "Swissair Gives MD-11 Mixed Marks at Midpoint of Phase-in Effort." *Aviation Week & Space Technology*, pp. 36–38, September 30, 1991.

"MD-11 Avionics Suite Developed by Joint Venture." *Aviation Week & Space Technology*, pp. 45–46, October 22, 1990.

SMITH, B.A., "Douglas to Accelerate MD-11 Flight Test Program." *Aviation Week & Space Technology*, pp. 36–38, January 29, 1990.

Smith, B.A., "Engine Makers and Douglas Work to Improve MD-11 Range." *Aviation Week & Space Technology*, pp. 70–71, August 6, 1990.

SMITH, B.A., "McDonnell Douglas Launches MD-11 Flight Test Program." *Aviation Week & Space Technology*, pp. 62–63, January 15, 1990.

SCOTT, W.A., "MD-11 Flight Testing Progresses Toward End-of-Year Certification." *Aviation Week & Space Technology*, p. 19, June 4, 1990.

VELOCCI, A.L., and J.T. MCKENNA, "MD-11 Deliveries Crucial to Company's Finances." *Aviation Week & Space Technology*, p. 34, July 15, 1991.

32

COMPARISON OF THE AIRCRAFT CASE STUDIES

The Design Difficulty and Resources scores for the aircraft case studies are presented in Tables 32.1 and 32.2 and in Figure 32-1.

TABLE 32-1   Summary of Design Difficulty Scores.

Metric	777	F-117	B-2	C-17	Learjet	MD-11
Design type	9	13	13	9	3	4
Knowledge complexity	6	8	8	6	4	5
Steps	9	8	9	9	6	9
Quality	9	7	8	6	5	6
Process design	4	4	5	4	3	4
Aggressive selling price	4	1	1	2	4	4
Design difficulty total	41	41	44	36	25	32

TABLE 32-2   Summary of Resources Scores.

Metric	777	F-117	B-2	C-17	Learjet	MD-11
Cost	12	9	12	10	9	10
Time	7	7	8	8	5	6
Infrastructure	8	8	8	8	6	7
Resources total	27	24	28	26	20	23

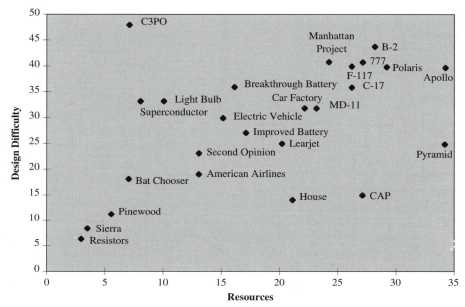

Figure 32-1   Design Difficult versus Resources for 26 case studies.

The Resources scores were similar for all the aircraft, as shown in Table 32-2. This is reasonable, in that all large and highly complex aircraft need most of the same types of components and subsystems and utilize much of the same supplier infrastructure.

The results of plotting Design Difficulty versus Resources, as was done in Chapter 23, are shown in Figure 32-1. This indicates that aircraft generally follow a linear relationship with regard to the two characteristics. For the most part, these six case studies fit into the expected regions of this plane. The Learjet and the MD-11 fall into the Consumer Products region and the three military aircraft fit into the Government region. However the Boeing 777 notably is out of the Consumer Products region. The Boeing 777 is probably the most ambitious commercial system ever designed.

The other metrics for the aircraft case study ratings are summarized in Tables 32.3 through 32.5. These scores were used to explore possible relationships between the characteristics of the system development process. Due to the limited number of data points, no strong conclusion can be made. However, there appears to be a positive relation between the *performance* scores and the *systems engineering fundamentals* scores for the aircraft development case studies. But before exploring this issue, let us discuss the cases in relation to one another.

The six case studies were presented in the order of the highest to lowest *systems engineering fundamentals* score, as indicated in Table 32-4. However, all six aircraft are successful, as indicated by the Technical Performance-Mature figure of merit in Table 32-3. Combining technical performance with the Cost and Schedule Performance figures of merit provides an effectiveness index of the overall system

TABLE 32-3   **Summary of Performance Scores.**

Metric	777	F-117	B-2	C-17	Learjet	MD-11
Technical performance—initial	8	8	8	3	9	3
Technical performance—mature	10	10	9	9	10	10
Cost performance	8	4	3	6	2	5
Schedule performance	10	4	4	5	4	4
Performance total	36	26	24	23	25	22

development process. The 777 development was the highest rated system, followed in order by the F-117, B-2, C-17, Learjet, and MD-11. Tables 32.4 and 32.5 clearly point out their main strengths and weaknesses in terms of the *systems engineering fundamentals* and *development environment*.

The Boeing 777's success is indicated by its on-time production and delivery of an aircraft meeting customer requirements. The 777 received the highest ratings of the six cases in *performance* (36) and *systems engineering fundamentals* (126), and second highest in *development environment* (96). Boeing effectively utilized the full range of systems engineering principles, tasks, and techniques. Boeing also created an environment that strongly supported the work and communication of the interdisciplinary design and build teams. The success is due specifically to thorough requirements generation, the close participation of the airline customers throughout the entire development, the advanced computer aided design and manufacturing system, and the longer planned full-scale engineering development (FSED) schedule that ensured development problems were worked out before the first customer delivery. The result was a development with no apparent areas of significant weakness.

TABLE 32-4   **Summary of Systems Engineering Fundamentals Scores.**

Figures of Merit	777	F-117	B-2	C-17	Learjet	MD-11
Requirements development	20	18	16	16	2	4
Incipient system design	18	18	16	14	14	10
Evaluating alternative concepts	10	10	10	8	6	6
Make-or-buy decision	10	10	9	9	8	8
Validation	9	9	9	8	5	6
Verification and integrated testing	10	8	10	8	8	7
Configuration management	10	9	7	3	7	4
Manufacturing considerations	9	6	9	6	5	6
System integration and technical management	10	10	7	4	7	5
Life-cycle considerations	10	6	10	8	7	7
Program management	10	9	7	3	6	3
Systems engineering fundamentals total	126	113	110	87	75	66

TABLE 32-5 Summary of Development Environment Scores.

Figures of Merit	777	F-117	B-2	C-17	Learjet	MD-11
Emphasis on the customer	10	9	9	7	6	6
Stability of requirements and configuration	8	7	3	2	3	4
Funding and work-force-level stability	9	10	9	2	8	6
Strong support	10	10	6	3	8	6
Continuity of core development team	9	10	8	2	10	5
Stability of organizational structure	9	9	9	1	9	2
Cooperation among stakeholders	9	9	9	3	8	5
Effective communication	9	8	7	4	5	5
Flexibility and autonomy	7	8	7	5	8	6
Work-force qualifications	8	9	8	5	8	5
Accountability for system performance	8	8	7	8	6	8
Development environment total	96	97	82	42	79	58

The next two aircraft, the F-117 and the B-2, are both revolutionary aircraft of high design difficulty that followed strong systems engineering practices to help develop the highly integrated designs. Both aircraft possessed strong technical performance from their introductions, and they have satisfied their Air Force customer. Schedule and cost performances, however, were not laudatory, especially for the B-2. The uncertainties surrounding the development of complex, breakthrough technologies certainly contributed to cost growth and delays, and the highly integrated nature of both designs generated many new issues to resolve. This is true despite the fact that both programs carried out extensive risk reduction activities prior to entering FSED. Furthermore, as classified military efforts, both were developed by highly skilled and motivated workers in highly stable environments that maintained strong funding and political support throughout most of their respective FSED phases. However, countering the favorable environment for the B-2 was a major requirements change from the Air Force early in FSED, resulting in a costly redesign and an extension in schedule. The momentum of the B-2 program was also affected by the Air Force's delay in starting FSED to accommodate the resurrected B-1 program. The F-117 did not experience a major change in customer requirements like the B-2, but its FSED schedule and budget were impacted by the crash of the first production aircraft due to an assembly error not detected during ground inspection and testing.

These aircraft were developed differently. While the smaller F-117 was designed and fabricated by a relatively small project team in accordance with the philosophy of the Lockheed Skunk Works, Northrop developed a new approach to develop the large B-2. Interestingly, most of Northrop's approach was later adopted by Boeing, a B-2 subcontractor, for its development of the 777.

Northrop and Boeing both created a digital "paperless" database, set up extensive in-house integration testing laboratories, utilized an avionics testbed using other aircraft, and planned for extensive flight testing beyond what was required for certification. One major difference was the way the efforts were organized. Northrop had a functionally oriented team that used an informal zone management structure to deal with interdisciplinary and interface issues, whereas Boeing developed formal integrated product development teams. Furthermore, Boeing's computer aided design and manufacturing system was also more advanced. It was able to perform virtual prototyping, thereby identifying interface problems on the computer. Therefore, Boeing essentially refined and successfully implemented the development approach that Northrop had pioneered. The B-2 and 777 case studies are significant in that they indicate the direction to which all aircraft development is moving to deal with increasing degrees of aircraft complexity and integration.

Of comparable design difficulty to the 777 was the C-17 military transport. However, its *performance* score of 23 is significantly lower. The initial technical performance was not acceptable, and cost and schedule performances were marginal. While the early requirements development and design work with the Air Force were commendable, actions by Douglas throughout FSED, as well as imposed conditions, resulted in great difficulties. Perhaps as its first mistake, Douglas contributed to its many eventual problems by accepting more stringent performance requirements than what the customer had originally requested.

Many of the *performance* shortfalls, however, were due to poor management on the contractor's part. Douglas's configuration and production management systems were inadequate, and its program management function was ineffective. These problems enhanced, as well as were enhanced by, a very volatile environment; much of it was defined by numerous design changes, high rates of repair and rework, a massive Total Quality Management System (TQMS) reorganization, opposition from Congress, acrimonious relations with the customer, and continuous turnover of the work force. Further contributing to some of the instability was the long, drawn-out schedule with a delayed FSED start. The C-17 development evidences many of the same problems as the MD-11, which was developed in the commercial sector by the same contractor during the same time.

The Learjet Model 60 was rated with a high technical performance score. However, as most of the other aircraft presented, the overall *performance* score was tempered somewhat by low Schedule and Cost Performance scores. For the relatively uncomplicated redesign effort, which was made by a small development team that carried out many of the fundamental systems engineering practices to a reasonable degree, this is unfortunate. Learjet's major shortcoming with the Learjet Model 60 effort was poor requirements development stemming from the lack of communication and coordination between the sales department and the engineering group. This situation resulted in a redirection after the initial design had been completed. Except for the changing requirements and internal communication problems, the small team development environment was quite conducive to systems engineering activities.

Like the Learjet Model 60, the MD-11 was a stretched version of an existing airframe with improved integrated avionics, engines, and aerodynamics. Also like the Model 60, one of the MD-11's biggest problems dealt with requirements development. The failure to develop a single, distinct specification for the MD-11 before FSED, and the attendant underestimation of the incipient system design effort, helped lead to the unanticipated systems and interface problems. Such problems were exacerbated by marginally effective mechanisms for configuration and production management, as well as a development environment not highly supportive of strong systems engineering activities. The situation worsened during the poorly executed McDonnell Douglas TQMS reorganization, thereby greatly impacting progress on the MD-11 effort towards the end of FSED. Consequently, the *performance* score reflects only a moderate overall success, having been downgraded by the schedule delays, cost growth, and problems with initially delivered aircraft.

The picture that emerges most prominently from the aircraft case studies is that poor requirements development, inadequate configuration management, and weak program and technical management appear to be the primary determinants of lower *systems engineering fundamentals* scores. Significant *development environment* instability is reflected in the scores of several of the cases as well, primarily in the categories of Stability of Requirements and Configuration, Funding and Workforce-Level Stability, Strong Support of Program, Continuity of Core Team Members, Stability of Organizational Structure, and Cooperation among Stakeholders.

Comparing the *systems engineering fundamentals* scores for the cases, the military programs appear to tend towards higher scores. This is probably due to the fact that the government usually mandates a high degree of systems engineering on its large system development efforts. However, a commercial program received the highest *systems engineering fundamentals* score.

An important question to consider now is whether or not the case study ratings suggest anything about a possible relationship between *systems engineering fundamentals* and *performance*. Figure 32-2 is a plot of the *performance* scores versus the *systems engineering fundamentals* scores. The plot illustrates a generally positive relationship between the two characteristics. If the scoring methodology is valid, then this would indicate that better systems engineering produces better performance.

The commercial aircraft and the military aircraft appear to lie on two separate lines. The 777, Learjet Model 60, and MD-11 fall on one line, while the three military aircraft fall on another. The F-117 and the B-2 were breakthrough designs and therefore had higher technical risk. Perhaps Design Difficulty could be used to generate a multiplier to adjust the *performance* scores and move the military aircraft closer to the commercial aircraft trend line. The C-17 is also below the trend line, but its Design Difficulty is not as high as the stealth aircraft. However, the deviation may be attributed to the program's volatile environment as reflected by its low *development environment* score. This again suggests that a multiplier, based on *development environment* scores, might be used to bring all six systems onto the same line.

However, the differences might simply be caused by inherent differences between government and commercial ways of doing business. Perhaps a single factor multiplier can be developed based simply on whether or not the development was a government effort. Since all three military efforts had marginal cost and schedule performance, this suggests that the development process for government aircraft is

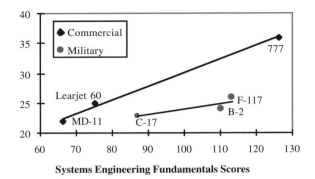

Figure 32-2   Performance Scores versus Systems Engineering Fundamentals.

inherently more prone to cost and schedule difficulties. By multiplying the government aircraft figures of merit scores by a factor of two, the resulting performance numbers bring the commercial and military aircraft data much closer together.

Whether such a factor or other potential factors mentioned is valid, is mere speculation without further data to analyze. Therefore, the impact of *design difficulty*, *development environment*, and government procedures in the system development process is an area requiring further study.

Figure 32-3 shows cost overrun as a function of the systems engineering effort for some space projects. We think these data were compiled by Werner Gruhl at NASA Headquarters in the early 1990s. We do not know what the acronyms mean, but we think these were all NASA projects. These data suggest that systems engineering helps minimize cost overruns. Almost all of these projects had cost overruns, which suggests that the U.S. government has traditionally been less concerned with cost overruns than commercial industry.

While much effort went into the development of our rating methodology, it is conceded that improvements can be made. Some ideas that may enhance the process are provided as follows.

The figures of merit for *systems engineering fundamentals* can be considered reasonably complete based on the existing systems engineering literature. However, they may be broken out in different combinations than what was presented. As for the *development environment* figures of merit, they could be refined in some instances to be more precise and measurable. Perhaps the most important issue that needs further attention is the relative weighting between the figures of merit within the system development characteristics. It may be appropriate to make modifications if justification can be found. Review of the characteristics, figures of merit, rating criteria, and scoring system by others in the fields of systems engineering, engineering management, organizational effectiveness, and decision analysis would be helpful in making improvements.

In addition to investigating possible refinements to the methodology, additional case studies are required to provide data to support or refute the methodology

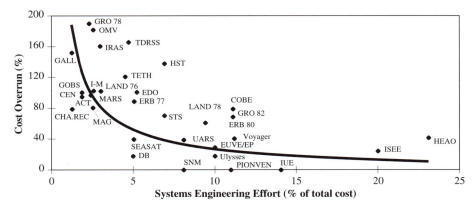

Figure 32-3   Cost overrun as a function of systems engineering effort.

presented and the assertions made earlier. Additional data points are needed to provide a statistically significant database to allow a more rigorous analysis to be conducted to test whether or not the results presented above represent more than coincidence. Furthermore, cases are needed from areas other than aircraft systems, to determine if the suggested positive relationship between *systems engineering fundamentals* and *performance* hold up for all categories of systems, from complex consumer electronics to large construction projects. Also, any further investigation should attempt to determine how design difficulty and the level of resources relate to the outcomes of the overall system development process. Additional work will help determine if the proposed methodology provides for a valid "apples-to-apples" comparison between widely different categories of systems.

VALIDATION OF METHODOLOGY

The case study evaluation and scoring methodology presented here was subjected to a validation trial. Ten engineers in Systems Engineering at the University of Arizona read the aircraft case studies and rated them according to the methodology. The scores were compiled for each metric, and for each case study; and the range, average, and standard deviation of each were used in comparing them.

The mean and variability of the engineers' scores were calculated as a way of assessing how clearly the cases were written and how well the metrics were defined. If the scores for a particular metric had a large variation for all the case studies, then that metric must have been poorly written. If the scores for a metric for a particular case had a large variation, then the portion of that case study that dealt with that metric needed to be rewritten. Of all the metrics, the Make-or-Buy Decision had the largest Standard Deviation of 1.8. Therefore we reformulated this metric as presented in Chapter 25.

33

OTHER METRICS

Lots of other metrics have been used. One that readily comes to mind is the Percent Co-Location of Team Members. It would be nice if all members of the Integrated Product Development Team (IPDT) had their offices in the same place. A distance of even 50 feet reduces interaction. Fragmentation of the IPDT often occurs because people are located according to their departments (e.g., Electrical Engineering or Test Engineering), whereas they do work according to the projects they are assigned.

Another useful metric is Simplicity of the Processes. The business and engineering processes should be well known, documented, repeated, and standardized. But it might be hard to collect data for this metric. The point being that it is easy to conjure up metrics, but they may or may not be useful. Recently many groups have started to study metrics. The purpose was to find out what metrics are being used and what makes a metric useful.

THE INCOSE METRICS WORKING GROUP

The International Council on Systems Engineering (INCOSE) has a working group that collects and evaluates systems engineering metrics that are being used in industry. Their *Metrics Guidebook for Integrated System and Product Development* can be ordered through the INCOSE world wide web home page (http://www.incose.org). In their *Metrics-In-Use Catalog*, they divided their metrics into the categories of Process, Progress, and Product.

In the *Process* Category they list: Knowledge Area Representation, Preparation Effort, Process Compliance, Review Rate, Systems Engineering Process Compliance, Systems Engineering Staffing Levels, Specification Errors, Specification

Productivity, Systems Engineering Staff Size, Systems Engineering Training, Systems Engineering Requirements Productivity, and others.

In the *Progress* Category they list: Cost versus Schedule Performance, Cost, Document Status, Interval, Normalized Cost Variance, Normalized Schedule Variance, Requirements Allocation Mastered, Requirements Analysis, Requirements Noncompliance, Requirements Processing Status, Requirements Stability, Requirements Validated, Requirements Volatility, Software Informal Test, Specification Accuracy, Specification Completeness, Spec-to-Spec Disconnect Resolution, Test Progress, Verification Requirements Closeout, and others.

And finally in the *Product* Category they list: Productivity and Quality (Defect Density).

To provide a flavor for these metrics, we will now present two of them.

Metric Name: Systems Engineer Training.
Purpose: Measure fraction of systems engineers trained and proficient in CASE tools.
Definition: Some fraction of systems engineers should be trained and proficient in CASE tools such as RDD, DOORS, etc., and should have access to the hardware and software.
Potential Usage: Assess tool use in Systems Engineering Department.
Collection Method: Quarterly assess the percentage of systems engineers who have proficiency in using CASE tools.

Metric Name: Requirements Stability.
Purpose: Provides insight into the stability of the program in relation to the requirements churn.
Definition: At specific collection increments, compute the ratio of the number of changes in the requirements to the number of requirements in the baseline. This is done throughout the program life cycle.
Potential Usage: Determine if different resources are needed: gives insight into cost, schedule, risk, and mitigation planning.

THE SAN FRANCISCO BAY INCOSE CHAPTER

The *National Council on Systems Engineering (INCOSE) Metrics Guidebook for Integrated Systems and Product Development* (1995) says that a good metric promotes understanding of progress, as well as processes, and helps improve the way we do business. They say the following are basic characteristics of a good metric:

1. It is meaningful to the customer.
2. It relates to organizational goals.
3. It is simple, understandable, logical, and repeatable.
4. It shows status over a period of time.

5. Its data are economical to collect.
6. It provides insight that drives action.

They go on to say that a metric package has three elements: the definition, the measurement process, and the metric presentation. The definition explains who, what, when, where, why, and how. It should contain:

1. an unambiguous description of the metric,
2. frequency of measurement,
3. source of data,
4. equations used in the metric,
5. definition of key terms,
6. description of the graphic that will be used to display the data,
7. the owner of the metric,
8. the owner of the process being measured,
9. the desired behavior of the measurements, and
10. the link between the process being measured and the organization's goals.

The second element, the measurement process, is the actual process of measuring and recording data. It translates data from the process being measured into meaningful information that will be used to improve the process.

The third element, the metric presentation, transforms the collected information into a summary, which is usually graphical, for presentation to a person.

We will now present an example of their Manufacturing Metrics Tree.
Primary management goal: Create Total Quality Management (TQM) teams to help make improvements in business practices.
Sub-Goal #1: Upgrade the parts ordering process.
Question: How many parts are ordered and when are they received?
Metric: Material Control Status Metric.
Measures:

1. Number of parts projected,
2. Number of parts ordered,
3. Number of parts received., etc.

We will also present their Material Control Status Metric.
Definition:

1. Total number of parts projected to be ordered for the project.
2. Number of parts ordered.
3. Number of parts received.

Analysis:

This metric shows a simple baseline for ordering parts. The number of parts projected to be ordered are determined from preproposal, proposal, and early life activities. After the contract is awarded, manufacturing starts ordering the parts. Times depend on the schedule and the need. This chart can be used to analyze and improve the process.

1. If the parts received fall behind those ordered, you should look at vendor response, vendor supply, your in-house ordering process, internal receiving, etc.
2. If the projected number of parts falls above or below the actual parts needed, you should look for poor requirements definition, frequent design changes, etc.

Finally, this metric concludes showing a graph of the total number of parts projected to be ordered for the project, the number of parts ordered, and the number of parts received as functions of time mapped on the project schedule.

The 1996 INCOSE Symposium had two sessions on metrics. The papers for these sessions (pages 987 to 1041 of the proceedings) list hundreds of metrics and discuss their strong and weak points. Two of the metrics presented by Goldense are presented here: Percent of Sales Due to New Products and Product Selection Success.

Percent of Sales Due to New Products. In the 1980s, competitive companies had around 30% of their sales due to products released in the last three years. In the 1990s, competitive companies had around 50% of their sales due to products released in the last two years.

Product Selection Success. Product Selection Success is the percent of products released that met their targeted profitability and performance goals after X period of time. For toy manufacturers the time period is less than a year, whereas for automobile manufacturers, the time period is many years. This is one of the most important metrics for modern manufacturers.

Metrics Used at AT&T Martin (1997) says there are three reasons for using metrics. First, you must be able to measure a process in order to improve it. Second, metrics provide data for planning and scheduling. Third, metrics provide data to compare projects, divisions, and companies. He lists the following types of metrics: Customer Satisfaction, Performance, Productivity, Cost, Time Interval, Process Maturity, Process Compliance, Process Improvement, and Product Maturity.

This chapter shows that metrics is a hot topic in the Systems Engineering field. It also shows that the topic is volatile and will change a lot in the next few years.

TECHNICAL PERFORMANCE MEASURES

A term closely related to, and often used interchangeably with, metrics is techni-cal performance measures (TPMs). They are used to mitigate risk. TPMs are mea-surements that are made during the design and manufacturing process to evaluate the likelihood of satisfying the system requirements. Because of their high cost, not all requirements have TPMs, just the most important ones. In the beginning of the design and manufacturing process, the prototypes will not meet the TPM goals. Therefore the TPM values are only required to be within a tolerance band. It is hoped that as the design and manufacturing process progresses, the TPM val-ues of the prototypes and preproduction units will come closer and closer to the goals.

As an example, let us consider the design and manufacture of solar ovens (Funk & Larson, 1994). In many societies, particularly in Africa, many women spend as much as 50% of their time acquiring wood for their cooking fires. To ame-liorate this sink of human resources, people have been designing and building solar ovens. Let us now examine the solar oven design and manufacturing process that we followed in a Freshman Engineering class at the University of Arizona.

First, we defined a TPM for our design and manufacturing process. When a loaf of bread is finished baking, its internal temperature should be 95° C (203° F). To reach this internal temperature, commercial bakeries bake the loaf at 230° C (446° F). As initial values for our oven temperature TPM, we chose a lower limit of 100° C, a goal of 230° C, and an upper limit of 270° C. The tolerance band shrinks with time as shown in Figure 33-1.

In the beginning of the design and manufacturing process, our day-by-day measurements of this metric increased because of finding better insulators, finding better glazing materials (e.g., glass and mylar), sealing the box better, aiming at the sun better, etc.

At the time labeled "Design Change-1," there was a jump in performance caused by adding a second layer of glazing to the window in the top of the oven. This was followed by another period of gradual improvement, as we learned to stabilize the two pieces of glazing material.

At the time labeled "Design Change-2," there was another jump in perfor-mance caused by a design change that incorporated reflectors to reflect more sunlight onto the window in the oven top. This was followed by another period of gradual im-provement, as we found better shapes and positions for the reflectors.

But, in this case, it seemed that we might not attain our goal. Therefore we reevaluated the process and the requirements. Bread baking is a complex biochemi-cal process that has been studied extensively: Millions of loaves have been baked each day for the last four thousand years. These experiments have revealed the fol-lowing consequences of insufficient oven temperature:

1. Enzymes are not deactivated soon enough, and excessive gas expansion causes coarse grain and harsh texture.

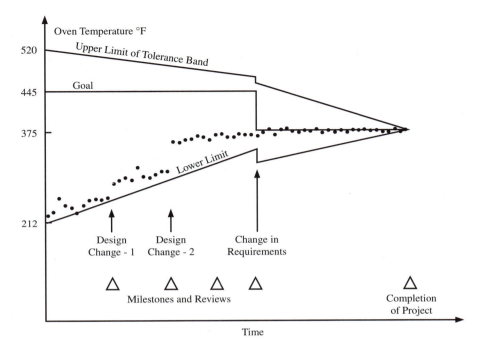

Figure 33-1   A technical performance measure.

2. The crust is too thick, because of drying caused by the longer duration of baking.
3. The bread becomes dry, because prolonged baking causes evaporation of moisture and volatile substances.
4. Low temperatures cannot produce carmelization, and crust color lacks an appealing bloom.

After consulting some bakers, our managers decided that 190° C (374° F) would be sufficient to avoid the above problems. Therefore, the requirements were changed at the indicated spot and our ovens were able to meet this TPM goal. Of course this change in requirements forced a review of *all* other requirements and a change in many other facets of the design. For example, the baking duration versus weight tables had to be recomputed.

If sugar, eggs, butter, and milk were added to the dough, we could get away with temperatures as low as 175° C (347° F). But we decided to design our ovens to match the needs of our customers, rather than try to change our customers to match our ovens.

Metrics are useful for designing systems. Thousands of metrics are available. Each company will have to select the metrics that are most appropriate for each project.

REFERENCES

FUNK, P.A., and D.L. LARSON, *Design features influencing thermal performance of solar box cookers*. Paper presented at the International Winter Meeting, No. 94-6546, American Society of Agricultural Engineers, 1994.

MARTIN, J., (Ed.), *Systems Engineering Process,* AT&T ATS Engineering Standard Process, 1994.

MARTIN, J.N., *Systems Engineering Guidebook: A Process for Developing Systems and Products*. Boca Raton, FL, CRC Press, 1997.

Metrics Guidebook for Integrated System and Product Development, INCOSE, 1996.

Metrics-In-Use Catalog, INCOSE Metrics Working Group, July 1995.

NCOSE Metrics Guidebook for Integrated Systems and Product Development, prepared by the SFBAC NCOSE Metrics Interest Group, 1995.

Systems Engineering Practices & Tools. Proceedings of the Sixth Annual International Symposium of the International Council on Systems Engineering, Volume 1, Boston, Massachusetts, July 7–11, 1996.

The INCOSE world wide web site: http://www.incose.org

34

GENERAL COMMENTS

Students in a graduate level systems engineering course at the University of Arizona studied the cases in this book and made the following remarks.

An important area that was not stressed in this book is project risk. To assess project risk, we would have to assess the value of the resources that go into the project, the potential value of the project result, and the probability of project failure. One of the chief benefits of using systems engineering is to reduce project risk. Therefore, we would expect formal systems engineering procedures to be used on high-risk projects, but not on low-risk projects.

Projects like Learjet, which did not completely determine their requirements early in the process, often found that unknown system performance requirements can cause large setbacks in the engineering design effort, and much of the work already performed may become useless. Time and resources are wasted developing products that do not match the desires of the customer.

Small projects and those that were simple redesign used less formal systems engineering. However it is important to consider system requirements, interfaces, and the make-or-buy decision, etc., even for redesign. Redesign presupposes that this design effort was previously performed properly. However, design flaws in the historical design are likely to be carried over into the new design without the engineering design team recognizing that these problems exist.

The system engineering process is NP-complete. With a seemingly infinite number of ways to perform any task, it is impossible to guarantee that any design is optimal—rather, the systems engineering team has to acknowledge that they have not, nor ever will, create the best design to meet the given set of requirements. But it is this fact that allows room for breakthrough discoveries like the superconductor and Edison's light bulb. There is always something that has not been tried yet that, when discovered, will launch the design into an entirely new realm.

Company policy and environment can affect the outcome of a project negatively, as shown by the MD-11, or positively, as with the Apollo project and the SIERRA.

Systems Engineering is more of an art than a science. In a perfect world, all designs would be like the Resistor Networks, where there was essentially one objective. Reaching that objective may or may not be possible, but it is easy to know when you have reached it. However, projects do not have to get much more complicated before designers have to start thinking about multiple, conflicting objectives, vague or incomplete requirements, and limited resources.

Every project can benefit from a systems engineering approach. The case studies where good systems engineering processes were used, seemed to make the stakeholders happier than similar cases where poor systems engineering was performed. The mantras of systems engineering "requirements development," "alternative concept evaluations," "validation," "verification," and "system test," are all necessary components for increasing the likelihood of a successful design.

The purpose of Systems Engineering is to increase a system's probability of success and reduce its risk of failure. But in times of downsizing, Systems Engineering is often one of the first activities to be cut, because it seems like overhead and its value is not obvious. However Figure 32-3 shows that spending money on Systems Engineering greatly decreases the risk of cost overruns. Figure 32-2 shows that better Systems Engineering produces better performing systems. We believe that it also reduces the risk of schedule delays. Therefore, it seems that investing in Systems Engineering produces better systems.

INDEX

A

Activities documentation
  systems engineers and, 130
Aggressive goals
  selling price and, 2, 3, 5
Aircraft case studies
  Boeing 777, 8, 37–40, 148–159
  comparison of, 230–237
  cost overrun, 237
  design difficulty scores, 230
  design difficulty vs. resources, 231
  development environment scores, 233
  Learjet Model 60 Business Jet, 206–214
  Lockheed F–117 Stealth Fighter, 160–171
  McDonnell Douglas C–17 Military
    Transport, 187–205
  McDonnell Douglas MD–11
    Commercial Airplane, 215–229
  methodology validation, 237
  Northrop B–2 Stealth Bomber, 172–186
  performance scores, 232
  performance scores vs. systems
    engineering fundamentals, 236
  resource scores, 230
  systems engineering effort, 237

  systems engineering fundamentals
    scores, 232, 236
Algorithms
  branch and bound, 109
  integer programming, 109
  NP–complete, 104–106, 109
  polynomial, 109
  system design process and, 106–113.
    See also System design process
  tree search, 108
Alternative concepts evaluation
  systems engineering fundamentals
    and, 139
Alternative designs
  systems engineers and, 126
American Airlines scheduling, 8, 27–29
  computer scheduling results, 28
  critical path invention and, 102
  design difficulty scores, 96
  design life scores, 103
  design strategy used, 118
  design type rating, 115, 116
  formal systems engineering and, 98
  recyclability design, 104
  resource scores, 97
  risk mitigation and, 99
  Supercollider effect on, 100

Analyses
  reliability, 129
  sensitivity, 126
  system, 128
Apollo moon landing, 8, 41–46
  concept selection and, 42
  critical path invention and, 102
  design difficulty scores, 96
  design life scores, 103
  design strategy used, 118
  development of rockets for space
    program, 43
  flight tests for space program rockets, 44
  formal systems engineering and, 98
  recyclability design, 104
  resource scores, 97
  risk mitigation and, 99
  Supercollider effect on, 100
Automobile factory, 9, 56–59
  critical path invention and, 102
  design difficulty scores, 96
  design life scores, 103
  design strategy used, 118
  design type rating, 115, 116
  development time for various producers,
    56–57
  formal systems engineering and, 98
  hours for various producers, 57
  recyclability design, 104
  resource scores, 97
  risk mitigation and, 99
  Supercollider effect on, 100
  team approach and, 58

B

Baldridge Award criteria
  product quality and, 4
Bat Chooser, 8, 16–18
  critical path invention and, 102
  design difficulty scores, 96
  design life scores, 103
  design strategy used, 118
  design type rating, 115, 116
  formal systems engineering and, 98

  recyclability design, 104
  resource scores, 97
  risk mitigation and, 99
  Supercollider effect on, 100
  systems engineering mistakes, 17
Batteries for electric vehicles, 9, 63–67
  critical path invention and, 102
  design difficulty scores, 96
  design life scores, 103
  design strategy used, 118
  emissions data vs. gas–powered engine,
    63, 64
  existing technology comparison, 65
  formal systems engineering and, 98
  goals for advanced batteries, 64
  recyclability design, 104
  resource scores, 97
  risk mitigation and, 99
  Supercollider effect on, 100
Boeing 777, 8, 37–40, 148–159
  critical path invention and, 102
  design difficulty scores, 96, 158
  design life scores, 103
  design strategy used, 118
  development environment, 154–156
  development environment scores, 157
  development history, design, and
    performance, 149–151
  formal systems engineering and, 98
  performance scores, 157
  recyclability design, 104
  resource scores, 97, 158
  risk mitigation and, 99
  767 design and build schedule vs., 39
  summary, 156–158
  Supercollider effect on, 100
  systems engineering fundamentals,
    151–154
  systems engineering fundamentals
    scores, 157
Branch and bound algorithms
  system design process and, 109
Breakthrough design model
  superconductors and, 30
  system design process and, 106
Building a house, 8, 47–49
  critical path invention and, 102
  design difficulty scores, 96

design life scores, 103
design strategy used, 118
design type rating, 115
formal systems engineering and, 98
recyclability design, 104
resource scores, 97
risk mitigation and, 99
Supercollider effect on, 100
systems engineering mistakes, 49
Bulb
  incandescent light, 8, 33–36. *See also*
    Incandescent light bulb

C

Cars. *See also* Automobile factory
  batteries for electric, 63–67
  electric, 60–62
Case studies. *See also* Aircraft case studies;
    individual case studies
  aircraft comparisons, 230–237
  American Airlines scheduling, 8, 27–29
  Apollo moon landing, 8, 41–46
  approach to, 2
  automobile factory, 9, 56–59
  Bat Chooser, 8, 16–18
  batteries for electric vehicles, 9, 63–67
  Boeing 777, 8, 37–40, 148–159
  building a house, 8, 47–49
  Central Arizona Project, 8, 50–52
  consumer products region, 1–2
  C3PO, 9, 68–69
  design difficulty scores, 95, 96
  design difficulty vs. resources, 1–2
  electric vehicles, 9, 60–62
  Great Pyramid at Giza, 8, 53–55
  Hubble Space Telescope, 9, 87–94
  incandescent light bulb, 8, 33–36
  Learjet Model 60 Business Jet, 206–214
  lessons learned from, 95–121
  Lockheed F–117 Stealth Fighter,
    160–171
  Manhattan Project, 9, 71–80
  McDonnell Douglas C–17 Military
    Transport, 187–205

McDonnell Douglas MD–11
    Commercial Airplane, 215–229
  metrics summary tables and, 95–104.
    See also Metrics summary tables
  moon landing region, 1–2
  Northrop B–2 Stealth Bomber,
    172–186
  Pinewood Derby, 8, 19–23
  Polaris Program, 9, 81–86
  regions of, 1–2
  resistor networks, 7, 10–12
  resource scores for, 95, 97
  score validation, 95–96
  Second Opinion, 8, 24–26
  seven wonders of the ancient world
    region, 1–2
  SIERRA train controllers, 8, 13–15
  star wars region, 1–2, 68–69
  superconductors, 8, 30–32
  system design process and, 104–119.
    See also System design process
  Velcro, 9, 70
Central Arizona Project, 8, 50–52
  critical path invention and, 102
  design difficulty scores, 96
  design life scores, 103
  design strategy used, 118
  formal systems engineering and, 98
  geographic information system and, 50
  recyclability design, 104
  resource scores, 97
  risk mitigation and, 99
  Supercollider effect on, 100
  systems engineering mistakes, 51
Childhood Stuttering: A Second Opinion,
    8, 24–26. *See also* Second Opinion
Columbia University
  Manhattan Project and, 74
Competition
  Boeing 777 and, 8, 37–40
Components to complete a design
  design difficulty scores and, 2, 3–4
Configuration management
  systems engineering fundamentals
    and, 141
  systems engineers and, 129
Consumer products
  design process and, 1–2

Continuous improvement design model
  system design process and, 105
Cost
  resources scores and, 6
Cost overrun
  aircraft case studies, 237
Cost performance, 137
C3PO, 9, 68–69
  critical path invention and, 102
  design difficulty scores, 96
  design life scores, 103
  design strategy used, 118
  formal systems engineering and, 98
  recyclability design, 104
  resource scores, 97
  risk mitigation and, 99
  Supercollider effect on, 100
Critical path invention
  case studies and, 102
  metrics, 101–102
Customers
  development environment and, 143
  product quality feedback and, 4
  systems engineers and, 123–124

D

Decision support system
  Second Opinion and, 24
Deming's 14 points
  product quality and, 4
Design compliance
  verification of, 140
Design continuum
  system design process and, 105
Design difficulty, 1–9. *See also* Case
      studies; Resources
  aggressive goals for selling price, 2, 3, 5
  Baldridge Award criteria and, 4
  case study approach, 2
  case study regions, 1
  components score, 2, 3–4
  customer feedback and, 4
  Deming's 14 points, 4
  design type score, 2, 3

ISO–9000 and, 4
  knowledge complexity score, 2, 3
  process design, 2, 3, 4–5
  quality circles and, 4
  Quality Function Deployment and, 4
  quality product score and, 2, 3, 4
  resources vs., 1–2, 101, 231
  scoring for, 3
  Six Sigma and, 4
  steps score, 2, 3–4
  Taguchi methods and, 4
  total quality management and, 4
  Zero Defects and, 4
Design difficulty and resource scores
  American Airlines scheduling, 29
  Apollo moon landing, 45
  automobile factory, 58
  Bat Chooser, 17–18
  batteries for electric vehicles, 66–67
  Boeing 777, 39
  building a house, 49
  Central Arizona Project, 51
  C3PO, 69
  electric vehicles, 62
  Great Pyramid at Giza, 55
  Hubble Space Telescope, 93
  incandescent light bulb, 36
  Manhattan Project, 80
  Pinewood Derby, 23
  Polaris Program, 86
  resistor networks design, 12
  Second Opinion, 26
  SIERRA train controllers, 14–15
  superconductors, 32
  Velcro, 70
Design difficulty scores
  aircraft case studies, 230
  Boeing 777, 158
  case studies and, 96
  Learjet Model 60 Business Jet, 214
  Lockheed F–117 Stealth
      Fighter, 170
  McDonnell Douglas C–17 Military
      Transport, 203
  McDonnell Douglas MD–11
      Commercial Airplane, 229
  metrics summary tables, 95, 96
  Northrop B–2 Stealth Bomber, 185

Design evaluation
  system design process, 113–118
Design life metric, 102–103
Design life scores
  case studies and, 103
Design metrics
  usefulness of, 96–101
Design process, 104–119. *See also* System
    design process
  strategies used, 117–118
Design reviews
  systems engineers and, 128
Design system, 128
Design type
  design difficulty scores and, 2, 3
Design type rating
  case studies and, 115
Development environment
  autonomy, 146
  Boeing 777, 154–156
  core development team continuity,
    144–145
  Customer emphasis, 143
  effective communication, 145
  flexibility, 146
  funding, 144
  Learjet Model 60 Business Jet,
    211–212
  Lockheed F–117 Stealth Fighter,
    166–169
  McDonnell Douglas C–17 Military
    Transport, 198–202
  McDonnell Douglas MD–11
    Commercial Airplane, 224–227
  metrics for, 143–147
  Northrop B–2 Stealth Bomber,
    181–183
  organizational structure stability, 145
  performance and, 134, 136–138
  scores of components, 147
  stability of requirements and
    configuration, 143–144
  stakeholders cooperation, 145
  strong support, 144
  system performance accountability, 146
  workforce and, 144, 146
Development environment scores
  aircraft case studies, 233

Boeing 777, 157
Learjet Model 60 Business Jet, 213
Lockheed F–117 Stealth Fighter, 170
McDonnell Douglas C–17 Military
    Transport, 203
McDonnell Douglas MD–11
    Commercial Airplane, 228
Northrop B–2 Stealth Bomber, 185
Documentation of activities
  systems engineers and, 130
Droid design
  C3PO and, 68–69

E

Edison, Thomas Alva
  incandescent light bulb and, 33–36
Electric vehicle
  design type rating, 115, 117
Electric vehicles, 9, 60–62
  batteries for, 63–67
  critical path invention and, 102
  design difficulty scores, 96
  design life scores, 103
  design strategy used, 118
  formal systems engineering and, 98
  recyclability design, 104
  resource scores, 97
  risk mitigation and, 99
  Supercollider effect on, 100
Engineering
  systems, 122–131. *See also* Systems
    engineering
Engineering fundamentals
  Boeing 777, 151–154
  Lockheed F–117 Stealth Fighter,
    164–166
Engineering Notebook, 130
Engineering systems scores
  Boeing 777, 157–158
  Lockheed F–117 Stealth Fighter,
    169–170
European car design approach
  Japanese vs., 56–59
Evaluating the designs, 113–118

F

Figures of merit
  systems engineers and, 125
Fleet Ballistic Missile program, 81–86.
  See also Polaris Program
Formal systems engineering
  case studies and, 98
Functional decomposition
  systems engineers and, 126–127
Funding
  development environment and, 144

G

General Motors
  electric vehicles and, 60–62
Geographic information system
  Central Arizona Project and, 50
Great Pyramid at Giza, 8, 53–55
  critical path invention and, 102
  design difficulty scores, 96
  design life scores, 103
  design strategy used, 118
  formal systems engineering and, 98
  recyclability design, 104
  resource scores, 97
  risk mitigation and, 99
  Supercollider effect on, 100

H

Hardware controllers
  SIERRA train, 8, 13–15
House construction. See Building a house
Hubble Space Telescope, 9, 87–94
  costs, 89
  critical path invention and, 102
  design difficulty scores, 96
  design life scores, 103
  design strategy used, 118

formal systems engineering and, 98
jitter, 93
life–cycle, 91
primary mirror, 91–92
recyclability design, 104
requirements, 89–91
resource scores, 97
risk mitigation and, 99
science instrument specifications, 90
Supercollider effect on, 100
system description, 88–89
systems engineering mistakes, 93
total life cycle cost, 89

I

Incandescent light bulb, 8, 33–36
  critical path invention and, 102
  design difficulty scores, 96
  design life scores, 103
  design strategy used, 118
  formal systems engineering and, 98
  recyclability design, 104
  resource scores, 97
  risk mitigation and, 99
  Supercollider effect on, 100
Incipient system design
  systems engineering fundamentals and,
    138–139
INCOSE metrics working group, 238–239
Infrastructure
  resource scores and, 6, 7
Integer programming
  system design process and, 109
Integrated Product Development Team
  metrics and, 238
Integrated testing
  systems engineering fundamentals
    and, 140
Integration system, 129
Interfaces
  systems engineers and, 128
Invention of the critical path metrics,
    101–102
ISO–9000
  product quality and, 4

J

Japanese car design approach
American/European vs., 56–59

K

Knowledge complexity
design difficulty scores and, 2, 3

L

Learjet Model 60 Business Jet, 206–214
design difficulty scores, 214
development environment, 211–212
development environment scores, 213
development history, design, and
performance, 207–209
performance scores, 213
resource scores, 214
summary, 212–214
systems engineering fundamentals,
209–211
systems engineering fundamentals
scores, 213
Lessons learned
case studies and, 95–121
metrics summary tables and, 95–104
system design process and, 104–119
Life–cycle
systems engineering and, 123
systems engineering fundamentals
and, 142
Light bulb
incandescent, 8, 33–36.
See also Incandescent light bulb
Lockheed F–117 Stealth Fighter,
160–171
design difficulty scores, 170
development environment, 166–169
development environment scores, 170

development history, design, and
performance, 161–164
performance scores, 169
resource scores, 170
summary, 169–170
systems engineering fundamentals,
164–166
systems engineering fundamentals
scores, 169
Los Alamos
Manhattan Project and, 76–77

M

Make–or–buy–decision
systems engineering fundamentals and,
139–140
Management. *See also* Systems engineering
configuration, 129, 141
program, 142
project, 130
risk, 129
technical, 141–142
total quality, 129
Manhattan Project, 9, 71–80
alternatives, 72–75
analysis, 77–79
chain of command for, 79
Columbia University and, 74
configuration leading to U–235
production, 78
critical path invention and, 102
description, 72
design difficulty scores, 96
design life scores, 103
design strategy used, 118
formal systems engineering and, 98
Los Alamos and, 76–77
objectives, 72
recyclability design, 104
requirements of, 72
resource scores, 97
resources, 71
risk mitigation and, 99
Supercollider effect on, 100
uncertainties, 75

Manhattan Project (*cont.*)
  University of California at Berkeley
      and, 74–75
  University of Chicago and, 73
  Westinghouse Research Laboratory,
      Pittsburgh, and, 74
Manufacturing considerations
  systems engineering fundamentals
      and, 141
McDonnell Douglas C–17 Military
      Transport, 187–205
  design difficulty scores, 203
  development environment, 198–202
  development environment scores, 203
  development history, design, and
      performance, 188–193
  performance scores, 202
  resource scores, 203
  summary, 202–203
  systems engineering fundamentals,
      193–198
  systems engineering fundamentals
      scores, 202
McDonnell Douglas MD–11 Commercial
      Airplane, 215–229
  design difficulty scores, 229
  development environment, 224–227
  development environment scores, 228
  development history, design, and
      performance, 216–219
  performance scores, 228
  resource scores, 229
  summary, 227–229
  systems engineering fundamentals,
      220–224
  systems engineering fundamentals
      scores, 228
Methodology validation
  aircraft case studies, 237
Metrics, 132–147, 238–246
  attributes of, 103
  development environment and,
      143–147
  INCOSE metrics working group,
      238–239
  Integrated Product Development
      Team, 238
  Percent Co–Location of Team
      Members, 238

San Francisco NCOSE Chapter,
      239–242
  Simplicity of the Processes, 238
  systems engineering fundamentals and,
      138–143
  systems engineers and, 126
  technical performance measures,
      242–243
Metrics summary tables, 95–104
  critical path invention, 102
  design difficulty scores, 2, 3, 12, 15, 17,
      23, 26, 29, 32, 36, 45, 49, 51, 55,
      58, 62, 66, 69, 80, 95, 96, 99, 158,
      170, 185, 203, 214, 229, 230
  design life scores, 103
  formal systems engineering, 98
  recyclability design, 104
  resource scores, 95, 97
  risk mitigation, 99
  score validation, 95–96
  Supercollider effect, 100
Mistakes
  systems engineering. *See* Systems
      engineering mistakes
Mitigation
  risk, 99
Model 60 Learjet. *See* Learjet Model 60
      Business Jet
Models
  system, 127–128
Modification management
  systems engineers and, 129
Moon landing
  design process and, 1–2

N

Networks
  design difficulty and resource scores, 12
  resistor design, 7
  resistor design case study, 10–12
New car factory, 9
Northrop B–2 Stealth Bomber, 172–186
  design difficulty scores, 185
  development environment, 181–183

development environment scores, 185
development history, design, and
    performance, 173–177
performance scores, 184
resource scores, 185
summary, 184–185
systems engineering fundamentals,
    177–181
systems engineering fundamentals
    scores, 184
NP–complete algorithm
system design process and, 104–106

O

Optimization procedures
system design process, 110

P

Percent Co–Location of Team Members
    metrics and, 238
Performance
    cost, 137
    schedule, 137
    scores of, 137
    systems engineering fundamentals and,
        134, 136–138
    systems engineers and, 125
    technical, 136
Performance measures
    technical, 242–243
Performance scores
    aircraft case studies, 232
    Boeing 777, 157
    Learjet Model 60 Business Jet, 213
    Lockheed F–117 Stealth Fighter, 169
    McDonnell Douglas C–17 Military
        Transport, 202
    McDonnell Douglas MD–11
        Commercial Airplane, 228
    Northrop B–2 Stealth Bomber, 184

Pinewood Derby, 8, 19–23
    critical path invention and, 102
    design difficulty scores, 96
    design life scores, 103
    design strategy used, 118
    design type rating, 115
    formal systems engineering
        and, 98
    recyclability design, 104
    resource scores, 97
    risk mitigation and, 99
    schedules for, 20, 22
    Supercollider effect on, 100
    systems engineering mistakes,
        22–23
Polaris Program, 9, 81–86
    analysis, 85–86
    communication, 84
    crew rotation cycle, 84
    critical path invention and, 102
    design difficulty scores, 96
    design life scores, 103
    design strategy used, 118
    formal systems engineering and, 98
    fuel, 83–84
    guidance/navigation accuracy, 84
    launch alternatives, 84–85
    objectives, 82
    recyclability design, 104
    resource scores, 97
    resources, 81–82
    risk mitigation and, 99
    Special Programs Office, 82–85
    Supercollider effect on, 100
    technical organization of, 86
    warhead (thermonuclear), 84
Polynomial algorithm
    system design process and, 109
Probabilistic jumps
    system design process, 112
Problem stating
    systems engineers and, 124
Process design
    design difficulty and, 2, 3, 4–5
Product quality
    design difficulty scores and, 2, 3, 4
Program management
    systems engineering fundamentals
        and, 142

Project management
  systems engineers and, 130
Pyramid at Giza
  construction of, 53–55

Q

Quality circles
  product quality and, 4
Quality function deployment
  product quality and, 4
Quality of product
  design difficulty scores and, 2, 3, 4

R

Recyclability design
  case studies and, 104
Reliability analyses
  systems engineers and, 129
Requirements
  systems engineers and, 126
Requirements development
  systems engineering fundamentals
    and, 138
Requirements relaxation
  system design process and, 109–110
Requirements tracking, 129
Resistor networks, 7, 10–12
  all possible solutions, 11
  critical path invention and, 102
  design difficulty and resources
    scores, 12
  design difficulty scores, 96
  design life scores, 103
  design strategy used, 118
  design type rating, 115
  feasible solutions, 12
  formal systems engineering and, 98
  recyclability design, 104
  resource scores, 97
  risk mitigation and, 99

Supercollider effect on, 100
Resource metrics, 1–9. *See also* Case
    studies; Design difficulty; Resources
  metrics summary tables and, 95–104.
    See also Metrics summary tables
Resource scores
  case studies and, 97
Resources, 6–7
  case study approach, 2
  case study regions, 1
  cost score, 6
  design difficulty vs., 1–2, 231
  infrastructure score, 6, 7
  metrics summary tables and, 95–104.
    See also Metrics summary tables
  scoring for, 6
  time score, 6–7
Resources plane
  design difficulty vs., 101
Resources scores. *See also* Design
    difficulty and resources scores
  aircraft case studies, 230
  Boeing 777, 158
  case studies and, 95, 97
  Learjet Model 60 Business Jet, 214
  Lockheed F–117 Stealth Fighter, 170
  McDonnell Douglas C–17 Military
    Transport, 203
  McDonnell Douglas MD–11
    Commercial Airplane, 229
  Northrop B–2 Stealth Bomber, 185
Reviews
  design, 128
Risk management
  systems engineers and, 129
Risk mitigation
  case studies and, 99
Robot design
  C3PO and, 68–69

S

San Francisco INCOSE Chapter, 239–242
Schedule performance, 137
Schedules

American Airlines and, 27–29
Boeing 777 vs. 767 design and build, 39
Pinewood Derby and, 19–23
Scores. *See also* Engineering systems
　　scores
　validation of, 95–96. *See also* Metrics
　　summary tables
Second Opinion, 8, 24–26
　critical path invention and, 102
　design difficulty scores, 96
　design life scores, 103
　design strategy used, 118
　design type rating, 115–116
　formal systems engineering and, 98
　recyclability design, 104
　resource scores, 97
　risk mitigation and, 99
　Supercollider effect on, 100
　systems engineering mistakes, 25–26
Selling price
　aggressive goals for, 2, 3, 5
Sensitivity analyses
　systems engineers and, 126
Serendipity
　Velcro and, 70
Seven wonders of the ancient world
　design process and, 1–2
　Great Pyramid at Giza, 53–55
SIERRA train controllers, 8, 13–15
　available components in lab, 14
　critical path invention and, 102
　design difficulty scores, 96
　design life scores, 103
　design strategy used, 118
　design type rating, 115
　formal systems engineering and, 98
　recyclability design, 104
　resource scores, 97
　risk mitigation and, 99
　student solutions, 14
　Supercollider effect on, 100
Simplicity of the Processes
　metrics and, 238
Six Sigma
　product quality and, 4
Space telescope
　Hubble, 87–94. *See also* Hubble Space
　　Telescope

Stability of requirements and configuration
　development environment and, 143–144
Star wars
　C3PO and, 68–69
　design process and, 1–2
Steps to complete a design
　design difficulty scores and, 2, 3–4
Strategies
　design, 117–118
Summary tables
　metrics, 95–104. *See also* Metrics
　　summary tables
Superconductors, 8, 30–32
　critical path invention and, 102
　design difficulty scores, 96
　design life scores, 103
　design strategy used, 118
　formal systems engineering and, 98
　history, 31
　recyclability design, 104
　resource scores, 97
　risk mitigation and, 99
　Supercollider effect on, 100
System design/analysis
　systems engineers and, 128
System design metrics
　usefulness of, 96–101
System design process
　algorithms and, 106–113
　branch and bound algorithms, 109
　breakthrough design model, 106
　conclusions, 118–119
　continuous improvement design
　　model, 105
　design continuum, 105
　design strategies used, 117–118
　designs evaluation, 113–118
　lessons learned from, 104–119
　NP–complete algorithm and, 104–106
　polynomial algorithm, 109
　probabilistic jumps, 112
　3–Opt optimization, 110
　traveling salesman problem and,
　　106–113
　tree search algorithms and, 108–109
　types of design, 105–106
System engineering fundamentals scores
　aircraft case studies, 236

System integration
  systems engineering fundamentals and,
    141–142
  systems engineers and, 129
System life–cycle
  phases of, 123
System models
  systems engineers and, 127–128
System performance accountability
  development environment
    and, 146
System requirements
  systems engineers and, 124–125
System testing
  systems engineers and, 129
Systems engineering, 122–131
  activities documentation and, 130
  alternative concepts and, 126
  configuration management and, 129
  customer needs and, 123–124
  design analysis and, 128
  Engineering Notebook and, 130
  figures of merit and, 125
  formal, 98
  functional decomposition and,
    126–127
  interfaces and, 128
  life–cycle phases, 123
  metrics and, 126
  modification management
    and, 129
  performance and, 125
  personnel selection for, 130
  problem statement and, 124
  project management and, 130
  quantitative measures and,
    125–126
  reliability analyses and, 129
  requirement validation and, 126
  requirements tracking and, 129
  reviews and, 128
  risk management and, 129
  sensitivity analyses and, 126
  system integration and, 129
  system models and, 127–128
  system requirements and, 124–125
  technical performance measures
    and, 125

  tests prescribed and, 126
  total quality management and, 129
  total system test and, 129
Systems engineering effort
  aircraft case studies, 237
Systems engineering fundamentals
  Boeing 777, 151–154
  configuration management, 141
  evaluating alternative concepts, 139
  incipient system design, 138–139
  integrated testing, 140
  Learjet Model 60 Business Jet, 209–211
  life–cycle considerations, 142
  Lockheed F–117 Stealth Fighter,
    164–166
  make–or–buy–decision, 139–140
  manufacturing considerations, 141
  McDonnell Douglas C–17 Military
    Transport, 193–198
  McDonnell Douglas MD–11 Commer-
    cial Airplane, 220–224
  metrics for, 138–143
  Northrop B–2 Stealth Bomber, 177–181
  performance and, 134, 136–138
  program management, 142
  requirements development, 138
  scores of components, 143
  system integration, 141–142
  technical management, 141–142
  validation of requirements, 140
  verification of design compliance, 140
Systems engineering fundamentals scores
  aircraft case studies, 232
  Boeing 777, 157
  Learjet Model 60 Business Jet, 213
  Lockheed F–117 Stealth Fighter, 169
  McDonnell Douglas C–17 Military
    Transport, 202
  McDonnell Douglas MD–11 Commer-
    cial Airplane, 228
  Northrop B–2 Stealth Bomber, 184
Systems engineering mistakes
  Bat Chooser, 17
  building a house, 49
  Central Arizona Project, 51
  Hubble Space Telescope, 93
  Pinewood Derby, 22–23
  Second Opinion, 25–26

T

Taguchi methods
    product quality and, 4
Team continuity
    development environment and, 144–145
Team design approach
    automobile factory and, 58
Technical management
    systems engineering fundamentals and,
        141–142
Technical performance, 136
Technical performance measures
    metrics and, 242–243
    systems engineers and, 125
Telescope
    Hubble, 87–94. *See also* Hubble Space
        Telescope
Testing
    integrated, 140
Tests
    systems engineers and, 126
3–Opt optimization, 110
Time
    resources scores and, 6–7
Total quality management
    product quality and, 4
    systems engineers and, 129
Total system test
    systems engineers and, 129
Traveling salesman problem
    system design process and, 106–113
Tree search algorithms
    system design process and, 108–109

V

Validating requirements
    systems engineers and, 126
Validating scores
    metrics summary tables and,
        95–96
Validation of methodology
    aircraft case studies, 237
Validation of requirements
    systems engineering fundamentals
        and, 140
Vehicles
    batteries for electric, 63–67
    electric, 60–62
Velcro, 9
    case study, 70
Verification of design compliance
    systems engineering fundamentals
        and, 140

W

Westinghouse Research Laboratory,
        Pittsburgh
    Manhattan Project and, 74
Work–force stability
    development environment
        and, 144
Workforce qualifications
    development environment
        and, 146

U

University of California at Berkeley
    Manhattan Project and, 74–75
University of Chicago
    Manhattan Project and, 73

Z

Zero defects
    product quality and, 4